Meaning and Ideology in Historical Archaeology

Style, Social Identity, and Capitalism
in an Australian Town

CONTRIBUTIONS TO GLOBAL HISTORICAL ARCHAEOLOGY

Series Editor:
Charles E. Orser, Jr., *Illinois State University, Normal, Illinois*

A HISTORICAL ARCHAEOLOGY OF THE MODERN WORLD
Charles E. Orser, Jr.

AN ARCHAEOLOGY OF MANNERS: The Polite World of the Merchant
   Elite of Colonial Massachusetts
Lorinda B. R. Goodwin

AN ARCHAEOLOGY OF SOCIAL SPACE: Analyzing Coffee Plantations
   in Jamaica's Blue Mountains
James A. Delle

BETWEEN ARTIFACTS AND TEXTS: Historical Archaeology in Global
   Perspective
Anders Andrén

DOMESTIC ARCHITECTURE AND POWER: The Historical Archaeology
   of Colonial Ecuador
Ross W. Jamieson

HISTORICAL ARCHAEOLOGIES OF CAPITALISM
Edited by Mark P. Leone and Parker B. Potter, Jr.

THE HISTORICAL ARCHAEOLOGY OF BUENOS AIRES: A City
   at the End of the World
Daniel Schávelzon

LANDSCAPE TRANSFORMATIONS AND THE ARCHAEOLOGY OF
   IMPACT: Social Disruption and State Formation in Southern Africa
Warren R. Perry

MEANING AND IDEOLOGY IN HISTORICAL ARCHAEOLOGY: Style,
   Social Identity, and Capitalism in an Australian Town
Heather Burke

RACE AND AFFLUENCE: An Archaeology of African America and
   Consumer Culture
Paul R. Mullins

A Continuation Order Plan is available for this series. A continuation order will bring
delivery of each new volume immediately upon publication. Volumes are billed only upon
actual shipment. For further information please contact the publisher.

Meaning and Ideology in Historical Archaeology
Style, Social Identity, and Capitalism in an Australian Town

Heather Burke
University of New England
Armidale, New South Wales, Australia

Kluwer Academic/Plenum Publishers
New York, Boston, Dordrecht, London, Moscow

ISBN: 0-306-46066-1

©1999 Kluwer Academic/Plenum Publishers
233 Spring Street, New York, N.Y. 10013

10 9 8 7 6 5 4 3 2 1

A C.I.P. record for this book is available from the Library of Congress

All rights reserved

No part of this book may be reproduced, stored in a retrieval system, or transmitted in any form or by any means, electronic, mechanical, photocopying, microfilming, recording, or otherwise, without written permission from the Publisher.

Printed in the United States of America

Foreword

A major challenge facing historical archaeology is the construction of culture histories of the past 500 years that simultaneously recognize global-scale processes and respect the particular contradictions, tensions, and unstable resolutions characteristic of any particular place. Reading Heather Burke's monograph about Armidale, New England, Australia while sitting in another New England some 8,000 miles away made me all the more aware of the difficulty of this challenge and the importance of fulfilling it.

An important aspect of the story of the post-Columbian world is the development of capitalist relations of production. This complex process is manifested in similar ways in Burke's New England as well as in mine. Early stages of surplus production used large tracts of land to develop products for export into the capitalist world-economy. Elites made use of wage and nonwage labor relations to effect this production. These elites had to make their accommodation with others who used strategies based on mercantile accumulation. Over the long run, the impacts of a third set of capitalist practices—industrial accumulation strategies—were exhibited in the regions.

The action of these different moments of capital resulted in heterogeneous regional landscapes. Some areas were transformed into industrial cities; others kept a rural, yet novel, character. Between these poles emerged a middle landscape that reflected distinctive mixes of the forces of development. Armidale, New England, Australia seems to be one of these places, as does much of the Connecticut River Valley in New England, United States. In both, commercial and even industrial activities developed among capitalized rural landscapes. Wage-based marketing, manufacturing, and agricultural enterprises were enmeshed within regional and world-scale exchange systems. Family reproduction distinctively shaped the domestic landscapes scattered among these capitalist places of work. And especially by the twentieth century, institutions of cultural reproduction (schools, churches, and museums) became important for regional identity and prosperity.

The emerging wealth differentials associated with capitalist development were codified in the built environments of these middle landscapes. Grid patterns became the basis for buying, selling, and understanding property. Neighborhood segregations, based in part on class and in part on race, gave a pastichelike structure to cities and towns. Domestic architecture signaled the class position of residents. Especially among the elite, the codes of Georgian symmetries were replaced by Victorian asymmetries.

Though the parallels are significant, one would not want to end the story of these two places with just these similarities. As a result of the particulars of history, ecology, political economy, and culture, the textures of everyday life—especially in their built environments—are very different. Wood is the most common fabric for domestic structures in the Connecticut River Valley, porches rather than verandahs adorn nineteenth-century homes, and turned timber finials are nonexistent. The scale of settlement in the Connecticut River Valley is closer, resulting from the agricultural exploitation of a temperate forest ecosystem. Georgian styles predominate, in part because of their association with an earlier beginning to the process of conquest. It might be that comparisons to places in the North American West would yield architectural styles and settlement scales more similar to Armidale. And yet something important would be lost in an enterprise that only looked for places around the globe manifesting similarities with the eventual goal of reducing all these places to a single explanatory structure. Rather than reduction, a global culture history should recognize that places around the globe are caught at different points in similar fields of social forces, with the result that unique places crystallize these forces in informatively different ways.

An important force manifested in material culture is that of ideology, and it is with this topic that Burke makes singular contributions. Eschewing a structural approach, she works in the realm of semiotic analysis, entering into the discussion richly pursued by the likes of Leone, Little, Shackel, Beaudry, McGuire, Wurst, and Hall. Embedding what has often been a debate in historical archaeology within a sophisticated philosophical consideration of ideology, Burke adds a new dimension by drawing on anthropological archaeologists (such as Wobst, Conkey, and especially Wiessner), who have thought hard about the notion of style. Mapping out the relationship between style, identity, and ideology, she discovers in the details of the built environment symbolic moves made by various classes and class fractions during the twists and turns of capitalist class formation. In particular, the shifting contest between pastoral and mercantile elites, and the cultural pastiche of a relatively powerless but not totally dominated working class, emerge from studies of town settlement plan and architectural detail.

Style as ideology not only marks boundaries but also refers to

Foreword

symbolic themes, some of which are familiar in the post-Columbian world and some of which seem distinctive to Australia. Panopticism, spatial segmentation, and the construction of abstract from absolute spaces are all evident at Armidale. The familiar cult of the Georgian is also present, and it receives an interesting interpretation as a cult of British imperialism. Working-class façades are symmetrical and uniform, and yet Burke presents a thoughtful assessment of the multiple meanings and possibilities for subversion lying just inside the doors of these homes. Gender ideologies shaped these domestic settings, especially notions of masculine respectability and the cult of the gentlemen. Hints of white supremacy, wrapped in the notions of the moral ascendancy of pastoral elites, can be found in the expropriation Aborigine lands and the segregation of Aboriginal people to special zones within the town. Commenting on if and how these dimensions of meaning fit with the cult of domesticity, the cult of gentility and notions of Protestant salvation that so affected the North American landscape await further study.

Armidale emerges from Burke's analysis of the meaningfulness of space as a messy place, one in which no single capitalist ideology or accumulative strategy takes precedence, one in which no single tactic of resistance is manifest. Building on previous studies where the political economic dynamic and the ideology were more clearly polarized, she presents a method for understanding the unique conjunctions that mark places on the middle landscape. Places where a monolithic elite's ideas alone structure the built environment are certainly part of the landscapes of capitalism, but so too are places where elite ideas conflict and where the working and middle classes had room to maneuver. At these latter places, as Burke admirably points out, structures and settlements do not always conform to types and style can be a weapon of the weak.

The points of contrast between these antipodal New Englands, as well as other places on the globe, deserve more attention. Sometimes the differences will be recognized as merely the differences of local academic traditions masking processual similarities. And sometimes they will be recognized as the distinctive ways in which class, race, gender, and state formation were worked out at different places in the world-system. It is from studies such as Burke's that a global historical archaeology will emerge.

ROBERT PAYNTER

Department of Anthropology
University of Massachusetts,
Amherst
Amherst, Massachusetts

Preface

Capitalism and ideology are two theoretical topics that saturate much of the recent literature on historical archaeology, despite (or perhaps because of) the fact that they are seldom explicitly defined. In many instances, architectural style is used as the vehicle for moving between the theory and the data, without examining the nature of the complex relationships between capitalism and ideology, on the one hand, and style as a mediator of relative social identity, on the other. Ideology, in particular, is a term with a complex intellectual genealogy, and sometimes the mere mention of the term elicits a well-choreographed reflex of resistance.

An increasing focus on the twin issues of capitalism and ideology within historical archaeology has been precipitated, in part, by a concern for a more politically active and accountable archaeology, but is also a result of the "bandwagon" effect, where simply using these terms is thought to be synonymous with demonstrating theoretical content. As a result, while it is a relatively simple matter to point to the words "capitalism" or "ideology" within many archaeological texts, it is not as common to find them linked with particular unambiguous definitions. On many occasions the terms are not defined explicitly at all, and within the one treatment there can be many implicit definitions—not all of which are necessarily compatible.

Bearing these issues in mind, this study set out to develop a workable set of definitions for capitalism and ideology, which could then be applied to an investigation of the relationships between the development of capitalism in a region and the expression of ideological information within architectural style. My principal theoretical concern lay in addressing the complex issues of how style encodes meaning, and how, as a medium for the creation of identity, it might be related to the social contexts and relationships within capitalism, which are in turn related to the construction of ideology over time. One principal result is that both local-scale membership in a particular form of capital production, and larger-scale membership in a particular social class (as a relationship to the means of production), have been found to influence the stylistic construction of identity. Stylistic features come to be indexical of membership in particular groups, and subsequently symbolic of the relationship between that group and other groups. This semiotic process creates both notions of stylishness and of value, which in turn become incorporated into subsequent contexts of meaning, and thus implicated in the construction of ideology. In looking at these processes across a community, rather than simply within a single structure, it becomes possible to move the study of ideology beyond the sphere of a single wealthy individual and to identify not only how members of all classes saw themselves, but also to recognize their responses to the pressures placed upon them by others.

Acknowledgments

Many people are in various ways responsible for the final form and content of this book. At UNE, Iain Davidson was the source of many perceptive insights and often lengthy constructive criticisms, and both Jane Balme and Wendy Beck provided invaluable assistance and advice.

June Ross, Michelle Seignior, Alice Gorman, Rod Cliff, Claire Smith, and Wendy Beck all took on the repetitive task of recording buildings, and I can honestly say that the extent of June's social contacts within Armidale and the wider district is only exceeded by her generosity. Rob Gargett and Stephanie Lambretti provided a welcome place to stay, Katrina Macdonald willingly (and continually) shared her knowledge of Entrer Trois and Access, and Scott Cleland took many of the photographs in Chapters 5–8.

John Ferry of the History Department, UNE, made available his extensive knowledge of the history of Armidale and his original research into land titles and wealth distribution. Linda Bedford and Sally Maloney from the UNE Heritage Center gave me extensive help in negotiating my way through the collections and in allowing me access to closed collections. In the UNE archives, Chris Buckley and Jill Manuel ensured that my research was both pleasant and productive.

In the Department of Anthropology at College Park, Maryland, I owe a great debt to Mark Leone and Nan Wells, Lynn and Larry (and Louie) Jones, Mike Lucas, Mark Warner, and Abdul Mustafa. Thomas Patterson's kind invitation to lunch put me on a different track, although I'm not certain that I ended up in the direction he had in mind.

In the Armidale community, many people kindly gave me access to their properties and to their store of knowledge about their homes. I would like to thank particularly John and Jane Baldry, Cam and Judy Lawrie, Sally and Owen Croft, Graydon Henning, Arch and Erica Nelson, Roberta Cahill, Nannette Connock, Beth Mallam, June and Peter Atherton, Bertram Wright, Mary Bookallil, Jennifer Johnstone, Ann Dangar, and Ross and Penny King. Annette Gill kindly loaned me

Clarice Dight's photograph albums and a considerable stock of family history.

I have also incurred a debt to Matthew Johnson, Martin Hall, and Charles Orser, all of whom provided thought-provoking and constructive criticism, even though I know that not all of their suggestions have been incorporated into this book.

Contents

CHAPTER 1. Introduction 1

CHAPTER 2. An Anatomy of Ideology 11

What Is Ideology? 11
What Does Ideology Do? 17
Ideology and the Construction of Social Identity 19
Ideology, Social Identity, and Style 25
Style and the Semiotics of Social Identity 31

CHAPTER 3. An Introduction to Armidale 37

A History of Armidale and New England 40
Colonial Armidale 70
Ideology 71
Discussion 80

CHAPTER 4. Materials and Methods 83

Selection of Place 83
Selection of Structures 83
Selection of Variables 85
Variables Relating to Social Context 86
Variables Relating to Style 90
Variables Relating to Geographical Context 92
Variables Relating to Use 92
Data Collection 93
Location of Structures 94
Analysis 97
Biases in the Database 99
Limitations of the Study 99

xiii

xiv   Contents

CHAPTER 5. The Semiotics of Social Position 103

The Contexts of Production for Style in Armidale 103
Discussion 136

CHAPTER 6. Relations of Meaning and Relations of
         Membership 143

Creating Social Identity 143
Discussion 160

CHAPTER 7. Style in Space 163

The Contexts of Interpretation for Style in Armidale 163
The Space of Style 167
The Power of Style 174

CHAPTER 8. Styles of Ideology 181

Ideology from Artifacts 182
Ideology and Public Identity 194
The Material Constraints to Studying Ideology 213
Discussion 214

CHAPTER 9. Investments of Meaning 217

Context and Identity 219
Stylishness 220
Directions of Emulation 220
Dominant Ideology 222
Scales of Ideology 223
Persistence 224
The Commodification of Heritage 225
A Historical Archaeology of Ideology 226

Appendix: List of Structures 231

References 257

Index 267

Meaning and Ideology in Historical Archaeology

Style, Social Identity, and Capitalism in an Australian Town

Introduction | 1

Trust me, this will take time but there is order here, very faint, very human.
—MICHAEL ONDAATJE *In the Skin of a Lion* (1987), p. 146.

This study is about ideology. In many ways it is possible to argue that almost any archaeological text, particularly one created within the well-defined academic structure, is "about ideology" (see, for example, Tilley 1989, 1993), but it is explicitly true in this volume. When I began postgraduate studies, I intended to pursue the notion of adaptation, a largely undertheorized and uncritically examined category in Australian historical archaeology into which much research appears to have been "conveniently" placed. Initially I approached this from a relatively secure economics standpoint, asking: What is adaptation? What does it mean in terms of evolutionary theory? How has it been used by historical archaeologists?

However, in 1989 I read Russell Handsman and Mark Leone's article, "Living history and critical archaeology in the reconstruction of the past." As an examination of some of the alternative ways in which the same past may be constructed and how this reflects changing power relations, this paper altered my previous understanding of the ways in which Australian historical archaeology and the notion of adaptation are constructed, and hinted at the possible alternatives. It also raised the issue of the analysis of capitalism, which was firmly linked to ideology, and to the past and present uses of material artifacts.

Having decided to read more in this vein, the real impetus for my research sprang directly from Leone's detailed and insightful study of William Paca's garden, published in 1984. William Paca was a wealthy American landowner, lawyer, governor of Maryland, and a signer of the Declaration of Independence. In the 1760s he built himself an Annapolis residence augmented by a large, carefully designed garden, part Georgian symmetry, part wilderness, and entirely formal. In Leone's analysis of the garden's construction, layout, and appearance, his basic contention was that it embodied certain principles of order (grafting, transplanting, symmetry, formality, rules of geometry) and design (perspective through terracing and through gradation of avenues, appeals to antiquity in statues and architecture) that were an integral part of how Paca defined himself and his place in society, and which he could not help but represent externally (though not necessarily consciously). In other words, the garden, through its expression of order as control over nature and of perspective as control over space, *was* ideology, of which William Paca himself was also a part. Leone suggested that the garden was an articulation of the "quest for a fixed, natural order" and as ideology, its principles hid certain elementary contradictions within Paca's life and society: "The major contradiction ... was between a slave-holding society and one proclaiming independence in order to promote personal freedom and individual liberty.... The [hidden] contradiction ... is that between slavery for others and freedom for themselves" (Leone 1984, 33). It was the concealment of such contradictions that Leone saw as crucial to the definition of ideology. For him ideology was not simply a worldview or a belief but

> ideas about nature, cause, time and person ... that are taken by a society as given.... these ideas serve to naturalize and thus mask inequalities in the social order; [and] ... when accepted uncritically, serve to reproduce the social order. Ideology's function is to disguise the arbitrariness of the social order, including the uneven distribution of resources, and it reproduces rather than transforms society. (Leone 1984, 26)

As part of espousing this definition, Leone could not simply study ideology as an unspecified social process. His explicitly critical definition and his interest in the archaeology of the recent historical past led him to link ideology firmly to capitalism. Although some have argued that it is possible to link ideology to social forms other than capitalism (Gero 1987, 294; Miller and Tilley 1984), this has been the general tone that Leone has continued to follow.

Leone's 1984 study was one of the earliest attempts at reaching ideology through archaeological analysis. This study, and the volume of which it was a part, prompted the beginning of much debate, and many of the questions that I have attempted to deal with in this study are framed within the wider issues of this polemic. The most common criticism leveled at archaeological accounts of ideology is that "ideology" is too often taken to mean "the beliefs and values of the dominant"; ignoring the existence and responses of those segments of the population who are "ruled" in one fashion or another (see, for example, Johnson 1991; 1992; McGuire 1988; Paynter and McGuire 1991). Matthew Johnson (1989) had Leone's 1984 study particularly in mind when he argued that "Nowhere does Leone discuss ... how those who viewed the garden interpreted it, and how their interpretations differed according to class, gender, ethnicity, or other interests—in short, their goals as active

Introduction

social agents." Ian Hodder likewise insisted that "[i]t ... appears ... that the ideology is shared by all in society ... the extent to which people are duped by the ideas of the dominant class is remarkable in these accounts" (Hodder 1993, 67). He goes on to argue:

> There is no indication anywhere that the same material culture may have different meanings and different ideological effects for different social groups.... Different ideologies coexist in relation to each other and the dominant ideology is continually being subverted from other points of view.... William Paca's garden may have worked well for William Paca, legitimating his own social interests, but whether anyone else was taken in by it is less clear.... do subordinate groups ever visit or see the garden, do subordinate groups use such ordering in their own homes and gardens on a smaller scale or are their gardens very different? (Hodder 1993, 67, 70)

These are all positions expressly opposed to what has become known as the "dominant ideology thesis" (see Abercrombie et al. 1980; 1992), a shorthand for the assumption that the conscious values and ideals of the ruling group are automatically and naturally also those of the ruled. In other words, ideology arises solely from the position of the ruling class. In some quarters this valuable corrective has been expanded into a position that has crafted the notion of "ideologies of resistance" as the response (see, for example, Hall 1992; Beaudry et al. 1991; Paynter and McGuire 1991, 10). If Leone's 1984 position was concerned with identifying the process of manufacturing consensus or with how the dominant group incorporates itself, then the ideology of resistance approach sought to define and understand ideology in terms of how groups other than the dominant group react and "reply" to such attempts at incorporation (see McLellan 1986, 74).

In many ways the dominant ideology thesis has been overly caricatured in archaeology as a foil for debating purposes. Quite paradoxically, in using this as a basis for criticism, many responses run the risk of simply inverting the perceived hierarchy, rather than closely examining it. There is a danger here that the "ruled" will be so intently fashioned as "knowledgeable actors" that primacy will simply be accorded to their activities, rather than asking of each instance of resistance similar questions to those asked of instances of domination. The questions of how and why responses of resistance arise are routinely and often insightfully dealt with in archaeology, however, further questions beckon in relating them to the complicated schema of ideology. Are they themselves attempts to dominate others? If so, are there sets of responses to them? From whom? How does the engagement with instances of resistance affect the form and content of ideology? How might ideology be altered as a result? As Thompson (1986, 81–82) argues:

> The problem of ... dominant ideology is partly due to the tendency to look
> for a single dominant ideology, linked to a particular class, when what is
> needed is the careful mapping of the complex of discourses that articulate
> together to produce ideological effects.

Although it is laudable to attempt to isolate both ideology as the incorporation of a dominant group and ideology as a reply to such incorporation, this may not always be possible, particularly if the archaeological material under study relates directly to a single individual. It is impossible to articulate archaeologically the subordinate ideologies "resisting" William Paca's garden, if William Paca's garden is the only area that is studied (but see Orser 1996, 177–178). Precisely because Paca was part of the elite and lived a life well within the bounds of the hegemonic view, a dominant reading of his material artifacts is most appropriate as an analysis of the process by which his class attempted to incorporate itself as a class.

There are two key points about the importance of Paca's garden in relation to the ideology of class in that place (and at least in that time): As the underclass (in this case, slaves) built and worked in it, they became involved in a process by which they could not avoid its symbolism; and the sheer scale and position of it meant that the symbolism was overt. While Paca certainly subscribed to his own ideology, which linked him to a particular dominant social group, the monumental scale, position, and structure of Paca's garden was also designed to structure the world of the workers in such a way as to reinforce their perception of subordination.

It was against this background that this book is written. I was interested primarily in how the use of material artifacts to incorporate a ruling group might also be used to reinforce a perception of subordination in others, and how these boundaries, as exclusive coteries of status, might be broken down through the appropriation of these artifacts by the ruled. I was also concerned with how ideology is implicated in this process. The basic focus, as I first conceived it, was to understand the ideologies of capitalism as they may have existed in the past in the relatively small town of Armidale in New South Wales, Australia (Figure 1.1), and how this may be grasped archaeologically through the material objects that were made and used at that time. To this end I devised a historical account of the various forms of capitalism in Armidale during the nineteenth and early twentieth centuries, and how this might relate to various forms of ideology. I regard capitalism as a process, rather than a "thing," and attempt to approach it as "it unfolds through the production of physical and social landscapes" (Harvey 1985, xviii). In doing so I am assuming the utter dominance of capitalism as a

Introduction

Figure 1.1. The city of Armidale and the boundaries of New England, New South Wales, Australia.

social system in Western society, and the existence within it of underlying problems of political, economic, and social inequality. One of the main assumptions is that capitalism is a specific type of unequal relation (cf. Johnson 1993a; Potter 1994, 37).

My concern with capitalism and its relationship to ideology led inexorably toward a second focus. As an archaeologist, in considering what ideology might be and how it related to capitalism, I was forced to think through and then deal with several fundamental, but related, problems. Ideology is not a thing to be excavated like a pot or an ax, so what is an artifact of ideology? What is the chain of argument connecting definition, artifact, and interpretation? How are my definitions to be translated into a series of distinctly archaeological problems? Tackling these questions led me to focus on architectural style as a particular field of material artifacts, which may have marked different patterns of social identity relevant to the construction of capitalism in the past. In my analysis I have set out to address the successive links between style, the construction of social identity, the semiotics of social position within capitalism, and ideology.

There are problems with defining each of the key concepts of capitalism, ideology, and style. All have been used to mean many different things, not all of which are compatible; for my purposes it was necessary to formulate a specific definition of each. I will define capitalism as *a mode of production in which the means of production are individually appropriated as "property."* Capitalism thus both needs and produces the commodification of labor, the means of production, and the products of nature. The term itself is derived from capital, or all those accumulations of past labor that have not yet been expended, such as consumable goods, machinery, or authorized claims to material things (money). To be considered "capital," however, such accumulated wealth must be directed toward the primary capitalist goal of self-expansion, or of accumulating more of the same (Wallerstein 1993, 13–14). Capital is therefore not really a thing at all, but a social relation that appears in the form of a thing: In capitalist society the production of capital predominates and dominates every other sort of production.

The principal form of capitalist accumulation is based on legal rights conferred on property owners, who appropriate surplus value in a variety of ways, such as profit, rent, or interest. I regard capitalism as simultaneously a social process, a way of producing commodities, and a relationship between owners and producers by which both objects and the capacities of people are brought into definite social relations under the control of capitalists (Wells 1989, xiv). There are three central aspects to this control: control over things (nature—land, minerals, timber), control over the labor of direct producers (through the formation of wage labor with rights vested in the capitalist to alienate labor power), and control over production (over the productive process itself, and a right to control and dispose of the results) (Wells 1989, xii–xiv). It is important to realize that a definition of capitalism as a social process and a definition of it as a set of relationships are related systemically. In one sense capitalism *is* (and only is) the "narrow set of economic relations," which is reified to become the whole social process of classes and relations commonly associated with the economic formation.

Capitalism becomes related to ideology through the basic contention that societies with such an unequal distribution of resources are subject to potential contradiction within these relations. Within capitalism the principal contradiction lies between capital and labor, and

Introduction

reproduction of it entails both the reproduction of material means and wealth, as well as the reproduction of the principal contradiction and its social conditions. Although I argue that antagonisms other than that between labor and capital may also be part of ideological forms of domination (such as gender or ethnicity), the fundamental tension between capital and labor is the only contradiction that is necessary to the survival of the capitalist system *per se* (see Larrain 1994, 15).

It is this contradictory process that ideology conceals, thus, ideology is both the result and the condition of the reproduction of the contradiction between capital and wage labor (Larrain 1983, 157; 1994, 12–13). Through concealment, ideology prevents transformation and reproduces the social order. It mystifies, acquiring its meaning as a very powerful social force disguising the perpetuation of asymmetrical relationships and grounding exploitive relations and definitions in a sphere that seems beyond question (Leone 1982, 748–749). Ideology thus becomes the field through which the essential contradictions contained within a capitalist society are mystified, and either hidden from recognition as social products or removed from the realm of mutability. This is part of the process identified by Marx as alienation, whereby human powers, products, or processes escape from the control of human subjects and come to assume an apparently autonomous existence. Such estranged phenomena exert power, and people submit to what are, in fact, products of their own activities as though they are an alien force (Eagleton 1991, 70). In turn this is closely linked to reification: if phenomena cease to be recognized as social products, they are perceived instead as independent things, and accepted as being inevitable.

My understanding of style is firmly grounded in Polly Wiessner's contention that it is a medium for identification via comparison and a means by which people "negotiate and communicate personal and social identity *vis-à-vis*" others (Wiessner 1989, 59).

> Individuals in all cultures have been shown to possess a strong desire to create a self-image through social comparison and to project this to others ... Social identity is important in that individuals are unable to form self-images in the absence of an identity derived from membership in one or more groups. Conversely, an element of personal identity seems equally important and when put in situations of extreme conformity, individuals experience discomfort and strive to differentiate themselves from similar others.... Since style is one medium of projecting identity, one would expect both personal and social identity to be expressed in style. (Wiessner 1990, 109)

Taking this as her premise, Wiessner is able to argue, first, that style may in part be an indicator of the balance between the interests of the individual and the interests of society (Wiessner 1989, 59; 1990, 109), and, second, that in marking social distance, style may be linked to specific questions of status and power. Style may thus be studied in terms of how it is used in different social strategies.

Power is implicit in much of the discussion in this book. In understanding the variety of relationships between groups of people in Armidale, I have drawn on Wolf's (1990, 586) four modes of power:

1. Power as the ability of a person as potency or capability;
2. Power as the ability of a person to impose their will on another, in interpersonal social relations;
3. Power as the control of social settings in which people may deploy their capabilities or interact with others ("tactical power"); and
4. Power as the organization or orchestration of the settings themselves, as the deployment and allocation of social labor ("structural power")

The first mode is analogous to Miller and Tilley's (1984) "power to," and the last three to their "power over" (Little 1994, 23). Power as the orchestration of the settings themselves is relevant to descriptions of capitalism as a process; power as the expression of an individual's potency is equally distinctive of descriptions of resistance to that process. I am most often concerned with power in the third sense, that is, as control over the variety of social settings, such as those that exist within Armidale. Power in the third and fourth modes is squarely based on the distribution of limited resources (whether in labor, land, raw materials, products, or money), although, to some extent, power as the ability of a person to impose their will on another may also be based on this. When assessing the place of people within networks of power, I am not necessarily assessing their individual "potency or capability," although this becomes relevant if tackling the issue of resistance (see for example Orser 1996, 177–178), but their relative position within a landscape of limited resources. Stewart Clegg (1989, 219) argues for four circuits of power in such a landscape, which I have relied upon heavily in my analysis: mobilizing relations of meaning and of membership, and mobilizing techniques of production and discipline.

In terms of ideology, what is really at stake when the issue of power is raised is not simply the identification of a range of material signs or symbols and their possible signified meanings, but what these meanings accomplish within a given set of historical circumstances. Power is a set of relations between individuals and groups, yet a powerful group in one context may well be powerless in another. Whether or not signs

Introduction

are always held to be ideological, ideology is not just a matter of the signified meaning, but also of the *operation* of the signifier (Easthope and McGowan 1992, 6).

Given that this is a book about ideology, it would be remiss to ignore one last (though not final) issue that is highly germane to the archaeological debate over ideology: the commentary on contemporary contexts that such studies provide. The range of responses to a paper published by Leone, Parker Potter, and Paul Shackel in *Current Anthropology* illustrates this engagement. Whether it be in terms of recognizing how the present sociopolitical context of the researcher influences the agenda that is followed (Blakey 1987, 292); disentangling the ideological nature and implications of research into ideology (Bradley 1987, 292; Hodder 1987, 295; Levy and Silberman 1987, 296); examining the usefulness of the past in restructuring understandings of the present; or in undermining prevailing ideology or indicating the interest groups best served by particular reconstructions (Durrans 1987, 293; Gero 1987, 294), many archaeologists share a concern with how the present continually structures the creation, understanding, and uses of the past. It would be hypocritical to attempt to study ideology without also attempting to question the ideological bases of that research itself, although this is by far the most difficult implication of any project. As Blakey (1987, 292) persuasively argues, critical archaeological research, rather than "showing 'real relationships' or producing 'less contingent knowledge,'" can only be expected to yield *differently* contingent knowledge and relationships." Because it is the nature and implications of both this difference and this contingence that are at issue, there is also the question of to what criteria of acceptability such an exercise is answerable (Wylie 1987, 297). How should we value such studies as a means of characterizing the world today? This is neither a simple nor spurious exercise if archaeologists have any control over the accountability of the discipline or the intellectual investment in particular answers,

> for ideology is *justification*. It presupposes the experience of a societal condition which has already become problematic and therefore [which] requires a defense just as much as does the idea of justice itself, which would not exist without such necessity for apologetics. (Adorno, quoted in Kreckel 1985, 163, emphasis in original)

In the following chapters, I will attempt to deal with the problematic social conditions of capitalism in Armidale in the nineteenth and early twentieth centuries; how this may have given rise to ideology in the past; and the ideological basis for particular presentations of that past in the present.

An Anatomy of Ideology | 2

WHAT IS IDEOLOGY?

The study of ideology is an area of research that has long been acknowledged as part of archaeology in various capacities; however, there have been many different approaches to its study, corresponding to varying appreciations and definitions of the concept. The changing extent and ways in which archaeology has acknowledged ideology as an area for productive research are part of how archaeology itself has changed as a discipline. This is no simple or unidirectional process, of course, but is part of wider changes in the social sciences, in politics, and in society.

Terry Eagleton's (1991) recent comprehensive appraisal charts a complicated series of historical moments in the conception and definition of ideology. Within this framework, Eagleton (1991, 3) recognizes two primary mainstream traditions: an epistemological tradition descending from Hegel, Marx, and Lukacs, and a sociological tradition espoused by Althusser and Gramsci. The epistemological tradition derives from Marx's early use of the celebrated *camera obscura* analogy, which opposed "reality as it actually is" to ideology, which was an inversion of this reality. Ideology was an illusion (false consciousness) that could be combated by substituting true ideas for the false ones. This lent an eminently subjective character to ideology, and became one of the fundamental bases upon which the sociological tradition diverged from the epistemological (Larrain 1994, 61). Althusser in particular was critical of portraying ideology as a form of consciousness produced by, and therefore existing only in the minds of, individual subjects. The potential here was for ideology to be reduced to phantasm, and thus for it to be understood as a production of faulty cognitive processes in the human mind or as self-deception induced by a manipulative ruling class. Ideology is thus created as "... pure illusion, a pure dream,... nothingness. All its reality is external to it" (Althusser, quoted in Larrain 1994, 61). Instead, sociological interpretations are based on an intent to demonstrate that ideology indeed has some "external reality" that it is not spiritual, but based on actual material practices, experiences, and institutions; as a result it is not produced internally by any one subject, but instead shapes and constitutes all subjects.

As a result Eagleton (1991, 28–30) distinguishes at least six different possible ways to define ideology, and considers each as successively helping to refine the focus of the term:

1. *Ideology as "the general process of production of ideas, beliefs and values in social life."* This is possibly the broadest kind of definition and alludes to the way in which individuals live their day-to-day social practices, but is silent on the specifics of those practices themselves. Because of such breadth, ideology in this sense is analogous to the concept of "culture," and simply stresses the social determination of thought.

2. *Ideology as "ideas and beliefs (whether true or false) which symbolize the conditions and life-experiences of a specific, socially significant group or class."* This definition introduces a political element and begins to consider ideology in the sense of sectoral interests rather than as 'culture'; however, it still presents the concept of ideology in isolation and does not view it in either relational or conflictive terms within society. Such a definition is analogous to the concept of "worldview" or collective self-expression.

3. *Ideology as "the promotion or legitimation of the interests of social groups in the face of opposing interests."* Here a distinct element of conflict or contradiction is introduced, which enables ideology to be conceived of as a "discursive field in which self-promoting social powers conflict and collide over questions central to the reproduction of social power as a whole." This not only views ideology in relational terms, but links it more closely to questions involving reproduction of the social order.

4. *Ideology as "the promotion or legitimation of sectional interests, [in terms of] ... the activities of a dominant social power."* This definition continues the focus on sectional interests, but limits these firmly to those that are considered to be central to the social order. Because such a definition conceives ideology exclusively in terms of a dominant social power, it cannot help but consider ideology as homogenous and unifying, furthermore assuming that it helps to unify a social formation in ways convenient for its rulers.

5. *Ideology as "signif[ying] ideas and beliefs which help to legitimate the interests of a ruling group or class specifically by distortion and dissimulation."* This is very close in conception to definition number four; however, it gives greater consideration to the precise ways in which ideology might operate. Under definitions four and five, not all ideas of the ruling group need be considered to be ideological, as some may not promote its interests and some may not do so via the specific tactic of deception.

An Anatomy of Ideology

6. *Ideology as "false or deceptive beliefs [which arise] not from the interests of a dominant class but from the material structure of society as a whole."* This shift in emphasis, from dominant interests to the material structure of society in general, in part is a response to criticisms of accepting the ideology of the dominant group as the defining ideology for all of society (see, for example, Abercrombie et al. 1980). In this view, subaltern groups or classes retain a degree of autonomy, are often outside of the total control of the ruling group, and perhaps embody beliefs and values at odds with those of the dominant group.

In descending Eagleton's ladder, a concept of ideology emerges that has several significant implications. Most importantly, ideology is not a mere set of esoteric beliefs that are disconnected from daily life, but is instead fundamental to the social order, arising from the material structure of society as a whole. It therefore affects all members of a society, though perhaps not all in the same manner, and is connected to some minimum perception of social reality (cf. Feuer 1975, 96).

This means that, although ideology may include beliefs that are false or deceptive, "false" should not be understood here to mean "unreal" (as in a false reality, an imposed illusion), but as false in the sense of "untrue as to what is the case." It is perfectly possible for ideological discourse to be false at one level but not at another—true in its empirical content, for example, but deceptive in its force; or true in its surface meaning, but false in its underlying assumptions (Eagleton 1991, 16–17; Plamenatz 1970, 31). As Eagleton (1991, 15–26, emphasis in original) argues

> "Prince Andrew is more intelligent than a hamster" is ... probably true,... but the effect of such a pronouncement ... is ... likely to be ideological in the sense of helping to legitimate a dominant power.... while such utterances are *empirically* true, they are false in some deeper, more fundamental way.... [I]deology is no baseless illusion, but a solid reality, an active material force which must have at least enough cognitive content to help organize the practical lives of human beings ... and many of the propositions it does advance are actually true. None of this however, need be denied by those who hold that ideology often or typically involves falsity, distortion and mystification. Even if ideology is largely a matter of 'lived relations', those relations, at least in certain social conditions, would often seem to involve claims and beliefs which are untrue.

Eagleton's definition of ideology as false or deceptive beliefs arising from the structure of society as a whole (as well as his clarification of truth and falsity), firmly reconciles the potential of ideology to conceal with the question of how it can also relate to forms of lived experience. Ideology may well be misrepresentation, but it is not pure illusion. It is inextricably linked to the fabric of society and to the general reproduction of that society through the process of concealing antagonistic contradictions. This allows ideology to be understood as both something that masks (which presents false representations of life), and something that still makes some minimal sense of people's actual day-to-day life experiences. This suppleness is what gives ideology its power.

There is a distinct element of contradiction contained within the notion of ideology, either between classes in a society or between groups defined through other divisions. Ideology is thus seen to be a very powerful social force, which in part is used to contain contradiction in order to prevent it from becoming conflict (cf. Leone 1982, 748–749). This returns once again to the notion of ideology as being central to the general reproduction of the social order and to an appreciation of ideology as dynamic rather than static. Ideology does not function as an isolated body of thought, but as an ongoing social process; it is not a "possession" or a "state of mind," but is continually changing in response to its engagement in the world and the patterning of the relationships between given groups (Therborn 1980, 77–78). This raises interesting questions: Under what forces and at what rate does ideology change?

Ideology is best understood, not as simple and patronizing, in the sense of one (dominant) group always duping another (subordinate) group, but as sets of beliefs that enable *all* groups to live out their lives within a given social order, albeit a social order in which there may still be a considerable degree of inequality and conflict. Ideology is not a conspiracy of the ruling class, but an "organizing social force which actively constitutes human subjects at the roots of their lived experience and seeks to equip them with forms of value and belief relevant to their specific social tasks and to the general reproduction of the social order" (Eagleton 1991, 221). Ideology is not necessarily a systematic or coherently articulated body of ideas, but is related directly to practice, influenced directly by experience, and often uttered unreflectively as "common sense" (Rootes 1981, 43). For Eagleton, because ideology is not always directly equatable with outright systematic doctrine, and because it provides some minimal connection with material reality, it is implicated in much of the minutiae of day-to-day life experience.

Eagleton's six concentric definitions are clearly designed to narrow the definition of ideology towards an increasingly tighter account of the social processes involved. There are three movements here. First, each successive meaning is virtually a subset of the previous meaning, and as each is unpacked, greater attention is directed towards the issue of the imposition of ideology upon others and the power that is attached to this. But by the time the sixth definition is reached there is also a second shift—from questions of the imposition of ideology to questions of its

An Anatomy of Ideology 15

acceptance. The issue is no longer solely who imposes ideology upon whom, but also how this is received and what this process of reception might imply. Between the first and the second definition there is also a third shift, which in a sense ties both of the previous issues together: Once a notion of ideology as culture is rejected, the definition of groups itself becomes fundamental to the defining of ideology. Whatever particular attributes ideology may have then, it must be shared by a group of people, it must concern matters important to the group, and it must serve to hold the group together or to justify the activities and attitudes characteristic of its members (Plamenatz 1970, 31).

For the purposes of this study, my definition of ideology is *false or deceptive beliefs and presuppositions implicit in ordinary ways of thinking, speaking, or behaving in the world, which arise from the structure of society as a whole and the relations of the group to that structure, and which serve to reproduce that world by concealing contradiction and by perpetuating an unequal pattern of existing material relationships between and among groups. Because it is concerned with concealment, ideology necessarily serves particular interests and thus refers to the specific ways in which signs, meanings, and values help to incorporate and reproduce dominance as a social power and to manufacture consensus, while at the same time concealing the antagonisms resident at this point. Ideology may exist at more than one scale within the same society, or within the same individual.* It may exist as unsophisticated ideology or implicit "common sense," which is shared most widely and as sophisticated ideology; or as a more or less coherent system of explicit beliefs about the world that favors the interests or expresses the feelings of a more specific group in society, without the members necessarily being conscious of their belonging to that group.

One of the most difficult aspects of defining ideology is undoubtedly the permutations that are possible. Although this is one attempt at definition, it is not an attempt to provide resolution. Ideology may be all of the things in this chapter, but it is not reducible to any one of them. Eagleton (1991, 222) makes the point that ideology is impossible to define for all times and for all situations, "indeed it is doubtful that one can ascribe to [it] any *invariable* characteristics at all" (emphasis in original). My particular attempt at definition therefore has a number of specific historical roots. It is materialist rather than idealist in that it considers ideology to be anchored in real societal contradictions and to have some root in material "reality" (this may be also defined as a realist ontology, see Patterson 1994, 533). My definition is not so strictly materialist, however, that it reduces the position of ideology to one of subservience to the material base of society: Neither one is strictly determined by the other (it is therefore "dialectical" in the Marxist jargon). As a result my definition is also post-Marxist in the sense that it recognizes interests other than those that are strictly tied to production (i.e., between classes) as participating in ideological discourse. If ideology is the general process of masking contradiction and reproducing an unequal or conflicting societal form, then it would seem to be undoubtedly ideology in the service of particular interests. Because I conceive of power in a wider sense than Marx, these interests are not necessarily restricted to those of class. It is equally possible for ideology to refer to the specific ways in which signs, meanings, and values help to reproduce a dominant social power, as it is to refer to *any* significant conjunction between discourse and power (Eagleton 1991, 221). In this sense discourse is not reducible merely to language, but is instead the use of language for the production of specific effects, and is often a function of the relationship between an utterance and its particular social context (Eagleton 1991, 9).

> Ideology ... disguises not just forms of class domination but other forms too such as racial, gender and colonial repressions. This does not mean that such ideological processes are disconnected from or have no bearing upon particular forms of class domination—the colonial ideological construction of colonized peoples as inferior clearly plays an ideological ... role ...—but ... ideology conceals not merely class antagonisms but also forms of gender, racial and colonial domination which affect women, ethnic minorities and Third World peoples. (Larrain 1994, 15)

Undoubtedly some of the most important recent criticisms of treatments of ideology are those opposed to the existence of a single dominant ideology within society, targeting both the simplistic vision of society that this implies and the ideological nature of these arguments themselves. Like Larrain (1994, 13–15) I wish to widen the scope of the concept of ideology beyond the class and national context in which Marx primarily wielded it, and to consider a more general link between asymmetrical relations of power and situations of domination.

Despite disavowing strict idealism, my definition does allow for the participation of both an unconscious and symbolic element to the ways in which ideology functions. The choice to place the emphasis squarely on symbolic aspects should not be taken to imply that I consider ideology to be confined to the symbolic dimension of social life only, an implication that in turn encourages a link between ideology and idealism. As a result, I do not consider symbols merely in terms of esoterica, but in terms of the semiotic potential of *all* artifacts, from the mundane to the magnificent, to be symbolic or indexical of asymmetrical relations of power and situations of domination. I am not necessarily saying that

An Anatomy of Ideology

every artifact must always be symbolic, but that, depending on how an artifact is used, by whom, and why, it *may* be. Certainly, in terms of ideology, the potential is there.

WHAT DOES IDEOLOGY DO?

There is a complementary aspect to the definition of ideology that partially defines it according to what it *does*, rather than simply what it *is*. This expanded definition considers how ideologies operate: Ideology does not just *express* sets of ideas, beliefs, or values, but presents them in particular ways so as to remove them from contention. There is a distinction to be made here between the functions of the attitudes, beliefs, or ideas that compose ideology: They may well serve to describe and explain, but they may also justify and encourage behavior, or to condemn and discourage it. They are thus both descriptive and persuasive, and the same beliefs or attitudes may serve both functions (Plamenatz 1970, 70–71). Eagleton (1991, 45–59) has distilled six main strategies by which ideologies operate: unification, action-orientation, rationalization, legitimation, universalization, and naturalization (but see also Urry 1981 for a similar scale).

1. *Unification*. The process of unification strives to create a sense of community that may lend coherence to an otherwise internally differentiated society. Two examples are: creating a sense of national identity through patriotism or heritage, and the Australian Aborigines' creation of a national flag. Yet however much ideologies are used to homogenize, Eagleton points out that they are themselves rarely homogenous. Instead, they are usually internally complex, with conflicts between their various elements that must be continually renegotiated or resolved. The perception of dominant ideologies as unifying in particular contains an implicit paradox. A dominant ideology only exists in relation to other ideologies; therefore, it has to continually negotiate with these ideologies and cannot as a result achieve any kind of pure self-identity. As Eagleton notes, a concept of ideology as pure and devoid of contradictions is itself highly ideological.

2. *Action-orientation*. This relates to the ways in which an ideology may be used to express concrete social interests, rather than merely abstruse theoretical or metaphysical systems. This strategy attempts to translate ideology into practical states, capable of furnishing goals, motivations, prescriptions, and imperatives. Religions often function in this way, as did *Mein Kampf.*

18   Chapter 2

3. *Rationalization*. A strategy by which ideology is used systematically to provide plausible explanations and justifications for social behavior. This might be linked to other strategies, such as naturalization or legitimation.

4. *Legitimation*. The process of securing at least tacit consent to authority. Both rationalization and legitimation may refer to the conferral of respectability onto otherwise illicit interests, but may merely mean establishing one's interests as being broadly acceptable. Eagleton points out that legitimation is not necessarily normative (in the sense that a legitimated power is always internalized by its subjects), but sometimes pragmatic (the rights of the rulers are endorsed because the subjects can see no other realistic alternative).

5. *Universalization*. A strategy by which values and interests specific to a certain time and place are presented as common to all humanity and are rendered seemingly inevitable, as self-evident, anonymous, universal "truths." When, in August 1770, Captain James Cook (cited in Clark 1971) noted of the Australian Aborigines that, "They seem to have no fix'd habitation, but move about from place to place like wild beasts in search of food, and I believe depend wholly upon the success of the present day for their subsistence [sic]," his English shock at these behaviors presented European values through just such an ideological strategy.

6. *Naturalization*. As with universalization, naturalization is part of the tacit denial that ideas and beliefs may be specific to a particular place, time, or social group and presents them as natural or self-evident. "Science" is presented through such a strategy and rests upon a particular ideological conception of nature as being "massive, immutable and enduring" (which, Eagleton argues, in this age of technological dominance, it most certainly is not). Both universalization and naturalization present processes as things, "deleting agency and constituting time as an external extension of the present" (Thompson 1984, 131, 137). Essentially, both deny inequality by refusing the idea that it is a social product and by presenting it as though it was the result of distinctly nonsocial factors.

To these six might be added a seventh, as advocated by Thompson (1984, 137):

7. *Dissimulation*. A strategy that acts to conceal, deny, or block relations of domination, and to simultaneously conceal the process of concealment. This is ideology as a mask, for example by arguing that certain features of an order exist while others simply do not (e.g. affluence, freedom, and equality, not poverty, oppression, or exploitation).

The "end of ideology" thesis of the 1970s, which argued that people under late capitalism are too worldly and wise to be taken in by ideology, illustrates how ideology can be concealed by denying that it exists.

As is the case with essential definitions of ideology, although it is possible for ideology to operate via all of these strategies, it is not reducible to any one of them and many permutations are possible. Different strategies may be used successively over time by the same group of people, or the same strategy may be employed by completely different and separate groups.

IDEOLOGY AND THE CONSTRUCTION
OF SOCIAL IDENTITY

Implicit in discussions such as Eagleton's is a nexus between ideology and the construction of social identity, exemplified by descriptions of the patterning of groups as subordinate and dominant, male and female, Protestant and Catholic, or European and Aborigine, for example. Goran Therborn (1980, 28) argues that ideology at any scale consists broadly of two components: what constitutes "us" and what constitutes "them" and emphasizes the reflexivity inherent in making sense of your own place in the world through making sense of the relational place of others. For Therborn (1980, 18) there are three fundamental modes of ideological interpellation. The first qualifies subjects by telling them, relating them to, and making them recognize what exists, as well as its corollary, what does not exist: that is, who "we" are; what the world is; or what nature, society, men, and women are like. In this way "we" acquire a sense of identity and the world acquires structure. The second and the third are both consequent upon this, relating identity to what is good and what is not (i.e., what is right, just, beautiful, attractive, enjoyable), and its opposites. In this way, desires too become structured, as well as what is possible and impossible, "patterning a sense of the mutability of being-in-the-world and the consequences of change" (Therborn 1980, 18).

Whether or not one believes, as Marx did, that the proletariat is compelled to abolish itself, and is therefore conscious of both itself as a group and of its relative place in the rest of society, one strength of Marx's argument rests on his recognition that each group is only created as a group by reference to what it is not. Membership in a group (or groups) is created within the tensions of an unequal (in this case capitalist) society: In other words, who is and is not "proletariat" (or marginalized under some other distinction) can only be defined in relation to who is and is not "bourgeois" (or "elite" in some other sense). Ideology is thus a process that brings individuals and groups into certain power relations, and provides both social identity and knowledge about the world. Through ideology, which works to both include and exclude by suggesting standard sets of values against which everything can be measured, groups and individuals signify and respond to common arrays of values and beliefs.

John Plamenatz (1970, 17–18) took the premise of a connection between ideology and the construction of social identity and sought to reconcile an understanding of ideology as a general process of societal incorporation, with the obvious need to recognize the autonomy and heterogeneity inherent in human society. He distinguished between ideology in a sophisticated sense and ideology in an unsophisticated sense in order to approach the subtleties of individual identity. A sophisticated ideology is a "more or less coherent system of explicit beliefs about the world," an all-embracing philosophy or doctrine that may be shared by only a few members of society; an unsophisticated ideology consists of the "presuppositions implicit in ordinary ways of thinking and speaking about the things and persons, events and actions that constitute the world" and may be shared by all. A sophisticated ideology is not necessarily the vehicle for making explicit the presuppositions of an unsophisticated one (although it may be), but if all the members of a community or group are mutually to understand one another's "ordinary discourse," they must share an unsophisticated ideology (Plamenatz 1970, 18). Thus, while there may be only one unsophisticated ideology within a society, it is entirely possible for the same society to accommodate more than one sophisticated ideology.

Although Plamenatz chooses the words implicit and explicit to describe the way unsophisticated and sophisticated ideologies work, this should not be taken to imply any necessary equation with consciousness. Plamenatz (1970, 113–114) argues that it is entirely possible for a class or social group to have an ideology (beliefs that are widely held because they favor interests or express feelings shared by the group's members generally) without themselves being class- or group-conscious. In other words, they may have wants and feelings typical of that group, but not be organized to promote their interests or to act together as a group, or even be aware that they belong to a particular class or group. To a certain extent, what is definable as consciousness is dependent upon what the objective interests of the group are taken to mean:

An Anatomy of Ideology

> If we take a class (or other social group) and define it broadly in terms of some of the social relations in which its members stand, we can then perhaps discover aims typical of the class and define the conditions most favorable to their achievement, consistent with the class retaining its identity. These conditions we can call the 'objective interests' of the class and we can say that the class is 'class-conscious' when its members are effectively organized to further their interests and have beliefs (an ideology) which contribute to their furtherance. But if we define its objective interests and its class-consciousness as the aims and beliefs which its members would have if they understood the true significance of the course of history, we may be forced to conclude either that the objective interests and consciousness of all classes are the same or that no class ever achieves a full consciousness. (Plamenatz 1970, 121)

What Plamenatz distinguishes is the existence of ideology at different *scales*, either within the one social system, or even within the individual. Under this kind of approach, society at any given time will contain a variety of ideologies, unsophisticated and sophisticated, and analysis needs to focus upon the ways in which these ideologies articulate with one another to either promote or hinder different forms of social solidarity. Although the baseline Marxist emphasis rests upon how a social solidarity that allows capitalism to be reproduced is maintained, this maintenance may not be a result of a single dominant ideology incorporating all members. Rather, the reproduction of capitalism may be fostered as much by ideologies that effectively hinder, confuse, or divert the development of resistance as by ideologies that incorporate a ruling group.

Plamenatz' dichotomy is similar to the distinction between vulgar and non-vulgar ideology proposed by Meltzer (1981), and is echoed in a similar distinction formulated by Anthony Giddens (1979, 190–192). Giddens formulated a scheme for analyzing ideology as discourse that can be undertaken at two levels: ideology as strategic action and ideology as institutional analysis. Giddens' concept of strategic action encompasses ideology in its most conscious form, involving "the use of artifice or direct manipulation of communication by those in dominant classes or groups in furthering sectional interests" (Giddens 1979, 190). Political tracts and Machiavellian strategies are typical examples. Ideology as institutional analysis, however, is concerned with how forms of domination are sustained in the everyday context of "lived experience" (Giddens 1979, 191) and may be largely unconscious and deeply embedded, both psychologically and historically. For Giddens (1979, 193) the distinction depends upon a search for "the modes in which domination is concealed as domination, on the level of institutional analysis: and for

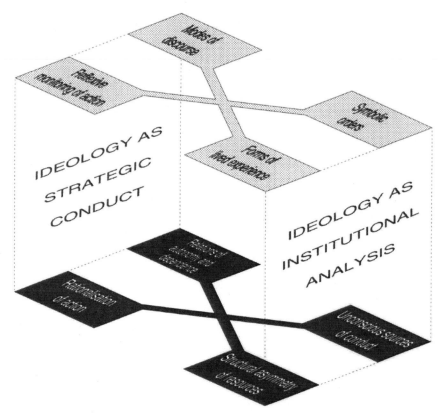

Figure 2.1. Anthony Giddens' scheme for analyzing ideology.

the ways in which power is harnessed to conceal sectional interests on the level of strategic conduct" (Figure 2.1).

Because, for Giddens, an analysis of ideology is contained within the broader theory of structuration, he is careful to point out that this distinction should not be taken to imply two different types of ideological elements, but rather two different levels of ideological analysis that are "connected via the duality of structure" (Giddens 1979, 193). An important strand that Giddens draws from his distinction is the relative degrees to which each ideological level may be penetrated and by whom: Ideology as strategic action is often ideology of the most easily penetrated sort and "by those who are the object of political manipulation— however subtle and clever the prince may be"; while ideology as insti-

An Anatomy of Ideology

tutional analysis contains the most "buried" form of ideology and is not easily penetrated by those who live it (Giddens 1979, 191–192).

Eagleton (1991, 50) has suggested that to study ideology is, among other things, to "examine the complex sets of linkages or mediations between its most articulate and least articulate levels." Perhaps what Eagleton would seem to suggest is that ideology at its least articulate is concerned with ideology as social practice, as opposed to ideology as carefully formulated political doctrine. In this sense then, archaeology will always be concerned with ideology at its least articulate levels, not because it is a recognition of the axiom that material artifacts are, by their nature, "mute," and it is the archaeologist who gives them "voice," but because archaeology, by definition, is routinely directed towards understanding daily material practices.

There would appear to be obvious similarities between Giddens' analysis levels, Eagleton's articulation levels, and Plamenatz's scales of sophisticated and unsophisticated ideology. In a sense these are all pointing in the same direction in order to intentionally highlight the complexity that faces any research attempt to analyze and contain ideology. Archaeology must also come to terms with this. Any contextual approach demands the same attention to the intricacies of ideology as to history or social context, while at the same time resisting a tendency to metaphorize and reify ideology as an organism in itself. Unsophisticated and sophisticated ideology are *only* articulated and made sense of through their continual reading and reception by people, and only expressed materially within the many different ways of life of the people who live them (Figure 2.2).

It is crucial to remember here that there is a close connection between unsophisticated and sophisticated ideology. Both are the process and the products of daily life. As Raymond Williams (1977, 70) suggests, to attempt to dichotomize ideology as either a label for formed, separable "ideas" or "theories," or as the general production of "real life," ignoring the links between the two, is "the persistent thread of error." This leads to a final rider on my definition of ideology. I also consider ideology to be dyadic, that is, existing simultaneously at two levels within one society, or even within one individual, and thus continually interacting and being negotiated as a result. Most importantly, my definition of ideology is firmly linked to questions of social power and to the negotiation of social identity.

Instead of a dichotomy, Williams proposes that it is the "fundamental signifying practices" of ideology as belief or theory that are an integral part of ideology as "real life," and it may well be the links *per se* that assume importance. It is this association between the "material

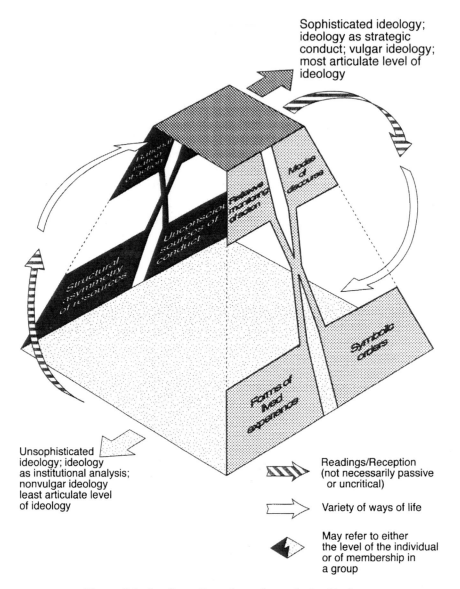

Figure 2.2. An alternative scheme for analyzing ideology.

social process" (the production of society through the interactions of and interrelations between groups) and signification (the production of meaning through signs) that is the key to understanding how ideology may be studied in archaeological terms.

IDEOLOGY, SOCIAL IDENTITY, AND STYLE

Identity is a central facet of ideology and a crucial aspect in allowing it to make at least minimal sense of people's position in the world, and thus their day-to-day life experiences. It is also expressed, sometimes deliberately, mostly unknowingly and often materially. Within archaeology, an argument linking identity, power, and ideology is applied not only to particular signs individually (see, for example, Handsman and Leone 1989; Thomas and Tilley 1993), but also to their manifestation as a collectivity, in other words, as "style" (see, for example, Earle 1990; Hodder 1990; Shanks and Tilley 1987).

My contention for a nexus between identity, style, and ideology is clearly expressed in Polly Wiessner's (1989, 58) argument that there is a single underlying behavioral basis to style, in the "fundamental human cognitive process of identification via comparison." Through this she views style as a component of non-verbal communication (although it is not reducible to such), which communicates information about aspects of relative identity at both an individual and a group level. Style thus becomes a medium for identification via comparison, and a means by which people "negotiate and communicate personal and social identity *vis-à-vis* others" (Wiessner 1989, 59).

Although style is non-verbal, it is a part of the construction of relative identity that is mediated by language and the symbolism that language entails (Noble and Davidson 1989; 1993). Just as language creates the potential for restricting access to information; thereby, separating groups who possess that conventional knowledge from those who do not, so too, style, as a physical and enduring manifestation of group, contributes to the construction and negotiation of this relationship between the "in-group" and the "out-group" (Davidson and Noble 1992; Noble and Davidson 1993). As Conkey (1990, 7, emphasis in original) has argued: "the word 'style,' like the rest of language works by difference, and we certainly have used the study of style as our *access to difference*." The advertisement of difference, of course, must still imply some convention of understanding of meaning across a boundary (Davidson 1995, 13). It is clear that I am subscribing here to a view of style as an inherently symbolic and purposeful behavior, which, whether consciously chosen or not, entails the choice of particular distinctive options of form from the range of alternatives available (see Sackett 1990, 35–36).

At the same time however, while the range of choices that create self-image may, in theory, be limitless, in practice, this creation is constrained by the range of choices that are seen to be possible as a result of culturally encoded experience. In other words, faceting a self-image through membership in one or more groups is directed by the range of groups that already exist, or that are able to be conceived as possible to exist. In this sense then, style both is the result of a fundamentally human cognitive process and at the same time is a *learned* behavior.

Like language, style is symbolic reference. It represents both individual and group identity in such a way that one thing, such as a particular pattern, shape, or range of colors, is made to stand for another, some grouping of people. In early approaches to style, representation was often used to refer to group on an extremely large scale, such as a supposed ethnic or geographic group. In the absence of absolute dates, style was thus used as a chronological marker (see Conkey 1990, 7–8). This type of approach viewed the limits to variation as extremely broad, and particular styles became labels for otherwise undefined groups of people, such as the Beaker folk and the Lapita culture. In turn, these groups came to be viewed as restricted in time, and labels for "cultures" also became labels for chronological periods, such as the Aurignacian or the Solutrean (Conkey 1990, 8). Because group was constructed at such a large scale, extreme variation within it was inexplicable, and was therefore often relegated to equally inexplicable realms, such as ritual. The recent criticism of such approaches has spawned work aiming to narrow down the focus of style in order to concentrate on the nuances of stylistic differentiation that are possible *within* a single group. The limits to variability have come to be understood in part as intragroup context: as the product of the social differences created between raw materials, between men and women, between the sacred and the secular, or between shadings of social status for example.

With this has come a recognition that style as an expression of social identity is necessarily complex. There are multiple facets to personal identity that are linked to membership in different social groups on a variety of scales, and group membership may be predicated on a wide range of aspects of social inclusion. A person may have many identities, corresponding to the many contexts of their social behavior. Identity consists of a variety of components with which individuals can construct aspects of differentiation in different social situations (Shennan 1989,

20). Thus, a woman may be simultaneously feminist, archaeologist, daughter, and mother. She may even be, in other times and at other places, a taxpayer, a Labor Party voter, and a collector of art. Ponzio (1993) refers to identity genres, in which rights and duties are determined separately. Profession, social status, political party, sex, age, nationality, and ethnic group are all genres that may inform a single person's identity. The expression of identity through style, then, may be as multifaceted as the expression of identity through group membership.

Understanding style as contextual also entails a more challenging proposition: that style is not necessarily always a deliberately communicative message, but often only has the *potential* to be received as a message, thus consideration must be directed towards the ways in which style operates and the productive contexts within which artifacts are given form and meaning (Conkey 1990, 11, 14). Although a contextual approach to style still begins with the analytical necessity of mapping the incidence of stylistic "messages," and thus plotting group boundaries, it attempts to then move beyond this to question the situatedness behind these boundaries. How do boundaries relate to each another? Are they fixed or are they fluid? What are the contexts in which these boundaries exist and change?

It is this successive movement "behind and beyond" that is advocated in Wiessner's (1990, 110) argument for a two-tiered approach to stylistic studies: Initially, at a superficial level, analyzing style according to the expression of similarity versus difference, or simplicity and uniformity versus complexity and diversity, and then at a deeper level, with attention being paid to the symbolism beneath these perceived patterns in order to grasp the underlying nature of social relations. The first level is what Conkey (1990, 15) refers to as pattern recognition, the process of describing observable patterns of artifact variability and relating them to group social relations. The second level, however, aims at questioning how that observable patterning might be generated, and asking why those groups in those patterns at those times or what those particular expressions of social identity might convey about the participant's construction of the world and the relative positioning of people within it. This is what Conkey (1990, 15) terms pattern generation, and it is at this level that Wiessner argues style is capable of revealing the "central metaphors" accompanying social relations; in other words, and in my terms, ideology.

Considering any study of style as social comparison in terms of these two levels begins to indicate the sheer complexity with which style may represent identity and the fluidity with which "group" might be understood as dependent upon the context in which identity is created. It is in this nexus between the systematic study of the relationships between style and context that style comes closest to answering questions concerning ideology. Ideology may refer to *any* significant conjunction between discourse and power (whether predicated on age, gender, ethnicity, or class), and thus is often closely related to context. I understand context to be the situation in which identity is activated, as indicative of the many facets that imbue identity. Style becomes one archaeological manifestation of ideology through its role as the material expression of aspects of contextual identity, and the negotiation through this of competitive strategies of status and power.

Conkey (1990, 10) has argued that archaeological analyses of style should take an understanding of context as their premise. Style, like meaning, is not a fixed property, but is anchored in the discursive activity of the members of a community. It is grounded in the shifting terrain of different constructions of group membership, but is expressed in material artifacts. By stressing the role of context as a creator of style, Conkey and others have fastened attention onto a specific range of questions. Conkey considers these to be questions of pattern generation: Why *that* style in *that* place? Why *that* style at *that* time? (cf. Conkey 1993, 106). As Smith (1994, 147) has phrased it: "[groups] ... are mobilized at particular times for particular purposes. The question that then arises is why are particular forms of group activated in particular contexts of interpretation?"

It is through such an approach that material artifacts are often described as a "text" or a "discourse" (or at least part of one), which implicates meaning in the process of creating and maintaining social context(s). Discourse is the set of positioning arrangements within which identity and group (and the inequities that surround this) are negotiated. To reiterate Eagleton (1991, 9, emphasis added): discourse is not reducible merely to communication, but is the use of communication for *the production of specific effects* and is a function of an utterance and its particular social context. If an "utterance" can be communicated as much through the form or use of material items as through speech, then artifacts become implicated in the discursive process by which ideology is reproduced. For example, if spatial constructs and architectural styles are components of a discourse (if texts), they may be examined both in terms of how discourse enters into their construction (how the practice of construction, and the inclusion and exclusion of objects relates to the rules and patterns of discursive formations) and how, in consequence, buildings or planned environments become statements (Hirst 1985). Power is implicated in the process of creating social identity by constituting the conditions by which certain constructions of identity can come to exist and perhaps persist in the face of others. Ideology masks the asymmetry behind these different forms of identity, as well as also masking the spheres of power that legitimate and are, in turn, reinforced by this pattern.

Forging a link between ideology and style and then approaching it through the medium of architecture is not a new direction. Style in terms of the analysis of architecture—whether the façade or the plan— has recently become a focus for much historical archaeological research (see, for example, Anderson and Moore 1988; Johnson 1992; Leone 1994; Markell 1994; McGuire 1991; Mrozowski 1991; Palkovitch 1988). Bringing architecture into an archaeological study creates a peculiar problem in the understanding of style: While both disciplines may study it, they do not necessarily use it to mean the same thing.

Both architectural and archaeological style begin in the same place, with the morphological description of features and the relationships between them. Questions of style in architectural terms are generally directed towards seriating changes in architectural features, a practice that uses style as a basis for creating artifact types and chronologies. Style thus becomes the shorthand for a series of physical and morphological characteristics that go together in a known scheme (i.e., the broad design principles that underlie historical types). These schemes are predicated on an accumulation of architectural wisdom and are also referred to as "manner" (for example, a house may be said to be constructed in the Gothic or the Georgian manner). If an architectural style or manner is the coherence of particular sets of formal elements, it is also *prescriptive*, in that the "known scheme" is bound by rules that guide composition. Thus the limits to variation are tightly established. Style prescriptions were a major export to the colonies of European Empire (Markus 1993, 8) and have become entrenched over the last three centuries in the descriptive and legislative ways in which people interact with buildings. Architects, when dealing with style, commonly work within such prescriptions, and thus orient their studies towards the known schemes. Not all buildings are designed by architects, however, and in a town the size of Armidale, focusing on style as the province of professional designers, or even of popular interpretations of their designs, would exclude the majority of buildings from discussion. Many buildings in Armidale are excessively plain and unadorned and, although typical of any range of buildings, are problematic because they are not identifiable to any coherent style. It is the *absence* of a distinct manner that renders these buildings distinctive.

"Style," like "art" or "architecture," can be an eminently subjective term, and as Noble and Davidson (1996, 83) have argued for the terms "culture" and "symbol," may be given oppositional connotations associated with either mundane or highbrow meanings. While highbrow meanings imply particular value-laden judgments (style as restricted to the province of professional designers or to the art gallery), mundane meanings imply the less romantic opposite (style as the choices all people make between different options of form). Style as used by architects means stylish, and has far more highbrow connotations than style as used by archaeologists. As a value-laden category, style-as-stylish can become the means by which something is judged to be (or not to be) "Art" or "Architecture." This is one of the major differences between architectural and archaeological style. Architectural style is fundamentally concerned with assessing how a particular building fits within a known scheme, without being able to answer the more interesting question of why it may or may not conform. Archaeological style is less concerned with how a building *should* look as with *why* it may look a particular way; in this case, variation from the known scheme is not merely aberrant, but relevant. Although I retain the term "architectural style," I wish to make clear that I wield it in an archaeological sense. In this sense, I am using architecture (with a small a) as a convenient label to describe structural features, rather than as a judgment of a building's value (Architecture, with a capital A). By the term architectural style, I mean style that is analyzable in external structural features, as opposed to style in other areas of cultural production that archaeologists may investigate, such as rock art or pottery. I do not use it to refer to style as a known scheme (manner), but to particular features or groups of features that may be communicative.

Sequences of material artifacts thus become understood as combinations of material signs, and archaeological expressions of ideology become the ways in which, and means by which, these combinations of signs are embedded in relations of power between social groups who are continually negotiating their social identity in the world. Thus, analyzing ideology as it is constituted in material artifacts is essentially to question the constructedness of the social contexts in which producers of meanings, recipients of meanings, and the material items that may be implicated in those meanings interact. Ideology is meaning in the service of power (Thompson 1986, 7). Power is implicated in the process of creating social identity by constituting the conditions by which certain constructions of identity can come to exist, and perhaps persist, in the face of others. Ideology masks the asymmetry behind these different forms of identity, as well as also masking the spheres of power that legitimate, and are in turn reinforced, by this pattern.

STYLE AND THE SEMIOTICS OF SOCIAL IDENTITY

Ideology and style are closely linked, in that both are implicated in the continual process by which people construct their relative social identity in relation to other groups. This is the route by which ideology has come to be understood in part as a semiotic process, involving the relations between signified meanings and the various groups involved in producing and receiving those meanings.

At the base of semiotics lies the concept of the sign as a relational element. Peirce's (1985[1931]) vision of semiotics creates a three-tiered notion of what may constitute a sign, depending on the particular relationship between the sign and the thing that it represents. Both iconic signs and indexical signs exist in a direct relationship with the thing they represent: An icon is constructed as an analogous image; while an index is linked to its object through certain secondary characteristics generally acknowledged to be causal. Thus, flame is an icon of fire, while smoke, as caused by fire (even if the fire itself is not visible), is an index. In contrast, a symbol is a sign that has no direct connection or resemblance to its object. The relationship between a symbol and its referent is wholly arbitrary, and depends upon convention for its understanding. While the roman numeral II is iconic for example, in that the sign bears some resemblance to its object, the Arabic numeral 2 is a symbol. A symbol can thus be seen as communicative, in that through common convention it is shared with other members of society (Chase and Dibble 1992, 43–44). Although strictly speaking under this scheme a symbol is only one of three possible forms of sign, it is possible to speak more generally of an icon and an index functioning symbolically, in that both may be substituted to stand for an absent object.

As a material marker of identity then, style becomes symbolic of group, in that it functions as an indexical marker of membership in particular groups, as well as of those groups themselves. Through this symbolism, style promotes a group's self-identity and cohesiveness, maintains its boundaries, and arbitrates its interaction with other such groups (Sackett 1990, 36; see also Davidson 1995). Style, by virtue of its arbitrary and conventional association with particular groups in society, comes to be indexical of them and subsequently symbolic of the set of relations between that group and other groups. This is not a linear relationship, of course, but a circular one. As well as signifying positions of wealth, style may also index positions of poverty, but in the process, it may also signify the ways in which, and means by which, this difference is subverted and thus new indexes of difference are created. At any particular period, those features that symbolize the status difference are deemed by those who have them as stylish, but only so long as they constitute a recognizable system of difference. When concepts of stylishness become appropriated into alternative contexts, how are group boundaries maintained?

If style as an indexical marker persists into later contexts, when the particular grouping of identity it characterized no longer exists, it becomes a symbol in Peirce's understanding of the term—a sign that no longer has any direct resemblance or connection to the object it once marked. These previous coteries of status become symbolic to later observers (up to and including the archaeologist), and may well become incorporated into later contexts of meaning. It is crucial to remember that, for style to function as a symbol, there must be observers to whom it is meaningful, and among whom there is a convention that it stands for another thing (Noble and Davidson 1996, 68–69).

It is by this route that it is possible to understand the archaeological record as a composition of signs, which function in communicative behavior between and among groups of people (see Noble and Davidson 1996, 160–194). Archaeologists routinely analyze artifactual variability in terms of the expression of individual and group difference, which is itself one step removed from conjectures about ideology. The "signs, meanings, and values" part of my definition of ideology is what the archaeologist is analyzing, studying the material artifacts as signs, in a semiotic process as the vehicle through which ideology may be realized.

The Meaning of Persistence

Through its role as a communicative component of human interaction, style, in part, mediates the process of constructing social identity that all humans undertake. As an accessory to ideology, style is the material expression of aspects of contextual identity; and ideology is a facet of the assignment of meaning behind that construction. Ideology is fundamentally about providing meaning for particular characterizations of social identity, including some and excluding others. Ideology masks asymmetry by placing this characterization beyond human control, thus one of its meanings denies that difference is a socially constructed category. The archaeological study of style, however, is directed explicitly towards the opposite, that is, identifying the ways and means by which difference may be created socially through competing constructions of identity. Ideology may be one means of accessing Wiessner's second level of analysis, but ideology as a central metaphor, may give a particular meaning to the construction of particular contexts, and thus to the structuring of style within that context. Considering how context structures style is the study of generative processes—meaning as it is invested in each act of creation. Its aim is to articulate the constellation of social relations that gave rise to the construction of identity that produced that style. This set of social relations is what Handsman and Leone (1989) and Conkey (1990, 14) refer to as productive relations or productive context, the patterning of groups that gave rise to the creation of particular styles and the use of styles in particular ways.

Subsequent to the creation of a style, or an object in its particular contexts of production, are the various contexts in which interaction with that object takes place. There is meaning in every successive act of interpretation, and the longer an object endures, the more opportunities arise in which to interpret it. This is the context of visibility to which Wobst (1977, 328–330, 334–335) refers, that is, the place that an artifact occupies within the visible landscape and the possibilities for interaction with it that arise from this location. "Meaning" as a relationship arising from the continual use of material items is thus complicated by the many successive contexts in which those objects persist. This has repercussions for an archaeological investigation of ideology through the multiple meanings of style. Houses, gardens, or street plans, for example, are both highly visible and fixed features in the landscape, which often survive substantially intact through many successive historical contexts. This may extend to a time when they become classed as "heritage," and thus not only are preserved, but their very preservation is celebrated. Where this occurs—in other words, where sets of material remains persist into subsequent contexts—the material expression of ideology in itself becomes a "frieze," the physical motif of a previous configuration of social relations that extends into, and becomes part of, the present. Such a frieze makes an ideologically determined structure persist beyond the social relations that produced it and in such a visible way that it continues to be interacted with, and thus acquire meaning within, later contexts of interpretation.

Following from this is the question of how the persistence of each previous pattern, or frieze, may come to structure subsequent patterns. This succession is a continuum, and by no means the static sequence that my use of the term frieze might suggest. In any sequence there are likely to be common linking threads that both bind and direct change. While context certainly structures the range of possible meanings that may be assigned to stylistic choices, it is also possible that the range of previous choices that endure into, and inform aspects of, later contexts might also structure choice. This is particularly relevant when considering style in architecture and the negotiation of social identity, when the semiotic markers of relative social position persist into later contexts and thus become symbolic of particular groupings of people in the past. It is possible that, as a frieze of a previous social landscape, those architectural features provide both a benchmark for subsequent constructions of stylishness and a reminder of previous social boundaries that have since been subverted and renegotiated. While context certainly structures style then, it is also necessary to question the reverse: How might style structure context?

A Note on Meaning

In connecting style to symbolic behavior through the vehicle of semiotics, my position holds that there is at least some emic meaning to be gained from the analysis of style. Style is not just "something that informs," although the term is sometimes reduced to this etic position, but also "something that mediates," a behavior that was intentionally created and manipulated by the participants, as much as by the observer. Chase (1991, 195) recognizes this duality when he separates the meaning of style as the intent to communicate from the meaning of style as the recognition of the material patterning produced by that intent. By meaning, I do not wish to imply that it is possible to get inside another person's head, nor do I hold that there is *a* meaning to be associated with a given material artifact. Just as there can be more than one meaning attached to an anecdote or to a person's actions, so too are there many possible meanings associated with an artifact implicated in the myriad strategies of human behavior. It is not the case that artifacts or sequences of artifacts constitute a single text of the meanings associated with them, since meaning clearly changes with context. Various people in different groups (remembering that group may change over time as well as across space) may well interpret the same object or arrangement of objects in completely different ways.

As Howard Morphy's (1991) analysis of Yolngu paintings illustrates, meaning is an often hierarchical and always slippery category. A single painting or a part of one may have many meanings that are not held in common by all members of society. Which meaning is held applicable by which person is fundamentally a function of that person's relative position; in other words, their social context in terms of such factors as their age, their gender, or their moiety. As Davidson (1995) has argued, this very slipperiness implies that a painting may be in turn iconic, indexical, or symbolic, depending on the relative identity and knowledge of the interpreter. Paintings with more iconic representations (for example figurative motifs) belong to a wider, less restricted context, accessible in at least some degree to outsiders and the uninitiated.

While there may be elements of iconicity in the more geometric paintings that belong to a restricted "inside" context, they are "primarily indexical and ultimately symbolic," in that their meanings are not so immediately associative (Davidson 1995, 890). The issue of meaning between inside and outside becomes not "how many?," as in either context there may be multiple meanings, but of "to whom does it mean?," and what criteria of group membership this knowledge marks.

This is a crucial aspect of archaeological style: How does it help to constitute groups? How is the construction of a group mediated by access to the knowledge and position associated with that style? This links style firmly to power and to the differential power relations involved in creating and maintaining in-groups and out-groups. It is along this route that style is most closely linked to ideology, particularly when ideology is envisioned as the mask behind which exclusion is negotiated. In other words, if ideology masks social asymmetry created through different patterns of inclusion and exclusion, then the material expression of this patterning—style—may be a reliable archaeological indicator of past ideology.

It is time to situate the theory within the particular historical and social contexts that informed the construction of Armidale. What groups of people lived here? How did they interact? How might they have constructed their own identity and that of others through the medium of style in architecture?

An Introduction to Armidale | 3

Armidale is a small city in the state of New South Wales, located approximately halfway between Sydney, the state capital, and Brisbane, the capital of the adjacent state of Queensland. The wider region that encompasses the city is known as New England, which sits astride a particularly prominent section of the Great Dividing Range. Because of its height above sea level, Armidale and its immediate environs are often referred to as the Tablelands.

The first white people to enter what became the New England area were, in characteristic colonial fashion, male explorers. Surveyor-General John Oxley traversed the region with his party in 1818, followed by later journeys by other explorers in the late 1820s and early 1830s. The site that would become the city of Armidale was a focus for activity as early as 1841. The population slowly increased until by 1851 Armidale was one of the three largest population centers outside of Sydney and its environs (Kass 1991, 9). It was officially proclaimed a town in 1849, a municipality in 1863, and a city in 1885.

My intention in presenting a history of Armidale is to give both a sense of the forms capitalism has taken there in the past, and a gross idea of the groups that have been involved in its construction. As with the rest of Australia, it is not the case that capitalism has existed as a singular entity through all of Armidale's history, but has instead taken on a number of forms. It has been in continual development and redefinition as various sections of the population developed, and as the role of Australia in the international economy changed. In line with this, the composition of the ruling group has also changed, as has the composition and nature of the work force. Connell and Irving (1992) break down Australian history into five periods, which roughly correspond to the situation in Armidale. Each of these periods is either characterized by a distinctive form of capitalism or by a major class mobilization that occurred in response:

1. Pastoral capitalism (1788–1840).
2. Mercantile capitalism (1840–1890).
3. The working class challenge (1890–1930).

38   Chapter 3

4. Industrial capitalism (1930–1975).
5. Monopoly capitalism (1975–present).

I will only deal with the first four categories in this hierarchy as they apply to Armidale, as monopoly capitalism is too recent to be relevant to the subsequent archaeological discussion.

Under pastoral capitalism, surplus value is appropriated through control over livestock, chiefly sheep and cattle, and their products. Until the 1840s, pastoral capitalism lacked the full technical (fixed capital) and social (wage-labor market) relations characteristic of other forms of capitalism (McMichael 1984, 150). Surplus value in mercantile capitalism, on the other hand, is appropriated through control over trade or credit, rather than through the ownership or modernization of the production process itself. Thus, mercantile capital is composed of areas of capitalist activity specializing in the purchase and sale of commodities, rather than in production (Wells 1989, xvi). As opposed to mercantile capitalism, industrial capitalism entails ownership over the production process itself. It is a developed form of commodity production that is based upon the use of machinery and non-human energy, and the application of a complex division of labor to achieve improvements in productivity and, thus, greater potential for surplus value. Industrial capital includes those areas of capitalist activity specializing in the actual production of commodities, as opposed to the financing or circulation of those commodities (Wells 1989, xv–xvi).

The categories in this hierarchy are both chronologically defined and theoretically distinct, and are designed to apply predominantly to the experience of capitalism as it took place in an urban setting. As they apply to Armidale and the New England region, both the chronological separations and the content of these categories must be revised. Capitalism in the New England region has moved through a similar sequence of forms in its 160 year European history—chiefly concentrating around pastoral, mercantile, and, to a limited extent, industrial (although this is largely restricted to small-scale manufacture) capital. Armidale is a small town that existed in this net of wider relationships that constructed capitalism. Armidale and its region were both embedded in the large-scale processes that informed these categories, although precisely how it articulated depended on particular processes that operated at the local level. As a heuristic device, Connell and Irving's categories not only provide a sense of the changing structure of the ruling class, as well as of the responses of the working class, but also of the forms of ideology that may have accompanied these categories. I will deal first with an outline of the composition and values of the groups themselves, before I move on to an introduction to their accompanying ideologies. As part of this process I will sketch the gross spatial elements structuring these relationships and their possible material manifestations.

It is worth a preliminary note to consider the distinction between class and status, which are two specific, but different, social relationships. Each of Connell and Irving's categories presents social relationships in terms of class rather than status; as a relationship between owners and non-owners of the means of production (Wild 1978, 3). In Connell and Irving's terms, class is viewed as a relationship between an individual and the control of investments and resources, decision-making, the physical means of production and labor power (see Wright 1978; 1989). While I recognize that class is a problematic analytical category (see discussion in Connell and Irving 1987, or Wright 1989, for example), it is a useful shorthand for expressing three crucial distinctions in the broad dichotomy of owners versus non-owners (see Wild 1978, 3):

- Between the propertied and the propertyless
- Between employers and employees
- Between the leisured and the workers

People are not always categorizable in terms of the black-and-white distinctions of owner or worker, particularly on the small scale that characterizes Armidale. There are two crucial points to Wild's three distinctions: their shading helps to place people in a continuum from those elite members of the community who are propertied, own the means of production, and do not work, to those at the other end who are propertyless and work for their living; and the position of a person on this continuum may in part be a contributor to the status with which they are accorded. Status is a relationship between people of disparate prestige, and a status group is one that shares a common lifestyle and generally accepted forms of conduct that are recognized as bases for interaction, such as dress, accent, or the application of membership sanctions in voluntary organizations (Wild 1978, 2). Not all people of the same class are necessarily accorded the same status, however, and this in part helps to explain ideological divisions among members of the same class. While in theory, for example, all members of the working class are placed in the same antagonistic relationship to capital, it is not necessarily the case that all members of the working class consider themselves to be in the same group. While some merchants in Armidale possessed equal wealth to some pastoralists, they did not necessarily recognize each other as similarly prestigious. Likewise, there were similar status distinctions operating between workers: A person may be simultaneously an employer and a worker; propertied and an employee. This returns to the complex issue of the construction of social identity and how this may inform the construction of ideology.

One of the crucial aspects to Connell and Irving's differentiation between types of capital is a differentiation between status groups. It is possible that status, as well as class, is a basis upon which ideology is formed, and even that status constructs different ideologies to class. Having said this, as part of sketching the gross relationships between owner and worker under each form of capitalism, I will also consider the relationship between status and class.

A HISTORY OF ARMIDALE AND NEW ENGLAND

Pastoral Capitalism: The "Squattocracy" of New England (1830–1890)

The form of capitalism that came to order colonial Australian society in the first 52 years of settlement, after development of a limited labor market and the organization of production along capitalist lines, was the sharply polarized structure centering on the assignment system within the pastoral industry (Connell and Irving 1992, 56–58). In many respects the emergence of a pastoral ruling elite was a direct reflection of the institutional centrality of the state, as pastoral capitalism initially emerged to provide the state with necessary supplies and was monopolized by a select group of officer-traders (Buckley and Wheelwright 1992, 34–36; Turner 1992, 161). Even after a "private" economy had developed, the state continued to be a major supplier of the means of production, in particular in the form of land grants and convict labor (Turner 1992, 161).

Initially pastoralism was restricted to the Limits of Location, first defined in 1826 in an attempt to control the spread of settlement in New South Wales by containing settlers within a manageable area.

Limited to the 19 counties surrounding Sydney, the Limits of Location stretched as far north as the Hunter Valley, encompassing an area of some 90,000 km². It was only within this area that the Government controlled the sale or leasing of land, and until 1836, no attempt at all was made to control occupation outside the Limits.

The Limits of Location were officially expanded under the 1839 Crown Lands Act, when Governor Sir George Gipps proclaimed nine newly formalized pastoral or squatting districts, one of which was New England (Atchison 1977, 173). Despite lying beyond the boundaries of officially sanctioned settlement until 1839, squatters eager to amass land and wealth were already present in New England, running mainly sheep, but also cattle, at least seven years earlier. "Squatter" is a peculiarly Australian term, originally applied to persons who had occupied land for pastoral purposes without official sanction. The term later took on a distinctive class meaning, carrying a capitalistic suggestion and encoding a particular level of social prestige (Buckley and Wheelwright 1992, 267). The pastoral boom of the 1830s and 1840s was the first of two major surges of capital inflow into Australia.

Between 1832 and 1836, the first large pastoral holdings were established in the New England region: Wolka by Hamilton Collins Semphill in 1832; Gostwyck by Edward Gostwyck Cory in 1833, acquired by Henry Dangar in 1834; Kentucky by J. Chilcott in 1834; Tilbuster by William Dumaresq in 1835; and Gyra by Peter McIntyre in 1836. There is some debate over the dates for establishment of the other early station, Henry Dumaresq's Saumarez, with estimates ranging from 1834 (Oppenheimer 1988) to 1836 (Atkinson 1987); however, it was certainly well established by the latter date.

The majority of these squatters were already holders of substantial land holdings in other parts of New South Wales (notably the Hunter Valley region to the south), and although their expansion into New England corresponds to the tail end of the period as defined by Connell and Irving, it was still very much an expression of pastoral capitalism. In terms of the original land grantees, wealth in the region was concentrated almost exclusively in land, stock, wages, and equipment. Occupying land beyond the Limits of Location, however, meant more than just voluntarily moving beyond the bounds of "civilized society": it also meant occupying land that was not officially recognized as "ownable." Although the government did not prohibit squatting beyond the Limits of Location, it did refuse to sell land there and technically the owner of all such properties remained the Crown. Squatters thus had no title to pastoral runs unless the land had been officially alienated through a grant. Most of the Hunter Valley properties belonging to the New England squatters were occupied as a result of the land grants system; however, the "ownership" of their New England runs was not so official.

By the 1820s, sheep and cattle running had become the most profitable land-based economic activities, and in 1840 Australia was providing 20% of all British wool imports, a figure that had risen to 53% by the late 1840s (Buckley and Wheelwright 1992, 80; Morris 1986, 8). The rapid expansion of the pastoral industry in Australia was closely geared to the industrialism of the English textile industry. Australian wool rapidly replaced the German and the Spanish product, and continued to do so throughout the nineteenth century (Morris 1986, 8–9). Pastoralism, or the export of wool, was unique in its possession of overseas markets. It has been estimated that by 1850 pastoralism constituted one of the largest concentrations of land ownership in the world, with 42 squatters holding 13.6 million acres out of a total of 73 million occupied in New South Wales alone (Buckley and Wheelwright 1992, 3). In essence, Australia was drawn into the world economy through the pastoral emphasis on wool production, the powerful pastoral class of wool producers establishing links to urban centers through merchant capital, and to world markets through the London banking system (Turner 1992, 162).

As a consequence, pastoralism was the dominant form of wealth in the colony, although there was a high cost of entry (Buckley and Wheelwright 1992, 81). In the 1840s, estimates for establishing a station ranged from £500 to £8,000, and as pastoralism often relied on patronage to secure the necessary land grants or convict labor, this virtually guaranteed that only established merchants or gentlemen with imported personal or family capital from England could gain entry (Connell and Irving 1992, 43–44). When the colonial government instituted changes to the system that regulated squatting lands, they were also deliberately manipulating the social structure and regulating who could and could not gain entry. In 1831 this was manifested in a decision within the Limits of Location to abolish the land grants system and to allow Crown Land to be alienated only by sale at a minimum price of 5 shillings an acre. This was a large enough sum to keep small graziers out, but not large enough to seriously hamper larger proprietors (Buckley and Wheelwright 1992, 49, 72). It also effectively excluded ex-convicts or non-moneyed free settlers from acquiring land, while allowing established landholders or emigrants with capital to monopolize ownership. Because of the high cost of entry, pastoralism was very much a gentleman's pursuit. It has been argued that in following this policy the state was seeking to concentrate pastoral society into a sharp division between landowners and proletarians through artificially maintaining the price of land (Turner 1992, 161): "it was not enough simply to arrange for laborers to go to Australia: in the interests of capital, they must remain laborers" (Buckley and Wheelwright 1992, 72).

Karl Marx (1902, 791–800) argued that the aim of these artificial prices was to transform the peasant into a wage laborer and the system was envisioned as a self-perpetuating one: The money accruing from sale of land was then used to assist the passage of emigrants from

An Introduction to Armidale

England—in other words, to import still more laborers for the benefit of employers, particularly graziers (Buckley and Wheelwright 1992, 75). Until 1836 the earliest pastoralists in New England (Semphill, Dangar, Dumaresq) were essentially acquiring large tracts of land for free, and would have been unaffected by these rulings unless they also occupied land within the Limits of Location. After 1836, a series of Crown Lands Acts saw the first attempts by the government to regulate the position of the squatters, in the institution of the system of Pastoral Districts under the supervision of Crown Lands Commissioners. After New England became a Pastoral District in 1839, squatters were required to obtain government licenses at a nominal fee. The Crown Lands Commissioner, George MacDonald, had the responsibility of policing this obligation and of defusing the friction between landholders caused by such unregulated competitive acquisition.

During the late 1840s, the power base of the squatters began to come under increasing threat from the Crown's attempts to regulate the land apportioning system in Australia. Governor Gipps' suggested reforms of the squatting system in the 1840s met with severe opposition from the squatters, and in 1847 their demands for preemptive leasing rights over pastoral lands were granted for a period of 8 to 14 years (Buckley and Wheelwright 1992, 92). These leases were exclusive for the term of the contract, as was the option to purchase, and the "rights" of the squatters were protected absolutely from other interference for that period. Upon expiration of this leasing system in 1861, the Robertson Land Acts came into effect. This series of acts was designed ostensibly to alienate all Crown Land for the purchase of any selector, and to regulate the amount of land that could be held by any one selector, large or small. Essentially they made land freely transferable, like other commodities in a capitalist society (Buckley and Wheelwright 1992, 117).

Prompted by the growing parliamentary dominance of the urban bourgeoisie, these land acts were intended as a political weapon against the economic power of the squatters (McMichael 1984, 245). Prior to 1847, the squatters' rights and titles to land had been technically unstable, but because of the close patronage connection between pastoral gentry and government, their power base had been virtually absolute. This situation was threatened temporarily in 1847, until squatter privilege was reestablished by long-term leasehold rights to their occupied land, although for a set period of 14 years (McMichael 1984, 245). After 1861 and the enactment of the Robertson Land Acts, pastoral rights and titles to land again became unstable in the face of what was intended to be more egalitarian competition.

Despite the increasing legal restraints on the occupation of land, established pastoralists were still able to accumulate or hold onto large estates and to circumvent free selectors acquiring significant portions of their leaseholds. Grace and Henry Dangar were able to accomplish this successfully for their Gostwyck estate in New England (Ferry 1988), as was Henry Arding Thomas at Saumarez (Ferry 1994, 220–239). Wells (1989, 74) sees the sequence of events from 1847 to 1861 as a conversion from pastoral dominance as a political right to pastoral dominance as an economic right based on secure tenure. Unlike the situation in England, the pastoralists lost their privileged political right to the use of landed property as part of this process, and the colonial aristocracy was placed increasingly on the defensive (Wells 1989, 74). Despite this, another boom in wool production lasting until the 1890s ensured that pastoralism continued as a dominant form of capitalism, and many wealthy pastoralists arrived in New England as part of this second wave. The top wealth holders in New South Wales throughout the nineteenth century were always pastoralists, and many of the graziers of New England were often included amongst this privileged elite (Ferry 1994, 300–301). The occupation of runs in New England was occurring against this background, and the social distance that this implied was clearly remarked upon in New England. Thomas Tourle, the owner of Balala station, commented to his sister in the early 1840s that, "New England is considered by far the most aristocratic part of New South Wales, almost all the young settlers are either Oxford or Cambridge" (quoted in Walker 1966, 24).

Wealth in terms of the original New England land grantees originated more in their privileged position within colonial society than with older family money. In New England, with three exceptions, all exploratory surveys and the pastoral expansion that subsequently followed hinged upon the presence of the Australian Agricultural Company (AAC) and the advantages that accrued to its employees (Atchison 1977, 140). A number of men involved with the AAC made good use of their knowledge, experience, and connections to establish or advance their own interests. Henry Dangar, for example, a surveyor with the AAC, made a number of early forays into the region and may have helped to facilitate the movements of both Edward Gostwyck Cory and Hamilton Collins Semphill into pastoral holdings on the tablelands (Atchison 1977, 146). Dangar possessed the added advantage of family money held in estates in Cornwall (Ferry 1988), and himself acquired large pastoral domains in New England. Henry Dumaresq, in particular, through his position as Commissioner of the Australian Agricultural Company and also as brother-in-law to Governor Darling, was able to amass large grants of land spread over a wide area of eastern New South Wales.

In turn, Henry often supported other family members in a variety of ways, including his brother William, who also squatted in New England (Atchison 1977, 146–147; Oppenheimer 1988). Later in the century, the White family's extensive pastoral holdings in the Hunter Valley and New England were also established as a result of James White's involvement with the AAC, and although the Whites were a part of the second wave of New England pastoralism, the pattern was familiar.

Under this gentrified social elite pastoralism created a hierarchical, patriarchal society, with a deep gulf of status, property, and power separating those with wealth from those without wealth. As a group, the pastoral social elite sought the traditional prestige of large land ownership and maintained cohesion through informal networks, such as marriage, women's contact (through correspondence, visits, entertainments, and a general "policing of gentility"), clubs, schooling, and the magistracy, rather than formal political organization (Connell and Irving 1992, 57; Denholm 1979). Largely because the system of transportation on which this attempt to create a pastoral ruling class was based came to an end in the early 1850s, a plantation-like structure of convict–pastoral relations did not come to dominate later Australian society (Connell and Irving 1987, 54; 1992, 58). Additionally, the squatting boom in the early 1860s caused further disruption to the assignment-based land-owning structure, although this did not signal an end either to pastoral capitalism or to attempts to create a hierarchical ruling society. The case in New England continued to mirror the situation in other parts of New South Wales, and in a sense was a smaller act in the overall drama. One of the key factors in promoting the rapid growth and dominance of pastoralism as a form of capitalism was the close connection between those who aspired to own large tracts of land and the government, both in the colony and abroad, that controlled it.

This symbiosis was nowhere more apparent than in the system of the magistracy. In 1858, for example, 9 out of 10 magistrates on the Armidale Bench were either squatters or station superintendents, the one exception being William Richard Bligh, who, although not a pastoral property owner in New England, was nevertheless a senior Government bureaucrat and the grandson of a former governor of the Australian colonies (Ward 1976). Connell and Irving (1992, 37) argue that the institution of the magistracy in particular articulated the scheme of partnership between state and pastoralists into a manageable system. The origins of this system dated from the 1820s, when pastoral capitalism expanded and the pastoralists themselves became an arm of the state, as a "a vast outdoor department of penal supervision," while the state in turn became a partner of the pastoralists, both supplying labor and guaranteeing its discipline. The magistrates responsible for the supervision and discipline of the convict labor force and the major pastoral landholders were one and the same individuals, a coincidence (though hardly coincidental) that reproduced the English combination of economic with legal power to create a local gentry (Connell and Irving 1992, 37–38).

The manufacturing of such a gentry was often facilitated by Governors who chose to exercise their patronage and select particular settlers to fulfill the magisterial and judicial functions traditionally performed in England by the aristocracy and the gentry (Denholm 1979, 166). In 1852 Godfrey Charles Mundy described Matthew Henry Marsh, of Boorolong and Salisbury Court, as "one of the many gentlemen of superior condition and education, university men and others, practicing bucolics in this country, who have gained for the squatters the title of the aristocracy of New South Wales." This image was reinforced through the interconnections between state and capital, between patronage and prestige, and between individual members and families of the "ruling" class itself. The idea of a pastoral aristocracy did not necessarily imply the unequal distribution of wealth *per se*, but rather the conception of an hereditary elite: Membership of the gentry was thus far more about status and forms of social power than merely about wealth. The intricacies of marriage networks typify the elite cohesion maintained by the colonial squattocracy through marriage with other powerful colonial families and with minor members of English nobility (Denholm 1985, 175). This characteristic pattern extended well into the New England region and the late nineteenth century (Figure 3.1).

Shepherds and Shearers: the Pastoral Workforce

Because the first settlers of New England acquired their property through the land grant system, which ran on patronage, there were two broad groupings of people during this time—a few propertied employers and a large group of propertyless employees. In 1841, for example, at a time when nearly half of the population were convicts, 71% of the New England population worked as laborers and 87% of these were employed as either shepherds or stockmen. In contrast, only 1% of the population were classed as "landed proprietors, merchants, bankers or professional persons." Although transportation of convicts to New England ceased in 1851, the number of people employed as laborers was to remain fairly constant throughout the nineteenth century (see Gilbert 1982, chapter 2 and accompanying tables). The emphasis, however, gradually shifted from shepherds and laborers, to shearers, stockmen, and boundary riders (Walker 1963, 79).

An Introduction to Armidale

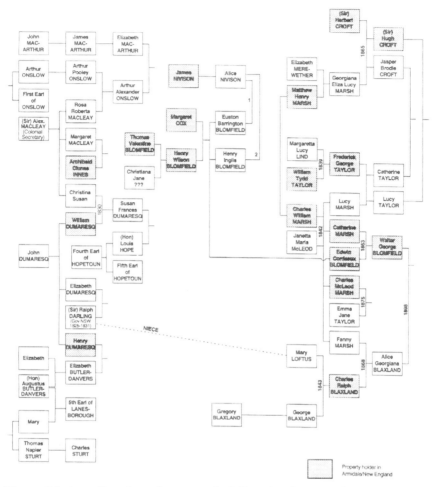

Figure 3.1. An outline of marriage networks influencing the pastoral presence in New England.

Although convicts formed the bulk of propertyless employees in the 1840s, Aborigines were also sometimes included within this grouping. Governor MacDonald noted in his series of annual reports that Aborigines were being employed as shepherds, stockmen, and house servants, and were paid in "wages as other ordinary servants" (quoted in Gilbert 1982, 29). The gold rushes near Armidale in the 1850s not only increased the demand for Aboriginal workers to be employed as "shepherds, grooms and ... house servants," but also their wages, as some were receiving payments "at the rate of £20 per annum" (quoted in Gilbert 1982, 29–30).

It seems that, although convicts and Aborigines were both forced to become part of a dispossessed propertyless class, convicts may have been part of a different status group than Aborigines. Particularly during the first half of the 1800s, the opinion that Aborigines were innocent and noble savages, while convicts were immoral degenerates, was current, prompting Commissioner Massie (MacDonald's successor) to point out to the Governor (quoted in Gilbert 1982, 30) "the bad example constantly set to the Natives by Stockmen and Shepherds ... from such a class of persons the Aboriginal can only get in exchange for their natural simplicity, a knowledge of the most degrading habits and vices."

This is a distinction in status that is accorded to each group by their employers, of course, and it is difficult to know how convicts and Aborigines regarded each other. Certainly both groups were often treated violently by squatters. Although there are many recorded instances of violent contact between Aborigines and squatters, particularly to the east of Armidale, and isolated recorded incidents on Salisbury Court (see Blomfield 1981, 37–38, 46–47; Rich 1990, 110), not all squatters had such a violent attitude to the Aborigines. Of particular note were the Everett brothers, who occupied Ollera, approximately 40 km to the north of Armidale, who not only employed Aborigines, but also successfully attempted to learn some of their dialects.

Pastoral Capitalism and the Construction of Space

The initial pastoral properties in New England were both extensive and poorly serviced. Many of them were first established by employees sent by pastoralists into new areas to claim land on their behalf, and most of their capital was invested in stock and wages. Goods were brought in by bullock dray and many pastoralists established private stores, inns, mail contracts, flour mills, and stock agencies to supply their stations (Oppenheimer 1977, 158). Henry Dangar, Henry Dumaresq, William Dumaresq, and the Dumaresqs' brother-in-law, Archibald Clunes Innes (who owned Furracabad to the north of Armidale and bought Kentucky from Chilcott by 1842), for example, all operated stores on their properties to supply their workers with basic goods and foodstuffs. The "scheming and enterprise" of William Dumaresq and Innes together prompted Alan Atkinson (1987) to argue that they may have been responsible for the site of Armidale becoming a major point in "a triangle of supply and communication" between their stations at

An Introduction to Armidale 49

Port Macquarie, the Hunter Valley, and New England. Innes established a store at the present site of Armidale in late 1841 to supply his other New England runs (Kentucky, Furracabad, Waterloo, and Beardy Plains) and expanded its interests by adding a postal service and mail run to the store's activities in 1843 (Atkinson 1987, 7–8). In the same year Dumaresq established an inn near the store to provide "decent" accommodation for travelers on the road (Atkinson 1987, 9).

The characteristic spatial patterning of the pastoral period was exemplified by a small nucleus of accommodation surrounding a head-station, with rudimentary service providers and several scattered out-stations. This pattern was repeated on each station and the work force was widely scattered. Many properties in the nineteenth century formed self-sufficient communities, complete with schools, public houses, and churches. Prior to 1852, the squatters and their stores were supplied with goods exclusively from either Sydney or Port Macquarie. Communications at this time were rudimentary: In the 1840s mail was carried in on a packhorse and all goods by bullock dray. Cobb and Co. did not begin passenger runs to the New England area until the late 1850s, and all the major overland roads were established by the mid-1850s (Figure 3.2).

Mercantile Capitalism: The Urban Middle-Class Alternative (1860–1890)

In the initial years of the colony, merchants and pastoralists were commonly one and the same and, as capital was easily transferred between land, stock, and trade, the merchants in no sense formed a separate class (Connell and Irving 1992, 59–60). Trade only became a more specialized activity after 1820, although most of it continued to be carried on by individuals or by private partnerships rather than by companies. This period opened with a surge of self-employment, with both the rapid expansion of capital markets during the gold rushes and a contraction in the degree of state intervention in the labor market. As the economy diversified, so too did mercantile capital, becoming organized on a variety of bases, such as banks, building societies, companies, business associations, and insurance companies (Connell and Irving 1992, 83–84). As most rural land had been appropriated by the squatters, the main avenues for private investment lay in the growth of the urban centers; the leading capitalists who emerged in this way were mainly based in the capital cities, although in towns like Armidale there was also a level of mobilization by country-town merchants and local manufacturers (Buckley and Wheelwright 1992, 8).

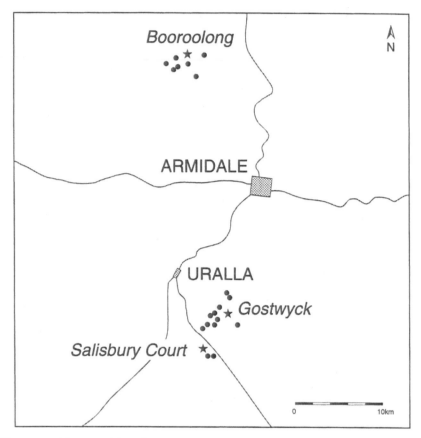

Figure 3.2. The spatial distribution of wealth and workforce under pastoral capitalism.

This growth in a new group and form of capitalism was so pronounced that by the 1840s a uniform colonial ruling class no longer existed and there was struggle for control of the state between rival social orders, that is, plantation/pastoral capitalism versus *laissez-faire* capitalism (Connell and Irving 1992, 94). Although Armidale and New England were hardly at the center of events occurring in the capital cities, they nevertheless experienced a similar struggle between competing forms of capitalism. Pastoral capital, entrenched in the rural hinterland, periodically clashed with mercantile capital, particularly over the direction intended for New England; this struggle was most frequently manifested through government. The squatters dominated the state parliament and some were often challenging political leadership through the particular issue of the revival of transportation. In 1852 the squatter of Salisbury Court, Matthew Henry Marsh, who was the only candidate to stand for New England in the Legislative Assembly in 1851, agitated not only for the revival of transportation, but also for the separation of New England from the rest of New South Wales and for its inclusion with Moreton Bay in Queensland. As a pastoralist, it was in his own interests to prolong the supply of relatively cheap convict labor; however, "the town" (i.e., the urban mercantile capitalists) was conscientiously opposed to this, and he lost the election.

In the early 1860s, this political struggle between rival social orders became solidified through the competing agencies of the Legislative Assembly and the Municipal Council. As a legacy of the magistracy, those individuals representing New England in the colonial legislature in Sydney were predominantly conservative squatters, while exclusive dominance of the Armidale Municipal Council (incorporated in 1863) was held by urban mercantile capitalists.

In Armidale, "mercantile capital" was never really "mercantile" in the same sense or scale as the leading merchants and financiers of the capital cities, who were directly linked to the London market. In Armidale, mercantile capital was concentrated more in terms of at least five fairly distinct groups of people: professionals and senior bureaucratic officials; small contractors; self-employed businessmen, such as shopkeepers or innkeepers; farmers; and gold miners (Figure 3.3). All of these occupations were established fairly early on, and there was often an interconnection between groups, with many individuals participating in more than one sphere. Mercantile capital in Armidale was mostly held by storekeepers and innkeepers, such as John Moore, John Trim, James Tysoe, Franklin Jackes, Joseph Scholes, John Richardson, and Edward Allingham or, later, the Hillgrove mine owners James Miller and Patrick McKinlay (Ferry 1994, 301). These urban mercantile capitalists have been variously referred to as "city fathers" or "self-made men" (Walker 1966, 102), and their wealth came close to rivaling that of the squatters, although never exceeding it (Ferry 1994, 300–301). Although half of all the deceased estates exceeding £6000 in Armidale and its surrounding area belonged to pastoralists, the remainder belonged to urban storekeepers, professionals, and mining entrepreneurs (Ferry 1994, 301).

There are many indications, however, that although New England pastoralists may have ranked among the top wealth holders in the state, urban capitalists within Armidale were relatively small scale compared to their counterparts elsewhere. There was a certain degree of

	William Palmer	Barnett Moses	John Richardson	John Trim	John Trim Jnr	George Nott	Joseph Scholes	John Moore	George Allingham	James Tysoe	Henry Mallam	Franklin Jackes	Richard Jenkins	Bernard Herzog	John Bliss	John Mather
Inn-keeping							1854-1858 Crown Inn / 1858 New England Hotel		1858-1896 New Daniel O'Connell Inn	1858-1870s? Freemason's Hotel / St. Kilda Hotel / 1889? Club Hotel						
Flour milling			1879 NE Flour Co. / 1880s?					1867 Steam Flour Mill			1874-1877 Partner NE Flour Co.					
Brewing /cordial													1865 ⇒ 1875			
Brick yards	1867					1901										
Tin/ iron factory														1866		
Tannery		1866 / 1872? Armidale Tannery	1872-?							1866 Armidale Tannery					1892-1897	
Boot shoe factory		1868									1870 Partner in Moses' factory					
Stores				1846 Commercial Store	1882 West End Stores			1857-1872 / 1878 New Store	1896 NE Co-op Butchery		1864 Chemist	1864 West End Store			1874 Great Northern Butchery	1846 Armidale Store
Other		1885 Partner in Armidale Gas Co.		1874-1877 Partner NE Flour Co.	Chaff Factory	Sawmill and Joinery works		Partner in Armidale Gas Co.								

⇒ Indicates change of ownership   Commercial Store Name or other description of property overlap here, of course, in that some pastoralists, such as Innes and Dumaresq, initially owned stores and inns within the town, and some urban mercantilists, such as Edward Allingham and Franklin Jackes, later became farmers and graziers (see Ferry 1994, Appendix 5.1).

It has been argued that one consequence of gold mining was the development of such urban capital, along with new markets that favored the development of an urban bourgeoisie in opposition to the pastoral class (McMichael 1984, 207; Turner 1992, 162). Although gold was "discovered" in New England and in the vicinity of Armidale as early as the 1850s, this did not appear to generate much commercial benefit to Armidale until the establishment of the larger finds around Hillgrove, which for a time proved extremely lucrative during the 1880s and 1890s (King 1963, 98; Steel 1990). By this time the schism between pastoralism and urban mercantilism was not as pronounced as it had been 20 years earlier. The period from 1860 to 1890 saw the second major surge of capital inflow into Australia. This was concentrated in three areas: accelerated urban development in the two main commercial centers, Melbourne and Sydney; railway construction throughout Australia; and the wool industry (Morris 1986, 12). Increased capital investment during this time can also be seen in rural centers such as Armidale, of course: The appearance of the town center was greatly affected by the heavy expenditure on public buildings in the 1860s (Walker 1966, 102), the railway reached the town in 1883, and several large pastoral holdings were established around Armidale in the 1880s.

Constructing Workers

Capitalism throughout this period was not just the meeting ground for a clash between rival social groupings, but also a process of incorporating an ever-growing work force. Under the pastoral assignment system, convicts were laborers for as long as their sentence lasted and had little grounds on which to bargain with their employers. As mercantile capitalism expanded, however, so too did a pool of "free" laborers, a factor with which capitalism in both mercantile and pastoral spheres had to come to terms. As Connell and Irving (1992, 106–107) have argued, there was a "hegemony in the making" during this time, which had little to do with the "benefits of civilization" or the "advances of progress," and much to do with incorporating workers into a system that relied utterly upon their labor, but not upon their individualism.

Investment in a building society or a bank, for example, was helping to create a hegemonic situation by drawing workers within the system and making them dependent upon it (Connell and Irving 1992, 107). In

1886, anyone buying a home through a mortgage was also acquiring "a stake in the country, and it is in his [sic] interest ... to avoid and fight shy of all revolutionary and disquieting or facetious movements, such as strikes, violent political agitation, or any[thing] calculated to hinder [the country's] advancement." (quoted in Buckley and Wheelwright 1992, 162). The key to hegemony, and hence ideology, is that people *participate* in it and the dominant group dominates, not through coercion, but through pursuing policies that can be represented plausibly as in the interests of everyone (Bocock 1986, 63).

The Schools of Art and the Mechanic's Institutes can also be viewed as part of this hegemonic process, as can the various friendly societies or benefit societies. The lessons to be learned here were essentially about self-government and order: "there was a great stress on rules, and on [the] penalties for breaching them, and on rituals and other formalities of meeting procedure, which inculcated orderliness and regularity" (Connell and Irving 1992, 106–107). The rituals may seem trivial, but they were a part of ordinary peoples' incorporation into a system of work.

Although he does not link it to capitalism, John Ferry has clearly articulated the stress that was placed upon respectability as a regime of rules during the 1860s and 1870s in Armidale, manifest in the increasing strictures on the behavior and conduct of bank employees, the tightening of legal sanctions governing a range of public order offenses, and the separation of the spheres of public and domestic life (Ferry 1994, 200, 202–204, 265–268). Hegemony was also constructed through a growing emphasis on colonial or national identification throughout this period. In contrast to the visions of the squatters, which were linked explicitly to English precedents as their wool trade was linked explicitly to English capital and markets (Buckley and Wheelwright 1992, 83; McMichael 1984, 243), urban mercantile capitalism expanded in tandem with spectator sports and organized sporting events (Connell and Irving 1992, 106). These played a large part in creating a colonial or national identity among workers and capitalists alike. In Armidale, organized horse racing appeared as early as 1842, and from this date spectator sport expanded rapidly. Cricket was played almost weekly from 1850 (Duncan 1951, 30) (often playing visiting overseas teams by the 1880s); by 1869 Armidale boasted the existence of the Armidale and New England Jockey Club (an athletic club), and in 1899 there was also the Armidale Golf Club (Gilbert 1982, 202–206). A growing sense of identity was commensurate with growing urban capitalism—at least one of the agendas of the shop assistants' holiday movement (ably directed by some of the leading urban capitalists) was steered towards a monthly holiday program of sports and picnics (Ferry 1994, 107).

An Introduction to Armidale

Mercantile Capitalism and the Construction of Space

Although there was a store and an inn on the site of Armidale by 1843, this was still an extension of pastoral capital. Both were owned by pastoralists and staffed by their representatives, established expressly to cater to the needs of fellow squatters (Atkinson 1987). An emerging urban focus for the site cannot be credited until six years later, when Armidale possessed five inns, four stores, a flour mill, a blacksmith, two churches, and a school. By this time Innes had gone bankrupt and John Mather had taken over his store. Although Armidale was first surveyed in 1846, a subsequent survey in 1849 records the growth of urban mercantile capital (Figure 3.4).

Most capitalists in early Armidale resided at the same location as their place of work: Robert Kirkwood beside his flour mill, Robert George Martin beside his inn, and John Mather beside his store, for example. There was a small scattering of workers around the edges of town and in the midst of the service providers (Figure 3.5).

In 1849, when Armidale was surveyed for the second time, it had only a rudimentary network of streets, mostly aligned to the major overland routes. One of the purposes of the 1849 survey was to establish the layout of the town proper and to regulate the future placement of buildings. Initially, the surveyor, Galloway, envisaged a rigid grid system oriented to the four compass points; however, his original proposal was objected to by the residents of Armidale "... in consequence of the streets running through all the public houses (five in number) and some private houses" (*Maitland Mercury* 12/6/1848). Galloway's grid ran directly through all the major concentrations of urban capital in town and the private houses of capitalists John Moore, Abraham O'Dell, and George Allingham. Not surprisingly, the public petition to the Governor resulted in Galloway being instructed to reorient the grid, resulting in the rotation of 8° from north, which characterizes the present streetscape (Figure 3.6).

Although one purpose of Galloway's grid may have been to establish the extent of the town proper, another of its purposes may also have been to promote public order through its network of straight streets (cf. Kostoff 1991, 230–232). It was certainly Galloway who remarked in 1849 that he was glad to hurry away from Armidale because of "the low debauchery of the place, which seduces them [his men] into great irregularities" (cited in Gilbert 1982, 79). In 1850, Galloway's design was acknowledged as having brought a "more regular and business-like appearance" to the town (*Maitland Mercury* 4/24/1850) and by the late twentieth century this ideological message had become firmly entwined with the rising fortunes of mercantile capitalism: "The 'more regular

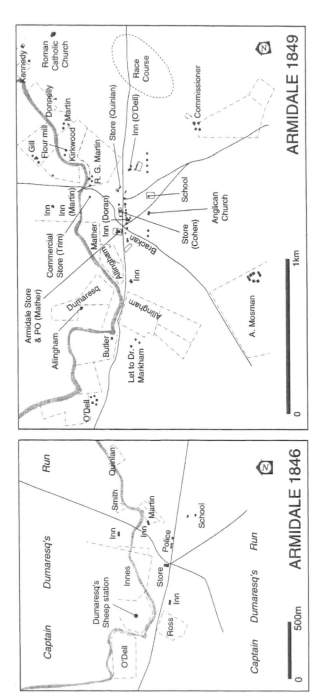

Figure 3.4. Two plans for Armidale—1846 and 1849.

An Introduction to Armidale

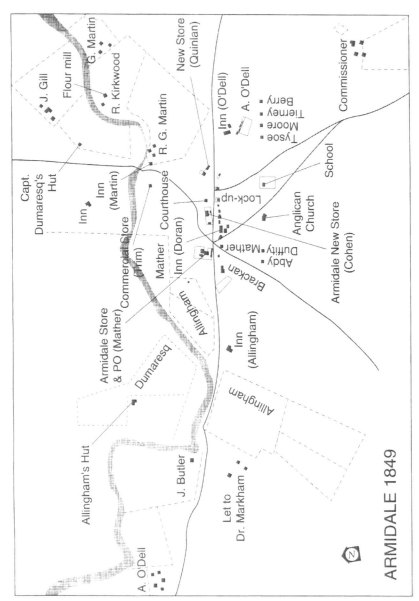

Figure 3.5. The spatial distribution of wealth and workforce under mercantile capitalism.

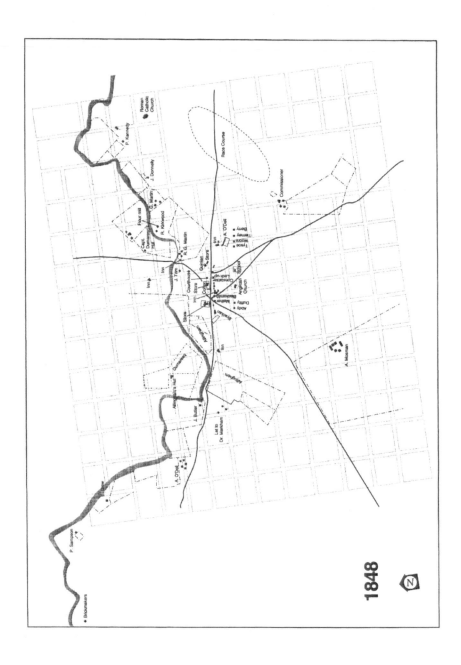

An Introduction to Armidale 59

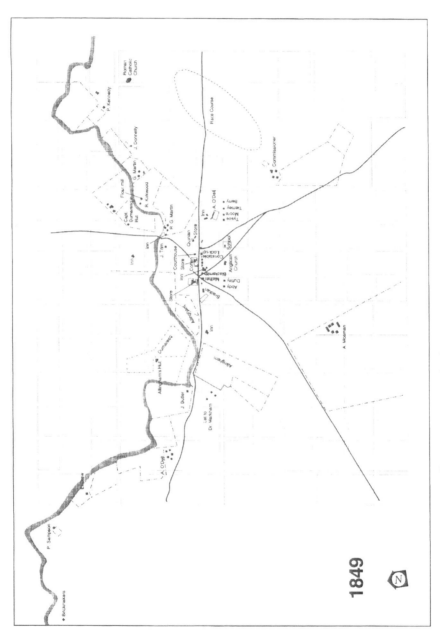

Figure 3.6. Galloway's original and subsequent street plans: May 28, 1848 and March 21, 1849.

and business-like appearance' of Armidale in 1850 was of course due to developments during the 1840s—not only the adoption of Galloway's tidy grid plan, but also the early and rather rapid development of trade, commerce, and industry" (Gilbert 1982, 82).

In contrast to pastoral capitalism, services were no longer provided exclusively on the properties themselves, but were beginning to center around Armidale and Armidale's proprietors. The extension of the railway line into Armidale in 1883 brought with it an alternative means of communication and goods, and passengers could now be transported more quickly and reliably. Prior to 1883 there were only two overland routes into Armidale: one via road from the coastal center of Grafton and one via rail to the southern city of Newcastle and from there via road into Armidale. Costs for transporting goods via either of these services ranged from £7–£9 and took from 15 days to 4 weeks delivery time (Harmon 1963). In contrast, when the railway finally reached Armidale, both time and costs were reduced so greatly that goods such as Adelaide flour could be imported for less than the cost of the local product (Harmon 1963). Horseback was still the predominant means of local travel and communication, although the telegraph line was connected to the Armidale Post Office in 1861 (Gilbert 1982, 47).

"Hydra-Headed Democracy": The Working-Class Challenge (1870–1930)

Unlike the other categories, the working-class challenge is not an exposition of a particular form of capitalism. Connell and Irving use this period label instead to refer to a "mobilization of the working class" (dating as a mass phenomenon from the late 1880s) against labor conditions, private property, and class structure. Most often this working-class mobilization occurred in a suburban setting, as rural workers were both widely dispersed geographically and highly mobile occupationally, as opposed to workers in the cities (Connell and Irving 1992, 127–129). Connell and Irving view the mobilization of the working class as an important phase, as it not only created a "form of power that is collectively based and experienced in the capitalist mode of production," but also because "it reflects the emerging collective forces of production and as such is a form of power which challenges capitalist relationships based on private ownership" (Connell and Irving 1992, 133). The working class challenge was thus a major expression of resistance to the capitalist structure and emphasized the contradictory experience of power.

While there were branches in Armidale of many of the organiza-

An Introduction to Armidale

tions that were a part of the working class challenge in Sydney or Melbourne by the 1870s and 1880s (the eight-hour-day association, the early-closing movement, the half-day-holiday movement, the shop-assistants'-holiday movement), there does not seem to have been any organized challenges to capital on a similar scale to that which was occurring in the capital cities. This may be due, in part, to the fact that the committees of many of these organizations in Armidale were not run by the employees themselves, but fronted by the employers—the urban mercantile capitalists—who often occupied the key positions of president, vice-president, and secretary (see Ferry 1994, 105–108). Such control over the shape and intent of such movements could not help but undermine their purposes. Isolated indications of a more antagonistic relationship between labor and capital did occur; Moses, in particular, as the only large employer of factory labor in Armidale, was the target of more than one act of sabotage. In 1879 two stacks of wattle bark in the grounds of the tannery were set on fire, leading ultimately to £1000 in damage. A year later three of Moses' dogs were poisoned with strychnine baits (Ferry 1994, 102–103; *Armidale Express* 1/31/1879, 10/22/1880). In 1881, a proposed strike by workers at his tannery was averted by a settlement, prompting the editor of the *Armidale Express* to affirm that Moses was not a hard taskmaster (*Armidale Express* 6/17/1881).

By far the most antagonistic relationship to develop between capital and labor in the region was between pastoralists and shearers, who in 1888 clashed over rates of pay as part of a national movement that polarized work relationships within the pastoral industry (Ferry 1994, 111–113). This pattern of events has led John Ferry to argue that organized resistance by the workers was relatively scarce in Armidale and more typical of "itinerant workers acting on agendas established outside the community" (Ferry 1994, 114). This pattern of worker resistance is partly a question of scale. The merchants and industrialists in Armidale were small scale compared to their counterparts elsewhere, but the shearers were members of unions operating on a national scale that were larger than any particular local grouping.

At first influenced by socialism, the most radical aspect of the working-class challenge—its anti-property stance—was stunted by some working-class intellectuals becoming property owners and separate in terms of property interests (Connell and Irving 1992, 138–139). Others were encouraged to enter parliament, their membership of a state organization thus separating them from the collective power of their class. Connell and Irving (1992, 138–139) argue that by the end of the 1890s there was a single milieu that stressed wealth, not ruling-class power, as the main characteristic of class structure, and that viewed change not in terms of revolution or radical change, but as "evolution," a gradual and peaceful process of mass education and enlightened legislation: "Henceforth, democratic citizenship was used to legitimate the actions of the main agencies of cultural control—the family, the churches and the Mechanics' Institutes" (Connell and Irving 1992, 104).

During the 1870s and 1880s the introduction of cheap, compulsory elementary education became part of a movement from church-dominated to state education, culminating in the Public Instruction Act of 1880, which withdrew all state aid to church schools (Connell and Irving 1992, 143; Madgwick 1962, 33). Education was often seen as the solution to the problems arising from the exploitative relationship of production, a remedy for the breakdown in "social responsibility" that was thought to originate in the factory system (Connell and Irving 1992, 144). Outside of Armidale, the increasing stress on compulsory education was linked with the establishment of the Factory Acts prohibiting child labor. A rise in the birthrate after 1865 had resulted in both child labor and loitering on the streets as growing problems of social control (Connell and Irving 1992, 143). In this sense then, schools also provided social control for workers' children. One strategy for combating this, as well as for defusing working-class antagonism, was the introduction of a special and separate system of technical education, designed to deliver non-elitist practical instruction that was both in tune with contemporary notions of progress and reinforced the idea of development through industrialization. Education in this context valued the spread of knowledge for its moral utility and further equated citizenship with self-discipline. Nor did education cease once the individual left school. Benefit societies, friendly societies, even unions and cooperatives, resembled schooling, with their stress laid on rules, regulations, and the penalties for breaching them, as well as on rituals and the formalities of meetings and greetings. All forms of education were designed to inculcate orderliness and regularity (Connell and Irving 1992, 107).

The number of schools in Armidale grew steadily over the nineteenth century (Figure 3.7). Although several of these were state-funded schools, there were also large denominational private schools, such as The Armidale School (TAS) and the New England Girls' School (NEGS). TAS was established almost exclusively by squatters, who also dominated its board of directors throughout the nineteenth century. NEGS was established by the sister of the Anglican Bishop, and also catered to pastoral families. An additional repercussion of the Public Instruction Act was to reinforce an association between church schools and pastoral landowners with financial resources, and between "selectness" and the charging of fees (Madgwick 1962), while at the same time reinforcing the association between state-funded education and the

An Introduction to Armidale 63

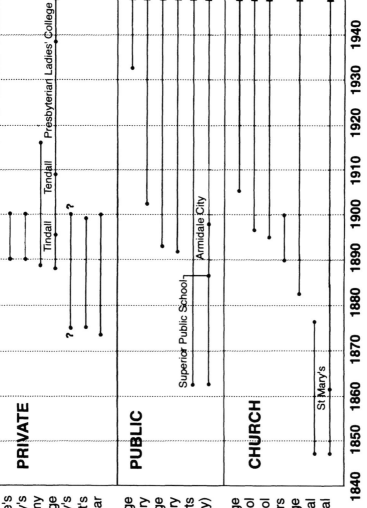

Figure 3.7. The growth in the number of schools in Armidale.

64 Chapter 3

working class. This linkage was nowhere more apparent than in Armidale. In 1918, for example, the Inspector of Schools (cited in Gilbert 1982, 180) commented that "there is an opulent station owning class and the manual worker between whom is a great social gulf. Of course there is a fair proportion of a well-to-do middle class ... this brings into existence a number of private schools which seem to depend largely on class distinction." In Armidale, there were also moves towards adult education in the form of the Mechanics' Institute and, later, the Technical College.

Working Class Armidale

Australian capitalism was a particular form of capitalism that influenced the character of the working class so that in many respects they were atypical of other groups of workers in more heavily industrialized Europe (Macintyre 1994, 126). Some sectors of the working class, such as convicts, miners, and pastoral workers with rural holdings, were not dependent on the sale of their labor in the labor market; a general shortage of labor and a greater degree of occupational mobility gave them exceptional characteristics (Macintyre 1994, 137). Nineteenth century Australian capitalism was always heavily based on pastoralism or on markets created by pastoralism, and on the small scale of most capitalist enterprise and its largely non-industrial character:

> The close contact between employer and wage earner stamped a deep imprint on the working class in the towns.... a compact between employer and worker ... intensified in the twentieth century;... Australian craftsmen were the first to win the eight-hour day, [and] during much of the second half of the [nineteenth] century they enjoyed what was probably a uniquely high standard of living. (Macintyre 1994, 137)

The working class as a group in Armidale are usually discussed as just that—a group, without reference to individual identities, unlike the case with references to pastoral or urban/mercantile capital. Often, those whom I would term "urban mercantile capitalists" are counted as "working class," and it is their identities that are often attached to historical accounts (see, for example, Wilson and Cooper 1991). The writing of history as a mainly middle-class pursuit with a tendency to focus on the wealthier or politically more powerful element makes it difficult to historically reconstruct just who comprised the working class in Armidale. Unlike pastoral capital or mercantile capital, this group is not definable in terms of property, but rather in terms of the opposite. It is precisely because the working class owned little or nothing that they are not customarily viewed in terms of contributing to the Armidale landscape (see, for example, Perumal Murphy 1991), and therefore given little prominence in historical treatments of the town. In 1861, the only year for which detailed population breakdowns have been

An Introduction to Armidale

prepared (see Ferry 1994, Appendix 5.1), the working class (i.e., men who either sold their own labor under the Masters and Servants Acts or who were self-employed in small single-operator enterprises, such as farmers, retailers, tailors, blacksmiths, or butchers) constituted approximately 27% of the total population. Of these, 14% were propertyless, owning nothing but their labor. Given that the number of workers is known to have increased after the arrival of the railway in 1883, there is no reason to assume that this proportion is unusual.

There is certainly a strong working-class element in the composition of the town, particularly as reflected in the location and identity of West Armidale, which has always been defined as a working-class neighborhood by both commentators and residents. In 1887, the Member of Parliament for New England described most of the residents in this section of town as "young married men employed at Mr. Moses' Tannery and Boot Factory, Mr. Palmer's brickyards, Mr. Trim's Chaff factory and at the Railway Station and Goods Shed" (quoted in Gilbert 1982, 178). It has been argued that there was a distinctive identity associated with residence in this part of Armidale (Wilson and Cooper 1991, 85), clearly manifested in the agitation for independent facilities and culminating in the existence of a separate Anglican church, public primary school, police station and lock-up, as well as numerous hotels servicing this section of town (Figure 3.8). Even Dumaresq Street and Beardy Street, which bisect Armidale from east to west, acquired separate identities as Dumaresq Street West and West Beardy Street, in order to differentiate the residences in this part of town.

Many of the workers who gave West Armidale its identity arrived in town as a direct result of the railway in 1883. Rather than being solely an opportunity for "business ... and increase in the value of land" (*Armidale Express* 2/2/1883), the extension of the northern rail line would appear to have been the catalyst for the consolidation and cohesion of West Armidale as a working-class focus. Between 1878 and 1883, 62% of all new buildings constructed in Armidale were located here, which Ferry (1994, 260) describes as "a building boom the like of which [Armidale] had never seen." In 1883, when £500 was the typical cost for a brick house and £150 the typical cost for a timber weatherboard house, and although most of the buildings existing in this section of town were virtually brand new, over half were rated at less than £25 and only 5% at more than £40 per annum (Ferry 1994, 260–262) (Figure 3.8).

Industrial Capitalism, 1860–1930

In the last quarter of the nineteenth century the economy was still technically preindustrial, as the factory system that emerged in the 1870s was designed to serve only a small domestic market (Connell and

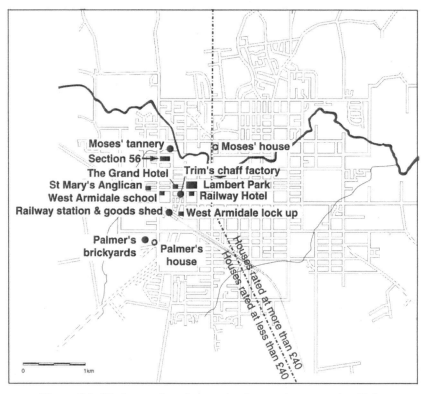

Figure 3.8. Workers and workplaces in nineteenth century Armidale.

Irving 1992, 98). The 1920s saw the beginning of a period of restructuring the economy around mass retailing and manufacturing however, which involved changes in the form of capital, as well as changes in the labor process and the work environment. Workers became more closely coordinated, new routines and regularity became necessary in the actual conduct of work, and labor became repetitious and constant. The social distancing that opened up within industrial capitalism also structured the space and style of the living arrangements of the workers. Part of the production process was redefining the relationship between time and labor, and work discipline came to reflect not only new work routines, but also new notions of efficiency and "economized landscapes" (Handsman and Leone 1989, 132). This structured the location of worker's housing and the lines of travel they followed to arrive at work, as much as it did the segmentation of a labor routine into repetitive and

An Introduction to Armidale 67

replicable units (Handsman and Leone 1989, 128–132). It was not only "efficient" for workers to live in close proximity to their place of work so that they minimized their amount of travel time, but in some cases also for the employers to create the workers' living space themselves (with the boarding house system, or the construction of company-owned worker communities). There was another element to the spatial segregation that accompanied industrial capitalism, this time on the part of the owners: As much as it was considered necessary for the workers to live in proximity to their places of work, so was it considered desirable for the owners to live away from it, or at least recognizably separate from it.

Industrial capital in Armidale was never as pervasive or powerful as either mercantile or pastoral capital, and certainly never reached the dimensions or complexity identified by Connell and Irving for other places in this period. An early and intense period of industrialization between 1840 and the 1890s focused on the manufacture of flour, and a later period from 1875 to 1977 concentrated on brewing and cordial manufacture; however, particular local industries were mostly small scale and short-lived (Figure 3.9). In 1871 local flour was exported as far as Queensland, but in the same year Adelaide flour was imported into Armidale (Harmon 1963). The coming of the railway in 1883 heralded the death of the local flour industry, as Adelaide flour could now be imported at a cost cheaper than the local product. Wheat, maize, barley, oats, fruit, and potatoes were other local products grown commercially in the 1870s and 1880s, some of which were exported to an extra-regional market.

The main and lasting exception to the small scale of local industry was Barnett Aaron Moses' tannery, established around 1866. It was the only venture in Armidale to produce consistently for an extra-regional market, and employed up to 100 workers at its peak in 1882 (Walker 1966, 107; Ferry 1994, 78). It closed in 1897, soon after Moses' death.

Moses was also one of the few capitalists who indulged in a physical form of paternalism for his workers. In 1880 he bought an entire town block opposite his tannery, subdivided it, and over the next two years sold most of the lots to his workers (see Figure 3.6). It is likely that there was strong enticement from Moses to encourage his workers to build their own houses. Almost without exception and within two years of buying a lot, each new property owner had taken out a mortgage with the New England Permanent Building Society (Land Titles Section 56, County of Sandon, Town of Armidale).

Because of the small scale of industry in Armidale, there was never anything approximating the scale or atmosphere of industrial towns,

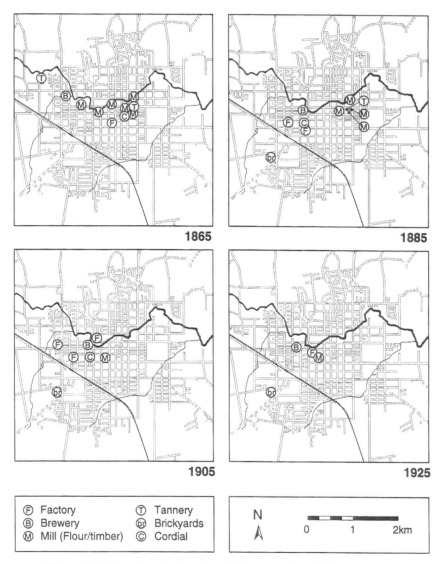

Figure 3.9. The changing location of industry in Armidale 1865–1925.

and it is debatable as to whether Connell and Irving's category applies to work relations as they were understood in Armidale. In addition, because of the often close relationship between industrial and mercantile capital in Armidale, industry in this context is perhaps best regarded as a facet of mercantile capitalism. Although in Armidale there were ex-

An Introduction to Armidale

tremely limited opportunities for movement across the division between a propertyless working class and a property-owning class (Ferry 1994, 316), the character of the workforce may have been much as Macintyre (1994) suggested. Armidale was largely non-industrial, except in very limited, small-scale terms and, if the example of Moses and his tannery and boot factory workers is any indication, there was often a close relationship between employer and wage earner. Many of the working class in Armidale were self-employed as shop keepers, boardinghouse keepers, or small farmers, and many also took seasonal work, such as shearing, if it was available. During the protracted and often bitter shearer's strikes of the early 1890s, many Armidale graziers preferred to shear with local, non-union shearers, many of whom were farmers with their own local land holdings (Ferry 1994). This should not be taken to imply that relations between capitalist and laborer were necessarily consensual, however, but rather that sharp dichotomies between rich and poor, or owner and wage-earner, may have been blurred in the specific context of Armidale.

Of course "democracy" was not at all democratic: In 1858 in Armidale the elector franchise was limited to a £10 householder fee, which effectively excluded all propertyless workers and women (Walker 1966, 154; Ferry 1994, 280–281). There was always poverty in any situation, and no matter how many stories of convicts or workers who "made it" are invoked, or how positively distinctive Australian capitalism is rendered, many large groups in colonial Australia, such as women, Aborigines, or the Chinese, are often excluded from discussion and antagonism was always present (see, for example, Stannage 1994). This was as true within the working class as between workers and employers, in fact one of the main goals of the trade union movement—that great bastion of supposed working-class mobilization—was the exclusion of cheap labor in the form of Chinese, children, and women (Lake 1994, 270).

This, then, is the setting that constructed capitalism in Armidale. To present the history of Armidale, however, without considering the presence and effects of the Aborigines who first inhabited that area, and later the margins and suburbs of the city, is to ignore an important group of people whose past and present became, whether they liked it or not, part of the development of capitalism in Armidale. What would at times seem an essentially straightforward description of the history of the "capitalists" and the "workers," is complicated by the existence of the Aborigines as something other than either, with a worldview totally apart from anything that encompassed capitalism, but who were forced to become a part of it regardless. For more than 50,000 years Australia was populated by people whose way of life did not encompass agriculture (or capitalism) until the arrival of European colonialism in the form

70   Chapter 3

of nearly 1,000 British citizens in 1788. Such colonialism appears to be an intrinsic element of capitalist expansion, reflecting the acquisitiveness and competitive nature of the capitalist experience and the ideology of appropriation that accompanied this. Although non-capitalist societies also colonized, it was not from similar needs or desires, and never at such a distance.

The societies established through the process of colonialism shared several features in common: They embodied the social relations of production characteristic of capitalism, depended for growth on large transfers of capital and labor from Europe, participated from the beginning in international trade, and as a result made large quantities of land available cheaply for settlers (Buckley and Wheelwright 1992, 27). In this context, the conflict between colonialist society and the indigenous people whose land they appropriated was inevitable and embodied the classic dichotomy between a fisher–gatherer–hunter and an agricultural society, between some degree of collective appropriation of nature and the individual appropriation of nature. When a system constructed on relatively undivided access to both land and resources comes into contact with a system that not only appropriates access to both, but also protects such "property" from further appropriation, the inevitable result would appear to be one of the alienation of fisher–gatherer–hunter people from their land and resources (Davidson 1989, 77). Thus "capitalism in Australia" not only connotes a history of white occupation of the continent and the development of the capitalist social form in this context, but also the myriad ways in which such development influenced the lives and traditional social structures of the indigenous population.

COLONIAL ARMIDALE

John Ferry's 1994 Ph.D. thesis, "Colonial Armidale. A study of people, place and power in the formation of a country town," is the only substantial document that attempts to isolate the precise groupings of wealth and power that form the social weave of nineteenth-century Armidale. Ferry (1994, 133–134) has divided the population of Armidale into four main strata: a middle, middling, working, and under class. The middle class, at one end of the spectrum, were in control of the means of production, investments, resources, and the labor power of others; the working class, at the other extreme, controlled nothing but their own labor power. Ferry (1994, 133–134) composed the middling class to account for people who lacked control over one of these basic attributes: those who incurred high levels of debt for instance, or those

An Introduction to Armidale

who had no legal title to productive assets, but who still maintained some control over the means of production or over the labor power of others, such as property managers, upper echelon public servants, or small entrepreneurs. The underclass, although holding no control over any aspect of production, can be contrasted to the working class in that it is composed of such unskilled workers that even their own labor power is not particularly sought after on the labor market. Also included in this grouping were those who were excluded from the labor market on other grounds, such as age, gender, or race, whom Ferry (1994, 133) terms the "chronic unemployed."

The main problem with Ferry's categories (which he himself recognizes) is that they place a large cross-section of the community into the one group—the middling class. Membership of this group ranges from pastoralists and large entrepreneurs (albeit with high ratios of debt), to managers, single-operator businesses, and small farmers. Ferry attempts to section this by grouping people into status rankings, which, when contrasted to Wild's three distinctions in class relationships, provides a framework for interpreting the groups present in Armidale in the past. In the following chapters I will distinguish groups in these terms (Figure 3.10).

The great strength of Ferry's formulation is that it allows for subtle distinctions to be drawn between grosser groups. Instead of pitting a working class against a middle or employer class in a stark dichotomy, Ferry distinguishes shading within each group, alluding to possible sources of tension *within* groups, instead of merely between groups. What, for instance, were the attitudes of the underclass towards the working class? Or the debt-encumbered middling class towards the middle class? Although Ferry's and my understanding of the working class and underclass coincide, his middle and middling class do not fit neatly into my understanding of the division between pastoral and mercantile capital. Although all pastoralists fell within the middle class, mercantile capitalists fell within both the middle and middling class. Although mercantilists such as Thomas Fitzgerald, Joseph Scholes, or James Tysoe fell squarely into the middle class, many equally well-known mercantile capitalists, such as John Moore, John Trim, or Edward Allingham, fell within Ferry's middling class.

IDEOLOGY

In order to link the previous section more closely with the aims of this research, it is necessary to isolate possible ideologies that may have accompanied the changes and development in capitalism in Armi-

WILD 1978	FERRY 1994
1. *Propertied leisured employers*	*Middle class:* Pastoralists, large-scale retailers, farmers, and successful mining speculators
2. *Propertied working employers*	*Debt-encumbered middling class:* Large-scale retailers with a high debt to assets ratio, senior public servants (e.g. district surveyors and school inspectors), station managers, high-ranking clergy
3. *Propertied workers, periodic employers*	*Middling class:* Small enterprise operators, clergy, local professionals (e.g., solicitors and doctors)
4. *Propertied workers*	*Working class:* Small farmers, skilled laborers (e.g., bootmakers and carpenters), white-collar employees (e.g. teachers, bank tellers, clerks, constables)
5. *Propertyless workers*	*Working class:* White-collar employees, skilled laborers (e.g. butchers, printers, blacksmiths, shearers), unskilled laborers (e.g. shepherds and station hands)

Figure 3.10. Ferry's status rankings in relation to Wild's class distinctions.

dale over time. Ideologies in this sense clearly refers to sophisticated ideologies—particular social strategies that produced and were produced by the different forms of capitalism that existed in the region. I will make no attempt here to elucidate an unsophisticated ideology of capitalism in Armidale, nor how sophisticated ideologies may have articulated with it. The sophisticated ideologies presented here have been extracted from general Australian historical literature, and discussion will focus on how closely these may be understood as representing the Armidale situation. There are three main sophisticated ideologies that may have articulated with the forms of capitalism in Armidale and New England, although all were no doubt closely related:

- Pastoral ascendancy and mercantile enterprise
- Progress, science and reason
- Respectability

Pastoral Ascendancy and Mercantile Enterprise

Pastoralism was not only a particular form of capitalism, but there was a highly specific sophisticated ideology that accompanied it. This ideology was unlike anything that came after it, but was not unlike that which existed in England, its parent. According to Connell and Irving (1992, 65), the dominant sophisticated ideology in the colony during this period was largely linked to the notion of moral ascendancy. The pastoral gentry were portrayed in direct contrast to the rise of ex-convict entrepreneurs, that is, both virtuous and moral and, as a result, with the legitimate franchise over the economic welfare of the colony lying in their hands. This was not so much a struggle against the workforce, but against another group of capitalists: the "virtuous," "respectable" (wealthy, pastoral) families with no convict taint, saw themselves as the "chief bulwark of social order against a sea of crime and immorality," as typified by those with a convict background (Connell and Irving 1992, 65–66). This ideology was obviously closely linked to the attempt by the colonial government and the incipient landed gentry to manufacture a social system with an enormous gulf between those with wealth and those without, which Connell and Irving (1992, 56–58) have likened to a "plantation-like oligarchy." It was obviously closely tied to the convict assignment system, not only literally in terms of the unequal labor relations necessary to effect this social system, but also metaphorically in that the gentry needed to manufacture an enormous gulf of social distance between themselves and the convicts in order to legitimize their power. The polar opposites of good and evil were not merely limited to church rhetoric, but closely linked to the maintenance of the social position of the pastoralists, and thus the fortunes of the state.

With the development and spread of mercantile capitalism, the ideological initiative of the pastoralists was challenged by an essentially urban movement that stressed respectability without hierarchy and economic development without ascendancy (Connell and Irving 1992, 66–67). This became translated into an ideology of progress, which, although based on the same system of private property as the ideology of ascendancy, explicitly linked property with enterprise and economic development with social prosperity. Thus, progress became identified with capitalist expansion, and the public good with the state of private profits in the leading industry. This opposition was basically a conflict between a plantation (squatter) style of social order, which unashamedly favored a revival of the set of relationships surrounding the assignment system, and an urban bourgeois social order, which favored a nationalistic, liberal individualism; a "free" labor market and a "free"

74 Chapter 3

society with profits and prosperity for all (Connell and Irving 1992, 94–96; Turner 1992, 162).

> Divisions between the conservative pastoralist class whose wealth depended upon land and sheep production, and an emerging urban industrial class, centred on the large cities, were also reflected in an ideological division between the ethic of social service and the ethic of hard work and profitability. The ideology of the pastoral gentry was based upon the notion of a moral ascendancy which distinguished the pastoralists from the ex-convict population by claims to moral value and inherited cultural superiority. The values of moral ascendancy emphasized the importance of social service and culture over and against both the degenerate convict and the money-grasping urban entrepreneur.... By contrast, the ideology of the urban capitalist class emphasized social progress, hard work, saving and the virtues of private property; this was an ideology for social mobility, not of inherited cultural and economic capital. (Turner 1992, 162–163)

The pattern of wealth inheritance in Armidale and district would suggest that there was a similar ideological division between the pastoralists and urban mercantile capitalists. There is a clear trend among pastoral families to bequeath wealth to selected sons (never daughters), tying lineage to pastoral property, and by various qualifications ensuring that land remained largely intact and in the family name (Ferry 1994, 310). In contrast, urban mercantilists typically distributed their property more evenly between (again) sons, and often before death in the form of cash gifts, effectively encouraging the next generation to establish themselves (Ferry 1994, 310–311).

> One set of inheritance practices was based on securing a position for selected sons; the other set was based on securing an advancement in life for all sons. One set was based on holding property and associated rights intact for the next generation; the other set saw merit in a changing economic world where the advantages of parental wealth would secure an assured but unprescribed future for the next generation. (Ferry 1994, 311)

There would seem to be parallels in Armidale between an ideology of inherited ascendancy and lineage subscribed to by pastoralists and an ideology of social progress (and mobility) through individual achievement and initiative subscribed to by urban capitalists. From the point of view of urban mercantile capital, moral enlightenment thus became linked explicitly with the ideology of economic development and the plantation ideal of the pastoralists weakened as the public sector legitimated the ideology of development (as a "universal law of civilization") and as pastoral capital became absorbed into mercantile capital as the economy expanded on the basis of government activity (Connell and Irving 1992, 92). This was not a distant and often unconnected encounter confined only to newspaper pages or particular political and social

An Introduction to Armidale 75

issues. Connell and Irving argue it was this political struggle by the mercantile bourgeoisie against the conservative pastoral capitalists that was the strongest dynamic in the emergence of the commercial capitalists as the leading section of capital in the colony (Connell and Irving 1992, 98). Eventually the squatters found themselves the target of a decidedly anti-squatter alliance led by urban mercantile capitalists.

This anti-squatter push had a number of ideological underpinnings (Connell and Irving 1992, 102–104): In an age of "progress," the squatters were accused of hindering development through a lack of interest in the explicit and socially beneficial union between capital and science; they were seen as rejecting equality of opportunity stemming from the freedom of wage labor, and, ultimately, the question of order was given an explicit social dimension, by making "order" a goal of "democracy," rather than of inherited social "right." Mercantile capitalism was thus almost inextricably entwined with a liberal and secular ideology of progress, which equated property with enterprise and economic development with social prosperity (Wells 1989, 38). Progress as the equation between capital and science was very much a secular ideology, and during this the time direct role of the churches in the cultural sphere diminished. The Anglican clergy in particular were commonly regarded as supporters of a privileged upper class (Connell and Irving 1992, 106), although there was likely an element of ethnicity to this evaluation as well. Although religion was no longer the bulwark for the dominant social order, this is not to say that religion did not still play an important part in fashioning people's identity and mediating between them and an ideology of progress. In Armidale, religion was an important facet of social identity and, as in many other places, the broadest and deepest divisions ran between Protestants and Catholics. Ferry (1994, 273–274) has pointed out that Catholics always constituted the largest proportion of the working class, while only three New England squatters in the 1860s were Catholic. In the same decade, urban property owners in Armidale who were Church of England outnumbered Catholic urban property owners by more than two to one (Ferry 1994, 274).

It must be remembered that my definition of ideology is something that masks inequality in the social order by making it appear as anything but a human social construction. In this sense then it is possible to speak of working-class ideology. As a group, the working class still excluded Aborigines and women as valuable and productive members of society, yet masked this inequality in a variety of ways. Even the trade union movement, as an expression of resistance by the working class, was sophisticated ideology because it continued to mask inequality and displace it as a social product. However, it was also unsophisticated ideology; the trade unions were fundamentally based on the acceptance of capitalist economic relations, each assertion of working class influence involving them as partners of property (Macintyre 1994, 127).

It is possible to speak of a working-class ideology of masculinism, which fostered a distinct sense of identity among propertyless working class males and persisted in various masculine constructions of the bush and of the resourceful, self-reliant, and independent Australian pioneer. It is also possible, however, to argue that an ideology of respectability, which cut across class boundaries, yet effectively separated men from women, was also a facet to the construction of identity among the working class, although not definable as a strictly "working-class ideology." It is at this point that it becomes less convincing to express as ideology the dichotomy between mercantilists and pastoralists, or between employers and workers. Although these constructions of "right" are certainly valid and distinctive of particular historical groups, this is not all there is to ideology. There are other characterizations of ideology, and other facets to the ideologies already discussed, that do not focus so clearly on class position, yet that still provided a framework in which this position could be interpreted. People were not always grouped together by ideologies in the same way, yet groups at all scales had a part in the construction of identity. The liberal and secular ideology of progress and the ideology of respectability are excellent examples of this: Both effectively constructed groups in different ways, yet both were closely intertwined with each other and with pastoralist, mercantilist, and working-class ideologies.

Progress, Science, and Reason

The beliefs of many working-class intellectuals in the late nineteenth and early twentieth centuries were affected by general processes of late-nineteenth century capital expansion, which presented the Westernized spread of European and American capital as a law of civilization and pointed to hopes for the future as lying with "new countries" of European investment and settlement. Often the qualities of the frontier were eulogized, and freedom and democracy were accepted as natural in "new" countries, such as Australia (Connell and Irving 1992, 137–138). The romantic myth of individual opportunity in a "new" country was present in various writings by the middle of the nineteenth century, largely because this theme was central to the political settlement based on access to opportunity imposed by the liberal bourgeoisie in that period (Buckley and Wheelwright 1992, 60–61). Liberal ideology defined development as a universal law of civilization, and enterprise as the denominator of success, and, under it, continued colonization and pioneer resourcefulness became inextricably coupled with the ideals of progress and democracy.

Under the liberal ideology of progress, epitomized by the Robertson Land Acts, it became customary to represent Australia as an egalitarian country, where the old class divisions of England were abolished and where democracy and freedom were the basic right of all (for the classic historical formulation see Ward 1958). Colonization and expansion were the gateways to wealth, and much as development was regarded as a basic law of civilization, so too was science regarded as the basic mediator for its measurement. Science and progress were inextricably entwined and under their aegis many overt class distinctions were supposedly broken down. Public clubs and societies became venues for male bonding and for the establishment and expansion of male social networks. Freemasonry was, and is still, an example one of the most influential and wide ranging masculine associations, with its emphasis on responsibility, respectability, and brotherhood through skill. Freemasonry stressed the "masculine virtues of loyalty to the community, probity in business and responsibility for dependents" and was an "attractive arena for the expression of masculine independence" (Davidoff and Hall 1987, 427). As both a local and national organization, it provided a bridge between town and country, and in England between the aristocracy and the middle class. With value being placed on scientific education and rationality, however, women were customarily excluded from participation, other than as audience or observers (Davidoff and Hall 1987, 425–427). The Masonic lodge at Armidale, constructed in 1860, was the first building in New South Wales built explicitly for Masonic purposes, and within five years was followed by other similar groups. The School of Arts was founded in Armidale in 1859 and, despite its franchise to educate "working men," it became effectively a social club for urban middle-class males. Although the School of Arts was expressly dedicated to the "moral and social benefits of knowledge" and to general intellectual improvement, membership in it was limited to an annual £1 subscription fee, which excluded the working class (Raszewski 1988). In Armidale it failed to attract the interest of squatters, and became a venue for the urban mercantilists and the various church leaders, the "men of power and influence in the town" (Raszewski 1988, 39).

Respectability

The ideology of science and secular progress became linked with the ideology of respectability, which was aimed at the male character and the female role in facilitating it. Science and reason became constructed almost exclusively as male, either implicitly (through the belief in rationality and the disbelief in women's ability to exercise it) or explicitly (as with the Masonic constitution, which expressly forbade the participation of women). An ideology of respectability is often counterpoised to an ideology of wild masculinity, which stood in opposition to many of respectability's fundamental tenets. The particularly masculine construction of honor and prowess, epitomized by an excess of alcohol, violence, competition, and deliberately provocative language, was an ideology of masculinity that had strong class overtones and found particular expression amongst propertyless working-class males (Ferry 1994, 197). Perhaps because the only property they owned was their bodies, this masculinist ideology was centered exclusively on the male body and expressed through personal competition in pubs and on racetracks and through a complex code of honor centering on the ability to best all others. Respectability, on the other hand,

> took men in hand and sought to re-teach them. The essence of masculinity was no longer prowess,... but ... the male character.... It was no coincidence that the noble protector and gallant knight re-emerged in England at the time when women were forced into a greater dependency on men than had ever existed previously. (Ferry 1994, 198)

Marilyn Lake (1994) has suggested that the struggle between respectability and unrespectability was also a conflict between competing ideals of masculinity. In both ideologies the construction of male became a dominant ordering principle, and under the ideology of respectability, it was both women and men who participated in the construction.

The ideology of respectability is an excellent example of "inferiors"— in this case women—learning to characterize themselves in a particular ideological fashion. It is an illustration of how an ideology may be both hegemonic, but not necessarily entirely fostered by the dominant. The learning process involved in rendering the ideology of respectability hegemonic involved creating new roles for women and men primarily through literature, most of the writers of which were women (Davidoff and Hall 1987, 176). It was women who were insisting on the probity of motherhood and the values of family, and characterizing domesticity and sexual difference in particular ways (Davidoff and Hall 1987, 149, 176). It was not men who were imposing such ideals upon women, but women who were fostering them among themselves. Under the ideology of respectability, women were relegated (and relegated themselves) to a particular and private sphere (the home) and to a particular realm of duty (through exploring the ways in which such values could be translated into the daily routines of home, nursery, and kitchen).

It is no coincidence that Ferry uses the notion of the "gallant

An Introduction to Armidale

knight" to describe the central tenets of the ideology of respectability. As an ideology that defined separate spheres for men and women, it was closely entwined with ideas of chivalry and the "gentleman," both of which were also part and parcel of British imperialism (Girouard 1981, 220–230). The nineteenth century husband was both a gentleman and a knight-errant, subscribing to a particular image of marriage and wifedom:

> The accepted symbol of mediaeval courtly love was the knight kneeling at the feet of his mistress, as a superior and adored being. According to early Victorian practice the image was acceptable in courtship but not after marriage; the husband was expected to be tender, reverent and protective, but he was also undoubtedly superior. (Girouard 1981, 199)

The image of the husband as both protective and superior was an image that carried over into the doctrines of imperialism and as a settler, the British gentleman had similar duties to guard and govern the colonies as he did his wife:

> "We have another function such as the Romans had. The sections of men on this globe are unequally gifted. Some are strong and can govern themselves; some are weak and are the prey of foreign invaders and internal anarchy; and freedom, which all desire, is only obtainable by weak nations when they are subject to the rule of others who are at once powerful and just. This was the duty which fell to the Latin race two thousand years ago. In these modern times it has fallen to ours, and in the discharge of it the highest features in the English character have displayed themselves." ... The sources of imperialism and the sources of the Victorian code of the gentleman are so intertwined that it is not surprising to find this code affecting the way in which the Empire was run. The philosophy of imperialism was essentially élitist. It was not only that it saw the British people as a ruling race; within the British people it saw British gentlemen as leading, loyally supported by what it liked to think of as British yeomen; and within the ranks of British gentlemen it tended to create little individual "bands of brothers," conscious of their traditions or believing in their superiority (Girouard 1981, 221, 224)

During the period 1840 to 1890, Connell and Irving argue that domesticity itself became devalued, as an age of progress held an undisputed ethic of performance, resulting in the separation of the household from the process of production. Thus, not only were the means of successful performance removed from the sphere in which many women were confined (Connell and Irving 1992, 69), but the earlier positive connotations that had surrounded the traditional occupation of industry in the home (independent handicrafts, peasant farming) also became converted to the spheres of factory production and work (Buckley and Wheelwright 1992, 145). The loss of opportunities to earn increased the dominance of marriage as the only survival route for middle-class

80 Chapter 3

women: spinster originally meant "one who spins," but by the same route came to mean an unmarried or unwanted woman (Davidoff and Hall 1987, 272). (Bachelor, of course, originally meant an aspirant to knighthood, one who as yet has not chosen a particular order). Progress and housework were successfully redefined in such a way that the State began introducing provisions for the teaching of "domestic science" or "home economics" in New South Wales in 1912:

> Science and planning joined moral purity in the women's movement's recipe for national progress, and "domestic science" and "home economics" not only rationalised confining the working-class woman to the house but, in the form of labor-saving devices in the kitchen and the consumer market in household goods, it placated the "new" bourgeois woman, who was trying to combine home duties and a restricted career. (Connell and Irving 1992, 142)

Although both the ideology of science and progress, and the ideology of respectability, were most clearly participated in by the mercantilists and pastoralists, they also provided a particular framework within which the working class viewed themselves. The idea of linking colonization to pioneer movement, and both of these to progress, was given a refurbishment in the 1890s:

> reasserting economic independence as a basic value, as well as indicating ... preoccupation with the bush ... The idealisation of a bush ethos, stressing egalitarianism, resourcefulness, contempt for authority, sardonic humour, and so on, also had a long history before 1890 in English accounts of the bush. (Connell and Irving 1992, 145)

The Australian legend of the independent, self-reliant (and bachelor) stockman became a particularly well-defined aspect of the idealization of the bush with which many working-class men empathized. Boys came to consent to their futures as laborers because such work was associated with the cultural apprenticeship they received that stressed the masculinity of hard work and "really doing things" (Thompson 1986, 121). It promoted a particular model of masculinity that was unrelated to domesticity or marriage and regarded feminine home influence as emasculating (Lake 1994, 265–267).

DISCUSSION

This chapter has attempted to outline not only the chain of individual dated events commonly cited as constituting the history of Armidale, but also to examine them in terms of a number of themes that make sense of some of the connections between them. As part of this I have attempted to sketch an outline of the different types of capitalism that existed in Armidale in the past, as well as how they may have articulated, and, more importantly, to suggest some of the possible ideologies that may have accompanied this. Ideology in this chapter has been extracted exclusively from historical literature. There are two important points here: This literature is predominantly secondary, and its corollary, these ideologies are thus identifiable closely enough with a particular historical group of people, or else sufficiently separated in time from "us," to be distinctive. This is not all of what ideology is, of course, but only, by my definition, particular examples of sophisticated ideology. Some of the ways in which these sophisticated ideologies intersect may well be associated with their relationship to unsophisticated ideology, which is not articulated in any of this literature. Likewise, there may be other sophisticated ideologies existing in the past in Armidale, which may still relate closely enough to the pattern of daily habit today so as to remain indistinguishable and thus unarticulated.

Part of the process of learning to do or be anything involves an interaction with material objects. People learn through use. What then is the potential for identity, and subsequently ideology, in the past of Armidale to be embodied in material artifacts? How is social identity manifest in architectural style and how might both architecture and style mediate the learning process?

Materials and Methods | 4

SELECTION OF PLACE

Within the framework for capitalism presented in the previous chapter, Armidale and its immediate region is an interesting case study: There was not only an initially strong pastoral push by many wealthy and influential landholders already well-established in other areas (which has continued in one form or another to the present day), but also the subsequent establishment of mercantile (including small-scale industrial) capitalist interests. Unlike other population centers in the New England region, such as Tamworth, Armidale is largely a nineteenth century town. It retains a high degree of nineteenth and early-twentieth century features within its boundaries, and also continues to be a center for the pastoral holdings that surround it. Some of these pastoral holdings and the buildings on them are amongst the earliest in the region (Salisbury Court, Booroolong), while others date from the comparatively more recent acquisition of the Robertson Land Acts (Chevy Chase), as well as from later periods (Saumarez, Trevenna). Most importantly, in recent years "heritage" has become a strong focus for Armidale's identity and, as a consequence, there is a high level of awareness about heritage and heritage issues and a considerable amount of effort expended in the renovation and maintenance of heritage buildings. This is fortunate for a study such as this—not only are most nineteenth and early-twentieth century buildings in Armidale in good repair, but there is also a broad awareness of the history of the place, including the particular histories of individual buildings.

SELECTION OF STRUCTURES

The selection of buildings was mediated by a number of considerations drawn from the previous chapter's historical research: First, I needed to record the public buildings associated with the daily business of capital—the hotels, shops, banks, and government offices, as well as the private residences of owners and workers. Second, I needed to include other major types of buildings where these same people customarily interacted, such as the churches, church buildings, schools, and voluntary organizations. A range of types of capital was also necessary for comparison, and I needed to include buildings built from both pastoral and mercantile capital, along with the houses of workers associated with each of these industries. This produced five primary groupings of structures:

1. Public buildings, capital
2. Public buildings, service
3. Private buildings, pastoral capitalists
4. Private buildings, mercantile capitalists
5. Private buildings, workers

Within each of these groups, I could, of course, only record houses to which I was permitted access, or if not, for which substantial photographic records existed. The latter was the case with Palmerston, for example; although I was not permitted to visit the house, I was still able to photographically record it.

Finally, I have used 1930 as the cut-off date for structures, so that I could draw upon existing historical research into the class structure of Armidale, which is focused almost exclusively on the nineteenth century.

This constituted my initial database and the first overarching category of buildings: extant standing structures for which I could establish a minimum of social context information, such as the name of the person responsible for building it and their position within the community. To this I have added two other categories of buildings for comparison:

1. Structures with accompanying social context information, but that no longer exist (i.e., which have been replaced by other structures). Buildings in this category were identified and recorded purely from documentary sources.
2. Extant structures for which there is no known associated social context information.

Each of these three categories relates structures to particular aspects of ideology. Initially, it is only possible to seek connections between style and social identity if a minimum of social context information can be attributed to particular buildings. Following from this, however, if ideology relates to the construction of social identity that is mediated by style, then what are the ideological implications of buildings for which no known social context survives? What is the style of these buildings?

Materials and Methods

It was not possible to record all buildings within Armidale and its surrounds, which in 1994 numbered in excess of 6,000. Although objectivity is ostensibly the goal of any archaeological study, any selection of what constitutes "data" is mediated by the knowledge and goals of the researcher and, on any given occasion, what is recorded depends upon what is considered to be relevant. My completed database consisted of 222 structures from Armidale and its surrounding rural hinterland (Figure 4.1).

SELECTION OF VARIABLES

My data collection was directed towards recording four interlocking sets of variables:

- Variables relating to social context
- Variables relating to physical appearance (style)
- Variables relating to geographical context
- Variables relating to use

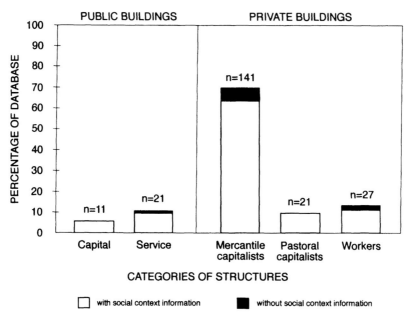

Figure 4.1. The range of structures recorded.

Although I was only able to record social context information for some buildings, for all others I have recorded variables relating to their physical appearance (style) and their geographical context. Geographical context is an attempt to record the physical location of the building within the city and the way in which it articulates with the city landscape (i.e., whether it is oriented to have a view or is located in a physically dominant position). Variables relating to use is a category that I have devised to account for the role that a building may play in the community and to question the ways in which change in a building's use may also alter both its "stylishness" and its relationship to ideology.

VARIABLES RELATING TO SOCIAL CONTEXT

These variables were all concerned with the date of the building and with information relating to the identity of the original owner (or whoever originally planned and paid for construction of the building). In terms of the identity of the original owner, I attempted to record his or her position within the power structure of the community, in terms of type of employment, religion, class (see below), gender, and the type of capital with which they may have been involved. Also included, when known, was the identity of the architect or builder who participated in the construction and the planned purpose of the building (see below). Social context information was extracted from a range of sources, including primary historical documentation, such as deceased estate files; "For sale/To let" notices; personal letters; and secondary historical sources, such as journal articles, theses, photographs, and personal interviews.

Collecting Social Context Information

Because I was interested in relating the style of a building to the possible ideology or ideologies mediating that style, I needed primarily to establish links between particular buildings and the identity of the person responsible for that building looking a certain way. By "responsible" I mean both who paid for the construction and who supposedly caused the building's final physical appearance. In some cases responsibility lay equally with the person or group who paid for the building and with an architect. In the case of public buildings in particular, an architect (either government or private) was usually involved throughout the construction process, even in the final selection of individual touches, such as cast iron. The same is true of the residences of many a

Materials and Methods 87

wealthy capitalist, who would also hire an architect to design him or her a distinctive house. In the case of government buildings, the architect worked as a permanent employee within a known system of power, and in any case was given certain specifications, presumably provided by the employer, to fulfill. I have assumed that in the matter of choice, it was the architect or the architect's designs that appealed to the employer, and which therefore related in some fashion to the employers' own sense of identity. This, of course, was not always true; for example, the many churches and cathedrals within the city were paid for by numerous subscribers, but not necessarily to their architectural specifications.

Often, one and the same individual paid for construction and "caused" the appearance of the building. For example, carpenter John Harper built his own house, as did builder Edmund Lonsdale. In contrast, there was not always a direct relationship between the first owner of a house and its form. Speculative builders, such as H. J. P. Moore, William Seabrook and John Brown, John Barnes, and William Cook, were solely responsible for both the location and the form of the final building, rather than the initial owner, who invariably purchased the structure either immediately or soon after completion. In these cases I attribute responsibility to the builder, rather than to the original owner, although I have also assumed that, as with architecturally designed houses, the form of the spec-built house in some way appealed to the buyer's own sense of identity.

The issue of the various degrees of responsibility held by the architect and the owner is redundant in considering the houses of the working class in Armidale. The final form of these houses was determined more by economies of scale than by extravagances of design, and was probably heavily influenced by the advent of mass production and the cheaper transportation costs offered by the extension of the railway. Unfortunately, I found no evidence for what caused the distinctive appearance of working-class houses in Armidale: no building contracts, discussions of taste, or product catalogues and pattern books. This does not mean that such things did not exist in the Australian colonies (pattern books, for instance, had come to Australia as early as 1809 in the form of Loudon's *Encyclopaedia of Cottage, Farm and Villa Architecture*) but simply that there were no local sources or, failing this, indications of which non-local sources may have been influential. In particular, the lack of pattern books and product catalogues restricted the interpretations that could be made of the architecture of working-class Armidale, and made it impossible to ascertain the extent to which the workers were able to control the stylistic elements that made up their own houses.

Class

I have attempted to take into account the relationship between an individual and the control of investments and resources, decision making, the physical means of production, and labor power (see Wright 1978; 1989), in terms of Wild's (1978, 3) three categories: properties and propertyless, employers and employees, and leisured and workers. Obviously, it was only possible to group structures by this variable if other aspects of social context were already known, namely the identity and profession of the person responsible. When assigning structures to one of these categories (see Figure 3.10), I have followed John Ferry's breakdown of the population. In some instances, named individuals from my database had already been placed in a group by Ferry; in others I have used his descriptions of the various groups as a guide.

The Purpose of the Building

Here I refer to the type of structure in question: capital, public buildings, service, public buildings, and domestic private buildings.

Dating the Construction of Buildings

The issue of establishing a date of construction for a building was particularly problematic. Perumal Murphy in the Heritage Study of the city of Armidale (1991) often sidestep this problem by assigning buildings to a "period" range. These periods vary from 8 to 18 years in length, and are based on arbitrary historical criteria such as "the coming of the railway" or "after the First World War." Often, as with Merici House, buildings are assigned to a date range within these periods based solely on their architectural style, which may provide a wildly inaccurate date.

In general, I found that social context information for public buildings was readily available, particularly for government- and church-funded structures. The problem of chronology was more apparent in the recording of private houses, whose date of construction was not normally recorded in prominent correspondence, but had to be extracted from title records. Because I am concerned with investigating a possible relationship between style, social context, and ideology, establishing a relatively secure date for a building is extremely important. The buildings that I have recorded were all contained within an 87-year capsule, yet my aim has been to try and distinguish between nuances of context within this. A difference of 15 or 20 years in the dating of a building may be decisive in relating it to its social context. A reliable date in my terms was, finally, one which could be narrowed down to a maximum range of 10 years.

Materials and Methods

For some buildings, a known history was already attached to the site or had been previously researched by others. Several publications in the *Armidale and District Historical Society Journal*, and many of the recording forms from the Armidale Heritage Study, were invaluable for this reason. For buildings where this information was not already recorded, I attempted to establish a relatively secure date of construction from searching chains of title for the allotment under question or from title information supplied by the present landowner. Before the conversion in the 1860s to Torrens title, the Old System title recorded all subsequent transactions for an allotment, starting from the name and date of the first purchaser. Often, the record of a mortgage having been taken out on a particular piece of land indicated the construction of a building on that site, and the size of the mortgage provided a fairly reliable guide to the size and construction material of the building. The main problem with using Old System title to date properties is that, once the property was converted to Torrens title, this chain ended. Because conversion was not automatic (it depended on the individual owner paying the required fee), it took place on various properties any time between 1866 and 1937. Drawing correlations between mortgages and the dates for construction of particular buildings was also complicated by the large loan amounts borrowed by richer property owners. Often many properties were offered as security for a single loan, and so were treated subsequently as a group, making it impossible to separate the treatment of individual blocks. John Moore, for example, took out a loan for £30,000 in 1887, which included numerous properties in Armidale as security.

Rate books and ratings maps are useful for cross-checking title information, particularly as rate books include a description of the ratable property, as well as the names of both owner and tenant. Unfortunately for Armidale, only one rate book survives from the nineteenth century, for the year 1883–1884, which supplies information for the years 1878–1884 inclusive. The only ratings map that survives is for the year 1866.

The other historical sources from which it was sometimes possible to reconstruct the date of construction for a particular building were advertisements or articles in the two main local papers, the *Armidale Express* and the *Armidale Chronicle*. Both contained "For sale" and "To let" sections, which sometimes identified the location of a building and provided a brief description (usually limited to size and construction material), as well as the name of the owner and, sometimes, the present or former tenant. These notices were particularly relevant when a building with a Section and Lot number was described as new, or when it was related to the location of other "desirable" buildings in the vicinity. Where possible I have also cross-checked title information, rate book information, and "For sale/To let" notices with deceased estate files. Because death duties were payable on each estate, these files entail lists of the real and personal properties comprising the estate, along with brief descriptions and valuations of each.

Of course, any linkage between specific individuals and specific buildings is fraught with other difficulties, such as change of ownership, tenancy, and subsequent modification to the façade. Consequently, I have also recorded possible variables relating to the degree of change over time to the building's fabric, what these changes entail, and who may have been responsible for them.

VARIABLES RELATING TO STYLE

In my recording I have attempted to take account of several interlocking sets of stylistic variables (after Apperly et al. 1989, 16):

- The scale of the building
- The shape of the building
- The space immediately around the building
- The materials of which the building is made
- The detailing of the building
- The textures visible externally
- The use or non-use of elements related to previous styles
- Ornament or its absence

My archaeological understanding of style is thus essentially a morphological one, and I have reduced this list to three articulating aspects of a building: scale, composition, and qualities between parts (cf. Layton 1991). Scale refers to the absolute size of the building, as well as to the relationship between the building and its immediate surrounding space; composition refers to the variety of morphological elements that combine to form a building's external appearance or its setting; and quality refers to distinctive relationships between elements.

Scale

Scale refers to the area of the building in square meters, the height of the building in stories, and the relationship between a building's area and the block of land on which it is situated (i.e., the proportion between a building and its grounds).

Composition

Because I was initially concerned with style as an expression of identity and with the construction of group over time in Armidale, I concentrated on the public areas and elements of a building, drawing particular attention to its exterior and façade. As a result, and following Blanton (1994, 118–119), I adopted a strategy of recording the structural elements of a building that would be seen by a person engaged in a formal visit, passing from the outside into the formal entrance leading to the front areas of the house. This consists of three decorative settings:

- Roof setting
- Façade setting
- Pre-entry setting

The inclusion of a pre-entry setting is a departure from the traditionally acceptable understanding of building style. Technically, although pre-entry elements located in the forecourt of a building are spatially divorced from the building itself, they constitute an important part of its exterior and should be considered in tandem with the decorative elements of the building proper. It would be misleading to assume that a building façade is communicative, while the appearance and use of entry spaces prior to reaching the house proper is not. I have termed this space "forecourt space" and have used it to include elements such as fences, gates, gardens, or landscaped yards within my analysis. These are all features that, although contributing to defining the spatial layout and public presentation of the building, cannot be accounted for within "roof setting" or "façade setting." Essentially, I regard these features as providing a scene in which the style of the façade may be set and interpreted, analogous to the border in a painting.

While many of these features, particularly gardens and statuary, are recent additions to the building and are not strictly archaeological, some elements, such as stairs, flanking piers, and old plantings of trees and fencing hedges are representative of the original appearance of the building. Because I was concerned with attempting to quantify how a building may have communicated aspects of contextual identity in the past, I regarded landscape elements as merely another medium of style, particularly those elements that either enhance the presence and presentation of a building (such as formally laid-out gardens or leading avenues of trees), or that mystify it (such as high fences or concealing hedges). While the implications of features enhancing the appearance of a building are routinely assessed in terms of historical archaeological treatments of gardens (see, for example, Leone 1989; Kryder-Reid 1994), features that obscure it, such as openness or visibility, are not. William Paca's garden is undoubtedly a statement, but what is the effect or intent of the wall that surrounds it? Given that ideology is concerned with metaphorical concealment, what might the physical concealment of particular buildings at particular times imply? For many structures, I was fortunate enough to be able to record original fence forms from photographs.

Each setting was broken up into discrete features (chimney, window, door, fence), that have then been recorded in terms of their form (i.e., their shape or other distinctive attribute), their material, and their constituent elements. For example the setting façade contains the feature "verandah," which itself contains the elements of columns, brackets, balustrade, and handrail. Each verandah element was then recorded in further detail using the same terms, i.e., to describe its form, material, and constituent elements.

Qualities between Parts

I attempt to assess the relationship between decorative settings or the degree of design formality between parts. I have assessed qualities in terms of the relationship between symmetry and asymmetry as evident in the building façade and forecourt space; formality or informality as evident in the construction of forecourt space, and the degree to which forecourt space is open or closed (i.e., visible to the passerby).

VARIABLES RELATING TO GEOGRAPHIC CONTEXT

Variables relating to geographic context encompass the location of each building within the city (according to the gridded block system laid down by the surveyor Galloway in 1849) and whether the building possessed a view, in other words, whether it overlooked, and in turn could be seen from, key positions within the city landscape. To record this, the location of each building and the size of its present allotment were noted on a section plan, which also noted the size and location of the original nineteenth century allotment.

VARIABLES RELATING TO USE

This is a more difficult category in that some allowance must be made for both past and present uses of a building. I have focused on

Materials and Methods

the original purpose for which a building was intended, any major change of purpose that it may have undergone (including identification of the subsequent purpose or purposes to which it has been put), and the dates and kinds of alteration that may have taken place. Who defined the first function? Who and by what authority was it transformed? What physical changes occurred? These last two variables are important for determining the proportion of original fabric that survives (and therefore which can be linked with the original owner) and the proportion of fabric attributable to subsequent owners and their intentions.

There is a complementary aspect of use that focuses on how buildings are either incorporated within, or excluded from, the public identity of the community, in other words, their "use" as physical containers for identity and as points of articulation for the historical narratives that construct this. As a consequence, I have also attempted to record any known associations between a building and particular historical figures, or between a building and particular historical events (either from historical narratives or extant oral histories within the community), including whether or not the building was recorded as part of the 1991 Armidale Heritage Study. As the most comprehensive study of the Armidale built environment and the link between this and the Armidale community and its history, the Armidale Heritage Study is one of the most prominent attempts to document (and of course to construct) a sympathetic and usable identity for the city (in terms of Council regulations and planning objectives), which is founded explicitly upon its buildings. Given that the total number of buildings existing within the city of Armidale in 1991 exceeded 6,000, and that the Heritage Study is directed towards only 207 of these, there is obviously a selective process here in determining what is or is not heritage. What are the consequences for this particular construction of heritage as representative of the Armidale community?

DATA COLLECTION

Each building was recorded individually and photographs were taken of each façade. Where owners of properties were willing and available, I also collected information relating to the known history of the building, including the date the building was constructed and who might have paid for it. Informally interviewing either owners or tenants also allowed me to collect oral histories for some sites, particularly associations between the building and local personalities or events. Although I was not able to physically visit some houses, I was still able to record them from photographs.

LOCATION OF STRUCTURES

The majority of buildings selected for recording were from five major geographic areas (Figure 4.2):

1. The conservation zone, which contains the largest concentration of nineteenth century private buildings within the Armidale city boundary, as well as both early-, mid- and late-twentieth century examples. Within the area of Armidale known as South Hill in particular, larger private residences were constructed by both mercantile and pastoral capitalists, as well as by upper-echelon public servants.
2. The west end of town, which contains the greatest concentration of worker's houses, as well as hotels and churches associated with this suburb.
3. The central business district and surrounds, which contains the majority of public buildings, including banks, hotels, stores, churches, and offices.
4. Domestic buildings associated with the pastoral industry on selected properties either in or surrounding Armidale. I have attempted to record buildings associated with both original pastoral stations and buildings associated with agricultural or smaller-scale rural properties. Such small-scale rural properties are exclusively associated with land tenure after the Robertson Land Acts came into effect in 1863, and are consequently later in date and associated with a different group of rural land owners.
5. Some buildings, such as the oldest surviving house in Armidale and the house built by B. A. Moses, the largest industrial capitalist in Armidale, which were located outside of these areas, were also included in the database.

It is worth noting that not all buildings within these areas were included in my study. Many buildings across Armidale have been heavily rebuilt, often by the addition of external brick veneer and "modern" aluminium sliding doors and windows (see Figure 4.3). As part of this, many have had their front verandahs enclosed to provide extra living space. In some cases, no original fabric at all remains visible on the façade, and where the façade of a building has been heavily compromised by such additions or alterations, it was excluded from the database. Although these alterations may well be informative in themselves, particularly the implications in converting the appearance of a weatherboard house to the appearance of a brick one through the use of

Materials and Methods

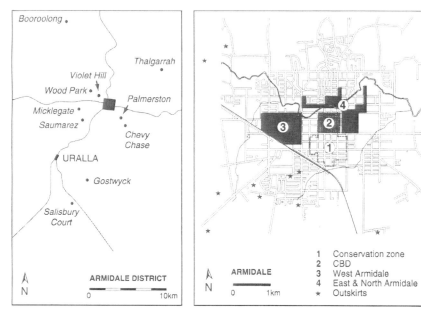

Figure 4.2. The geographical location of recorded structures.

veneer, I have assumed that any connection between the external appearance of these façades after alteration and the social context of the person who originally caused the structure to be built will be severely limited. Likewise, I have attempted to isolate the amount of reconstruction or renovation that each building has undergone (but see later).

In rare instances, nineteenth and early-twentieth century photographs of extant buildings exist, which I have used to record details of their original fabric. In some rare instances, the façade of a building has been completely rebuilt at a later date. Such was the case with Peter Speare's villa Denmark House, for example, which, although originally constructed in 1877 as a private house for a man who made his money from the Hillgrove gold fields, later became a convent for Ursuline nuns (Figure 4.3). It has been extended and altered partly as the convent and attached girls' college grew, and partly to conform to the early 1920s style of other Catholic church buildings. In this particular case, I recorded the building in terms of its original style and form, and attributed its style to its original owner, although the later religious purpose and style of the building can no doubt be read with as much intent.

A complete list of all buildings recorded for this study is contained in the Appendix.

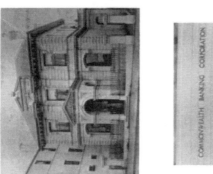

Figure 4.3. Alterations to the physical fabric of structures in Armidale. 1: Denmark House c1888 and 1996; 2: St. Ursula's College c1895 and 1996; 3: The City Bank of Sydney c1895 and 1996 (as the Commonwealth Bank); 4: "Modernizing" an old weatherboard house by adding brick veneer and enclosing the front verandah. (Original photographs of Denmark House, St. Ursula's College, and the City Bank, as well as the modern photo of the Commonwealth Bank, courtesy of the UNE Heritage Centre collections.)

ANALYSIS

All recorded information was entered into the Entrer Trois data-entry program and later transferred to a Microsoft Access relational database. My initial analysis was intended to gain an appreciation of the gross spatial characteristics of architectural style over time, and the relationship between this and possible status boundaries. Following this, I wanted to explore the manifestation of each aspect of architectural style in terms of each category of social context.

Given that my data was primarily nominal or categorical data, I have used the chi-square (χ^2) and Fisher exact tests to statistically examine associations between variables, except where I judged significance to be perfectly obvious, such as when either 0 or 100% occurrence of a feature occurred in a single social context. Choice between the chi-square and Fisher's exact tests was dictated by sample size and the size of expected frequencies: In cases where the chi-square test was inappropriate (i.e., where cell frequencies were less than 5 or $n \leq 20$) (Fletcher and Lock 1991, 118–119; Siegel and Castellan 1988, 123; Thomas 1986, 299) I have used the Fisher exact test. I have structured both the chi-square and Fisher exact tests to compare relative patterning in a feature with that in all other categories of the database. Ultimately, significance for all of the data was assessed in 2×2 contingency tables and most was calculated using Fisher's exact test.

Some initial sample sizes (i.e., structures in the date categories 1840–1860 and public buildings constructed by state capital for both of which $n = 7$) were too small to enable statistically meaningful conclusions to be drawn. Where possible in these cases I have combined categories to enlarge the sample size; thus, for example, the new analytical category "public buildings" contains both government, church, and bank buildings, and the category "early" contains all structures erected prior to 1880. In this fashion I have grouped several sets of scattered variables resulting in a complete list of 30 variables:

Symmetry	Parapet (verandah and main
Construction material	roof)
Brick bond (colonial, English,	Form of brick arch (flat,
Flemish, stretcher)	shallow, semicircular)
Decorative finishes	Finials
(polychrome brick, scored	Bargeboard
ashlar brick, and	Eave detail (bracketed)
weatherboard)	French doors
Quoins	Portico

Form of verandah roof (concave, bullnose, single pitch)

Timber verandah decoration (brackets, friezes, fringes)

Cast-iron verandah decoration (brackets, fringes, friezes, columns, balustrades)

Timber verandah columns (stop-chamfered or turned)

Fences

Hedges

Piers

Stained glass (in doors and windows)

Pilasters (beside doors and windows)

Label molds (over doors and windows)

Sidelights

Fanlights

Bay windows (square, faceted, oriel, round)

Formal name

Extras (tower, buttress, spire)

Design influences (classical, medieval)

View

Associated historical figures or stories

This process also resulted in three main chronological divisions, early (1840–1879), middle (1880–1899), and late (1900–1930), where previously there had been nine (one for each decade). Historically, the first two of these composite periods correspond to the main periods of ideological division: the early period between rival mercantile and pastoral capital and in the middle period between a consolidating mercantile/pastoral "privileged" group and outsiders. The final period constitutes the remainder.

Even these measures were not enough to raise some sample sizes. Although I would have liked more workers' houses in the database, these either did not survive or are impossible to link to social context. Small sample sizes also meant that I could not find significant associations between other categories of social context and style. Both gender and some indications of social status, such as membership sanctions in voluntary organizations, proved to be invisible as possible arbiters of style in this study. Although this prevented me from making statistically meaningful observations on any of these spheres, this in itself is data.

Finally, although graphs of the percentage occurrence of many variables suggested associations between style features and social context, when counts for the 30 variables were compared statistically in over 1,400 contingency tables, not all were found to have significant associations with capital or social class. I tested the frequency of occurrence of all variables at different time periods and for different social groups, but using a level of significance of 0.05 found only 43 statistically significant results (3% of the tests) (see also Table 5.1). Although this might indicate that these associations have arisen due to chance, very few additional associations become significant if the level is raised to 0.10, suggesting that they may, in fact, be real. In the next three chapters, rather than discussing the chronological and spatial distribution of all variables, I will discuss only those that were significant at either the 5% or 10% level (Figure 4.4).

BIASES IN THE DATABASE

Three kinds of biases occurred in the data. The first was the unequal representation of structures representing mercantile capital. Out of a total of 222 structures, 166 of these were either built by mercantile capitalists or by workers employed by them. Secondly, the survival rate of structures is clearly biased towards the 1880s, with very few structures surviving from the earlier decades of the 1840s and 1850s (see Figure 4.5). Lastly, most mercantile structures were geographically concentrated in a particular location, South Hill.

LIMITATIONS OF THE STUDY

As an historical archaeologist I have an enduring interest in standing structures and their place within the community. With the exception of the small sample of houses recorded purely from historical data, this creates two obvious problems: Only those individuals associated with property have been included within my study and, even more limiting, only those individuals associated with property that survives archaeologically are represented here. The focus on buildings as property effected a particular kind of social closure by automatically excluding a great number of people. In 1871, for example, only 13% of the total population of Armidale owned property, which obviously limits the proportion whose identity might be represented through architecture. Ferry (1994, 351–365) has already alluded to the proportion of working-class males who resided and worked, and no doubt had a stake in ideology, in Armidale, but who owned no property. To compound this problem, I was unable to find any information relating to who rented properties in Armidale, apart from a very few high-profile examples, such as when the Anglican bishop of Grafton and Armidale rented

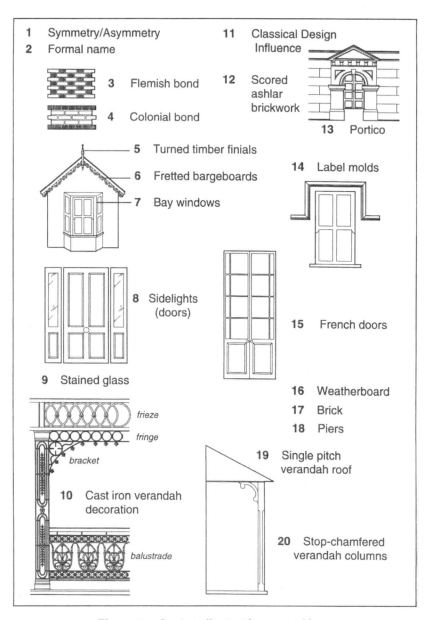

Figure 4.4. Statistically significant variables.

Materials and Methods

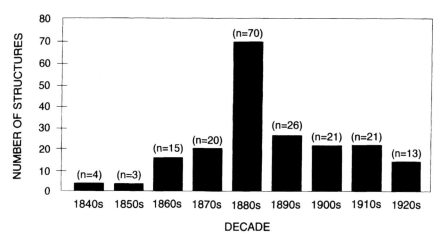

Figure 4.5. The survival rate of structures.

Henry Mallam's house in 1871. No information was available as to where or what properties working-class people rented.

Likewise, until the passing of the Married Women's Property Act in 1893, women's property belonged legally to their husbands, regardless of whether it was personal property (such as cash or stocks), real estate, or an inheritance coming to the wife during marriage (Ferry 1994, 148–149). In 1861, 43% of the population was classed as "residue"—those not working—and in terms of the ownership of property, women property owners constituted only a minuscule 4% of the total population. Although they resided, spent money, and used the facilities available in the town, their identity is much more difficult to establish through architectural style, particularly through the study of the external façade only; undoubtedly, women will be underrepresented in any predominantly nineteenth century study of the built environment. I was only able positively to identify seven buildings in my database commissioned by women, although there were undoubtedly more.

There are many other groups of people, such as domestic servants and white-collar employees, (school teachers, low-ranking clergy, police constables, and clerks), who likewise owned no real property and who are thus not represented anywhere in the built heritage of Armidale. And although I know that Aborigines in Aboriginal communities use and alter European houses in a particular way that renders them distinctive (and that often causes white people to complain), they are not represented here either for the same reasons.

Although Matthew Johnson (1993b, 10) has pointed out that to assume a relationship between wealth levels and house building is quite problematic, it is not really an issue in this study. Although it is undoubtedly true that "whether or not a household will invest its money in architecture as opposed ... to moveable goods or the Church, is a decision that will vary from culture to culture and from social group to social group" (Johnson 1991, 10), in Armidale, money was routinely channeled into standing structures, even by workers through mortgages offered by the New England Permanent Building Society.

Finally, because I focused on external façades, this left no room for discussing the expressions of identity constructed and displayed in private space (i.e., inside). While I assume that individuals also expressed their identity in private, and possibly in ways that ran contrary to their expressions in public (cf. Giddens 1979, 191), the inclusion of this data was beyond the scope of this study. It was also to a large degree irrelevant in a study concerned with the social construction of identity through the symbolic structuring of the public spaces of Armidale.

The Semiotics of Social Identity | 5

I have argued in Chapter 2 that style is a means of non-verbal communication that is implicated in the ways and means by which difference may be created socially through competing constructions of identity. In exploring this premise in relation to the architecture of Armidale, it becomes necessary to investigate both the types of group identity that may be constructed through style, as well as the changing scales at which this identity might be constructed. In other words, it is necessary to search for both similarities and differences in the context of production. How is similarity emphasized through the construction of groups? How are these groups then differentiated from others? Most importantly, how does this change?

In a general sense, it is obvious that the stylistic features of buildings in Armidale have changed over time. Some features occur for a short period only; others persist and are used over the entire time period covered by this study (Figure 5.1). In this chapter, I will discuss the statistically significant results as a prelude to the analysis in later chapters.

THE CONTEXTS OF PRODUCTION FOR STYLE IN ARMIDALE

The discussion in the following two sections relates exclusively to the occurrence of features in *new* structures being built in each period, ignoring the persistence of these features in subsequent constructions. Stained glass, for example, is incorporated into fewer public buildings in the 1880s and 1890s, despite the fact that public buildings with stained glass were still standing from earlier periods. Although it may seem misleading to discuss each new period of construction without reference to previously observed trends, I regard the persistence of features in subsequent contexts more as an issue of space, which will be discussed in the following chapter. For the same reason, while the stylistic elements of non-extant structures have been included as part of the gen-

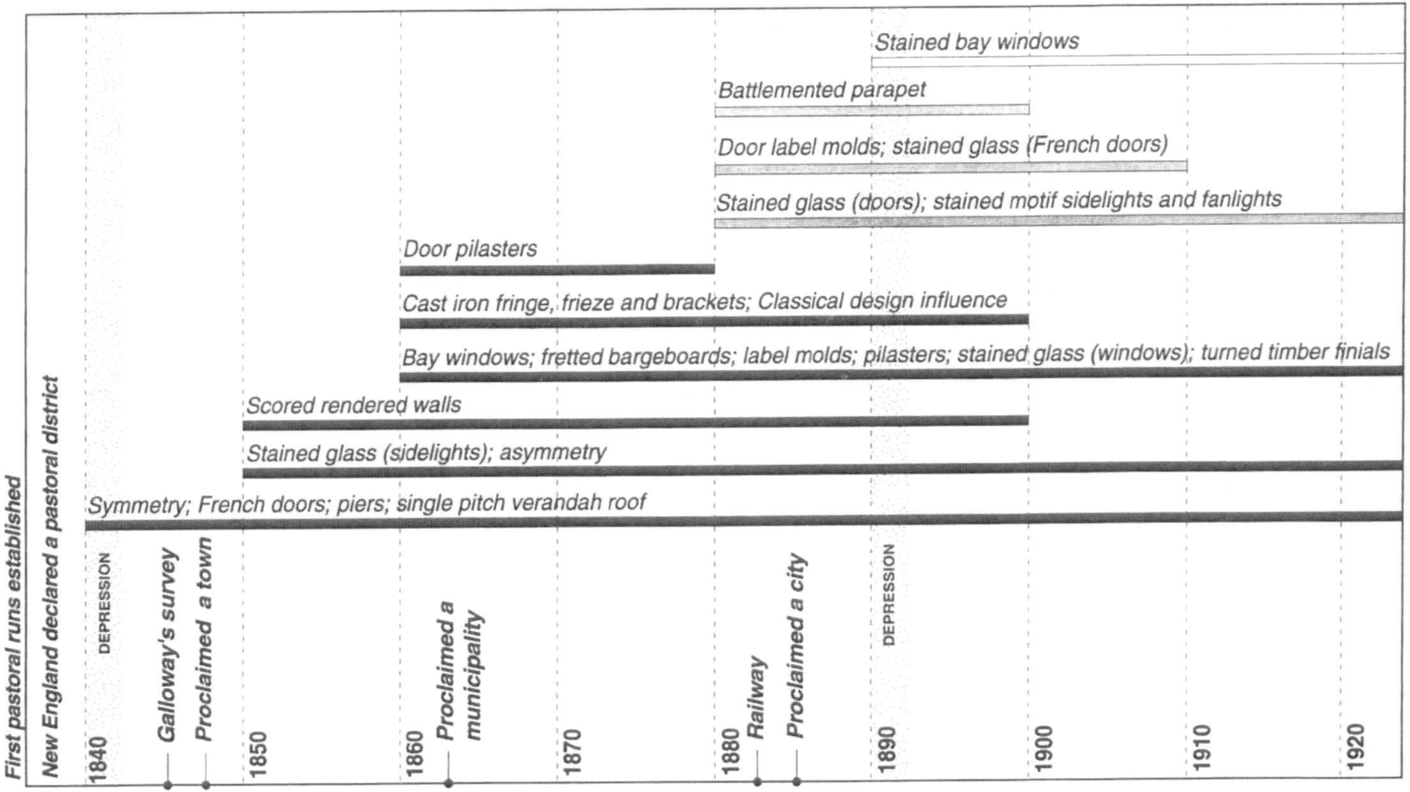

Figure 5.1. The changing use of style features over time.

The Semiotics of Social Identity

eral discussion in this chapter, I will separate them as a specific subset for discussion in the following chapter. For ease of reference, all statistically significant results have been summarized in Table 5.1. Throughout this analysis I will use the word "significant" to describe a level of statistical significance of 0.05 (5%), 0.01 (1%), or 0.001 (0.1%). The usual descriptive conventions are 0.05, significant; 0.01, highly significant, and 0.001, very highly significant. Unless otherwise stated, all tests are Fisher's exact tests.

Capital

Early Period: 1840–1879

The most obvious comparison to occur in the early period is between mercantile and public buildings in the influence of classical design elements (porticoes, pilasters, columns, etc.). Seventy-five percent of public buildings incorporate this feature, but only 14% of private buildings do (Figure 5.2). This difference of frequency is significant at the 0.03 level. Taking porticoes as a separate item, there are differences between their incorporation into public buildings, mercantile buildings, and workers' buildings (Figure 5.3). Seventy-five percent of public buildings have porticos, compared to only 14% of mercantile buildings and no workers' houses. The difference between public buildings and workers' houses is significant at the 5% level, and between public buildings and mercantile structures is highly significant at the 1% level.

In direct contrast to public buildings, no pastoral dwellings incorporate classical motifs, and although these design elements are evident in some worker's houses, there is no statistical evidence for a significant association.

Figure 5.4 shows significant patterning at the 5% level in the use of stained glass between public, mercantile, and workers' structures. Mercantile and public buildings are clearly separated in the occurrence of stained glass. The 75% of public buildings that incorporate this feature differ statistically from the 19% of mercantile structures that display this element. Stained glass also distinguishes public buildings from workers' structures, none of which incorporate this element.

Private pastoral dwellings have a high incidence of the use of French doors in this period (Figure 5.5). More than 83% of pastoral houses built in this period incorporate one or more sets of French doors, in contrast to 33% of mercantile structures (significant at the 0.05 level). No public buildings incorporate this feature, a difference that is also significant at the 0.05 level. Just as French doors are a differentiating feature between mercantile and pastoral capital, so too is the practice of naming

Table 5.1. Statistically Significant Results

Variable	Social context	Groups compared (n)	Test	df	p
Early Period (1840–1879)					
Classical design	Capital	Public (3) + mercantile (3)	Fisher's	1	0.031
elements	Capital	Public (3) + pastoral (0)	Fisher's	1	0.033
Portico	Capital	Public (3) + mercantile (3)	Fisher's	1	0.0011
	Capital	Public (3) + worker (0)	Fisher's	1	0.048
Stained glass	Capital	Public (3) + mercantile (4)	Fisher's	1	0.052
	Capital	Public (3) + worker (0)	Fisher's	1	0.048
French doors	Capital	Public (0) + pastoral (5)	Fisher's	1	0.048
	Capital	Mercantile (7) + pastoral (5)	Fisher's	1	0.043
Formal name	Capital	Public (1) + pastoral (6)	Fisher's	1	0.033
	Capital	Mercantile (12) + pastoral (6)	Fisher's	1	0.062
Formal name	Class	1 (8) + 2 (2)	Fisher's	1	0.014
	Class	1 (8) + 3 (6)	Fisher's	1	0.039
Symmetry	Class	1 (4) + 3 (10)	Fisher's	1	0.071
Middle Period (1880–1899)					
Scored ashlar	Capital	Public (3) + worker (0)	Fisher's	1	0.067
brick	Capital	Public (3) + pastoral (0)	Fisher's	1	0.003
Classical design	Capital	Public (3) + worker (0)	Fisher's	1	0.095
elements	Capital	Mercantile (14) + worker (0)	Fisher's	1	0.021
Cast iron	Capital	Public (4) + worker (0)	Fisher's	1	0.023
	Capital	Mercantile (13) + worker (0)	Fisher's	1	0.029
Symmetry	Capital	Mercantile (23) + worker (8)	Chi-square	1	0.0003
Label molds	Capital	Public (4) + worker (0)	Fisher's	1	0.023
Bay windows	Capital	Mercantile (14) + worker (0)	Fisher's	1	0.021
	Capital	Pastoral (4) + worker (0)	Fisher's	1	0.011
Stained glass	Capital	Public (1) + mercantile (20)	Fisher's	1	0.056
	Capital	Public (1) + worker (6)	Fisher's	1	0.069
French doors	Capital	Public (1) + worker (3)	Fisher's	1	0.040
	Capital	Public (1) + mercantile (20)	Fisher's	1	0.056
Brick	Capital	Pastoral (8) + worker (2)	Fisher's	1	0.0002
Weatherboard	Capital	Public (1) + pastoral (0)	Fisher's	1	0.0002
	Capital	Pastoral (0) + worker (11)	Fisher's	1	0.0002
Single-pitch verandah roof	Capital	Mercantile (10) + worker (7)	Chi-square	1	0.0448
Stop-chamfered verandah columns	Capital	Mercantile (8) + worker (6)	Chi-square	1	0.061
Fretted bargeboards	Capital	Mercantile (17) + pastoral (0)	Fisher's	1	0.043
Formal name	Capital	Mercantile (7) + pastoral (6)	Fisher's	1	0.037
Brick	Class	2 (7) + 4 (2)	Fisher's	1	0.0003
Flemish bond	Class	1 (10) + 4 (2)		1	

The Semiotics of Social Identity

Table 5.1. (*Continued*)

Variable	Social context	Groups compared (*n*)	Test	*df*	*p*
Middle Period (continued)					
Colonial bond	Class	1 (5) + 2 (0)	Fisher's	1	0.083
	Class	1 (5) + 3 (0)	Fisher's	1	0.005
	Class	1 (5) + 4 (0)	Fisher's	1	0.015
Classical design elements	Class	1 (6) + 4 (0)	Fisher's	1	0.033
Formal name	Class	1 (9) + 4 (1)	Fisher's	1	0.023
	Class	2 (4) + 4 (1)	Fisher's	1	0.025
Pilasters	Class	1 (0) + 2 (2)	Fisher's	1	0.055
Stop-chamfered verandah columns	Class	1 (2) + 4 (6)	Fisher's	1	0.029
Late Period (1900–1930)					
Symmetry	Capital	Mercantile (10) + pastoral (1)	Fisher's	1	0.049
	Capital	Pastoral (1) + worker (3)	Fisher's	1	0.069
	Capital	Pastoral (1) + public (3)	Fisher's	1	0.069
Asymmetry	Capital	Mercantile (8) + pastoral (7)	Fisher's	1	0.049
Piers	Capital	Mercantile (11) + worker (0)	Fisher's	1	0.045
	Capital	Pastoral (5) + worker (0)	Fisher's	1	0.081
Turned timber finials	Capital	Mercantile (0) + worker (2)	Fisher's	1	0.025
	Capital	Pastoral (0) + worker (2)	Fisher's	1	0.091
French doors	Capital	Mercantile (4) + worker (0)	Fisher's	1	0.042
Weatherboard	Capital	Public (0) + mercantile (6)	Fisher's	1	0.028
Stained glass	Capital	Public (2) + pastoral (8)	Fisher's	1	0.091
Asymmetry	Class	1 (11) + 4 (1)	Fisher's	1	0.021
Symmetry	Class	1 (2) + 4 (3)	Fisher's	1	0.091
Piers	Class	1 (9) + 4 (0)	Fisher's	1	0.014
	Class	3 (7) + 4 (0)	Fisher's	1	0.026
Sidelights	Class	1 (12) + 4 (2)	Fisher's	1	0.044
Stained glass	Class	1 (13) + 4 (3)	Fisher's	1	0.065
Bay windows	Class	1 (8) + 4 (1)	Fisher's	1	0.0035
French doors	Class	1 (7) + 4 (0)	Fisher's	1	0.053
Scored ashlar brick	Class	1 (0) + 3 (3)	Fisher's	1	0.067
Turned timber finials	Class	1 (0) + 4 (2)	Fisher's	1	0.065
	Class	3 (0) + 4 (2)	Fisher's	1	0.095

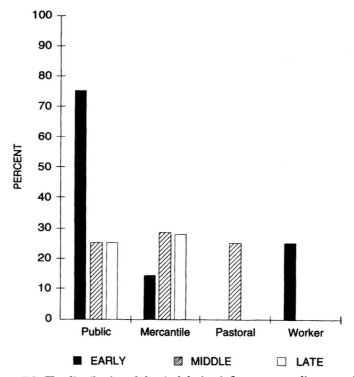

Figure 5.2. The distribution of classical design influences according to capital.

dwellings. In the early period all pastoral houses compared to 57% of mercantile dwellings have formal names (Figure 5.6).

Middle Period: 1880–1899

Public buildings in this period are defined by the use of scored ashlar brickwork to simulate the external appearance of stone, a more dominating and expensive building material. In both the early and middle periods, public buildings exhibited the greatest percentage occurrence of this feature, although it is only in the 1880s and 1890s that this percentage becomes statistically significant in contrast to both pastoral and worker's dwellings (Figure 5.7).

Unlike trends in the early period, a connection between mercantile buildings and public buildings began to be reinforced in the 1880s and 1890s. Both groups of buildings incorporate classical design elements in

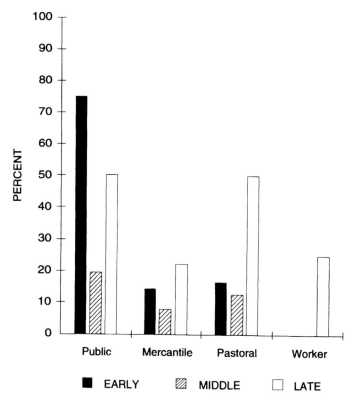

Figure 5.3. The distribution of porticoes according to capital.

the façades of their structures (see Figure 5.1), and both use cast iron as a decorative feature (Figure 5.8). The public buildings erected in this period were influenced by a classical worldview, a scheme that is echoed in the window pilasters and Corinthian pillar verandah posts in mercantile houses of the same period (Figure 5.9). The formal and distinctive appearance of the public sector of town was a deliberate attempt to represent the prosperity and progress of the mercantile sector of Armidale, and was affected by the heavy expenditure on public buildings in the 1860s (Walker 1966, 102).

In each of these examples, mercantile dwellings and public buildings are linked more by default than by an explicit association: In each, the relatively high percentage occurrence of these features is significantly associated with the concurrent absence of these elements from worker's cottages. In addition, a highly significant difference ($\chi^2 =$

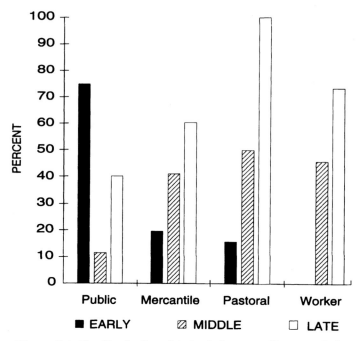

Figure 5.4. The distribution of stained glass according to capital.

0.0003) between mercantile and worker's buildings is evident in the use of symmetry in this period (Figure 5.10). Over 61% of worker's houses constructed in the 1880s and 1890s are symmetrical, compared to 48% of mercantile buildings.

As from the 1840s to the 1870s, worker's houses in the middle period are similarly characterized by the absence of stylistic features that render other structures distinctive. Significant at the 0.05 level is a difference in frequency between the 27% of mercantile buildings that use cast iron for verandah decoration (as brackets, fringes, balustrades, or friezes) and the complete absence of this characteristic in worker's cottages (see Figure 5.8). Likewise, the absence of cast iron in worker's structures is in direct contrast to its 40% use in public buildings, reinforcing the link between mercantile and public buildings (Figure 5.11). Other absences also characterize worker's cottages: label molds, which are prominent on 40% of public buildings and which distinguish ecclesiastical architecture, are absent from worker's dwellings (Figure 5.12), a difference that is significant at the 0.05 level; while bay windows are

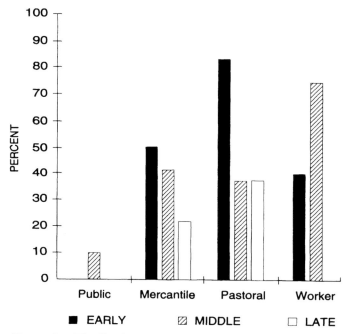

Figure 5.5. The distribution of French doors according to capital.

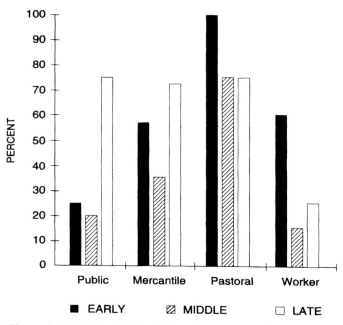

Figure 5.6. The distribution of formal names according to capital.

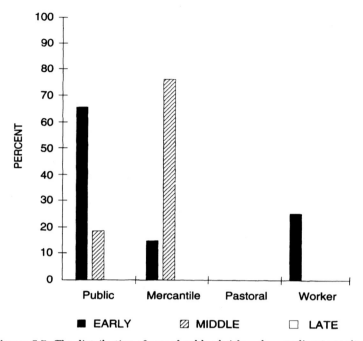

Figure 5.7. The distribution of scored ashlar brickwork according to capital.

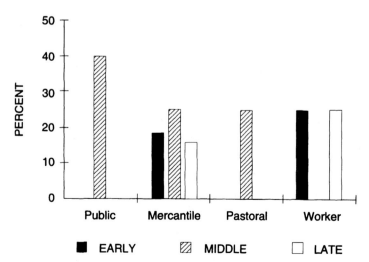

Figure 5.8. The distribution of cast-iron verandah decoration according to capital.

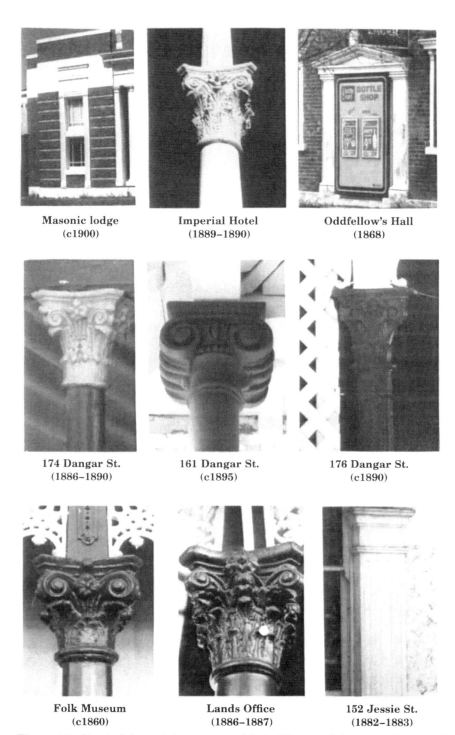

Figure 5.9. Classical design influences on public buildings and the private houses of mercantile capitalists.

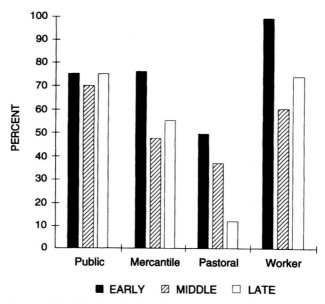

Figure 5.10. The distribution of symmetry according to capital.

used by 50% of pastoral and 30% of mercantile capitalists, but not by workers (Figure 5.13).

In contrast two exceptions appear to be in the use of stained glass and French doors in workers' houses vs. public buildings. Forty-six percent of workers' houses built during these decades display some form of stained glass in either windows or doors, in contrast to only 11% use of this feature in public buildings. Stained glass also separates public buildings from both mercantile and pastoral buildings, which use this element in 41% and 50% of cases, respectively (see Figure 5.4). Likewise, French doors are used in 75% of workers' houses, but only 10% of public buildings in this period (see Figure 5.5).

Two other elements are statistically associated with worker's buildings in the middle period. The 54% occurrence of single-pitch verandah roofs in workers' structures is not only the highest percentage occurrence of this feature in the middle period, but compared to its 20% occurrence in mercantile buildings, is significant at the 5% level (Figure 5.14). Stop-chamfered timber verandah columns are also associated with the style of workers' houses and are used in 46% of working-class structures, in contrast to 16.6% of mercantile buildings (Figure 5.15). This difference is significant at the 10% level.

A particularly noticeable difference is evident in the construction materials employed by workers and pastoralists: All pastoral houses

Folk Museum
(c1860)

78 Rusden St.
(1889–1893)

Folk Museum
(c1860)

131 Brown St.
(c1886)

134 Brown St.
(1883)

Bona Vista
(1884–1886)

Lands Department
(1886–1887)

Imperial Hotel
(1889–1890)

Loombra
(1880s)

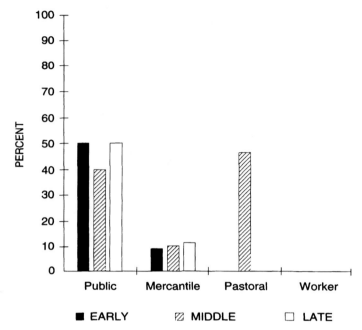

Figure 5.12. The distribution of label molds according to capital.

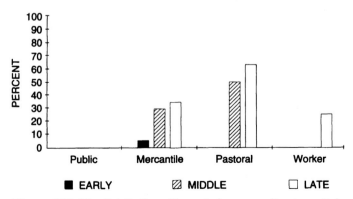

Figure 5.13. The distribution of bay windows according to capital.

The Semiotics of Social Identity

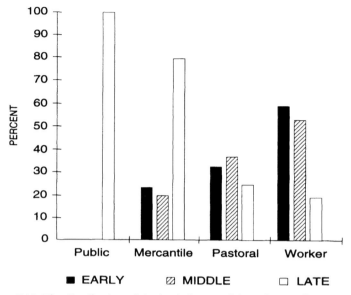

Figure 5.14. The distribution of single-pitch verandah roofs according to capital.

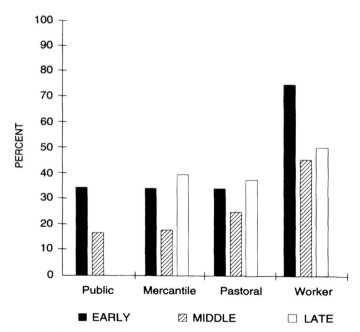

Figure 5.15. The distribution of stop-chamfered verandah columns according to capital.

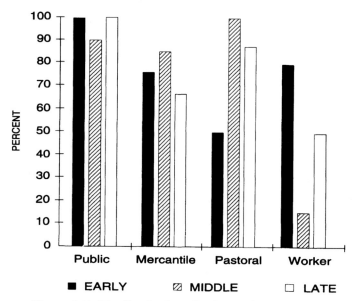

Figure 5.16. The distribution of brick according to capital.

built in the 1880s to 1890s were of brick, compared to only 15% of worker's structures (Figure 5.16). A decrease between the early and middle periods in the number of brick structures built by workers is understandable, as a result of the workers ceasing to reside exclusively on pastoral properties where the accommodation was provided for them by their employer. This difference is very highly significant at the 0.1% level. Likewise, over 85% of worker's dwellings were built from timber weatherboard, in contrast to no pastoral dwellings (Figure 5.17), a difference that is also very highly significant at the 0.1% level. The contrast between the workers and the 10% of public buildings that were built from weatherboard is also very highly significant at the 0.1% level.

The only other significant feature to characterize mercantile buildings is the use of fretted bargeboards across gable ends, which are found in 36% of mercantile buildings in this period (Figure 5.18). Compared to the absence of this feature in pastoral structures, this difference is significant at the 0.05 level. Elaborately fretted bargeboards are a part of the domestic gothic movement, symbolizing an attachment to a romantic image of a rural, vaguely medieval past (Apperly et al. 1989, 90). The significant use of this feature by mercantile capital in Armidale is in keeping with Kerr and Broadbent's (1980) observation that it was pri-

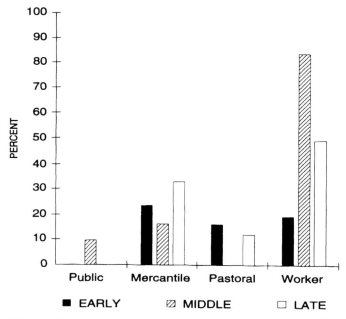

Figure 5.17. The distribution of weatherboard according to capital.

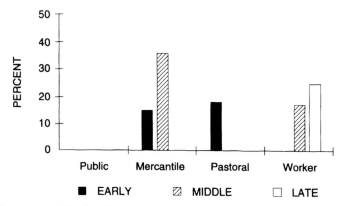

Figure 5.18. The distribution of fretted bargeboards according to capital.

marily taken up by the professional classes rather than the aristocracy, and was largely a function of middle-class taste (Campbell 1987, 33) (Figure 5.19).

Finally, an explicit link between mercantilists and pastoralists is evident in the practice of naming houses. Seventy-five percent of pastoral dwellings built during this period have formal names attached, compared to only 35% of mercantile structures (see Figure 5.6). This difference is significant at the 0.05 level.

Late Period: 1900–1930

During this period, a large percentage of mercantile structures (55%) were designed to be symmetrical, compared to only 14% of pastoral buildings, a relationship that is significant at the 0.05 level (see Figure 5.10). It is interesting to note that a statistically significant association is also evident in reverse, that is, between asymmetry as a feature of mercantile and pastoral buildings during this period (Figure 5.20). There is an example of association by default between mercantile

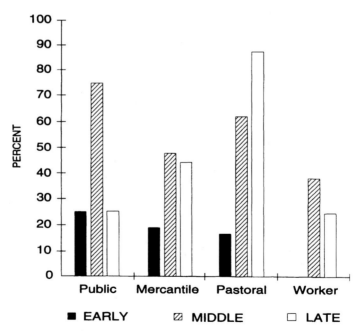

Figure 5.20. The distribution of asymmetry according to capital.

Figure 5.19. Fretted bargeboards on private mercantile houses

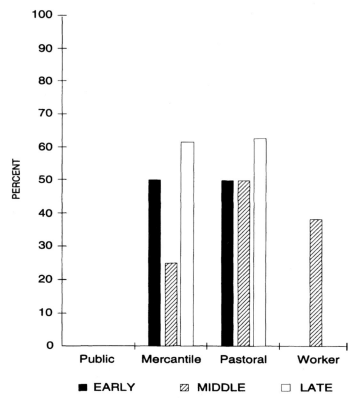

Figure 5.21. The distribution of piers according to capital.

and pastoral capital in the use of piers as a framing device for entries (see Figure 5.21): Both occur with relatively equal frequency (in 61% and 62% of cases, respectively) and both possess a statistically significant relationship to the complete absence of this feature from worker's houses (significant at the 5% level). Mercantile structures are also characterized by the use of weatherboard as a building material in the early twentieth century (see Figure 5.17). Thirty-three percent of mercantile buildings are of weatherboard, compared to no public buildings, a difference that is significant at the 0.05 level.

Turned timber finials are the one element that characterize worker dwellings in this period (Figure 5.22), with 50% of workers' houses possessing this feature. A statistically significant relationship is evident between this percentage and the absence of this feature from mercantile buildings (significant at the 0.05 level). In contrast to the

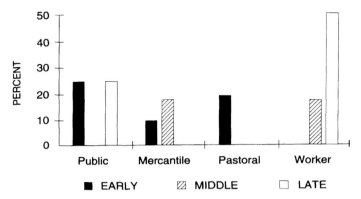

Figure 5.22. The distribution of turned timber finials according to capital.

previous period, workers' houses in the 1900s are no longer characterized by the use of French doors. Instead, compared to 37% of pastoral buildings, no workers' houses incorporate this feature (see Figure 5.5). This difference is significant at the 0.05 level.

As well as French doors, pastoral buildings in this period also show a heavy emphasis on the use of stained glass (see Figure 5.4). One-hundred percent of pastoral buildings incorporate some form of stained glass, compared to only 40% of public buildings, a difference that is significant at the 10% level.

Class

Most of the associations defined according to social class are gross differences between the leisured owners of Armidale (group 1) and the workers (group 4). Group 2 refers to working employers and group 3 to workers who are also periodic employers (see Figure 3.10).

Early Period: 1840–1879

Only two significant associations occur between 1840 and 1879 with respect to social class. The first occurs in the practice of naming structures (Figure 5.23). One-hundred percent of group 1 structures have formal names attached to them, compared to 34% of group 2 structures and 55% of group 3 buildings. Naming a house and an area of land creates links with the European model of landed estates and great houses, and many estates in Armidale and New England take their

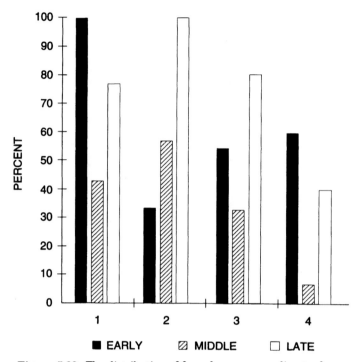

Figure 5.23. The distribution of formal names according to class.

names directly from European places and events (e.g. Salisbury Court, Saumarez, Waterloo, Cotswold, Arran House, Tintagel).

The second association is in the incidence of symmetry between group 1 and group 3 structures. Compared to 50% of group 1 buildings, 90% of group 3 buildings are symmetrical (Figure 5.24).

Middle Period: 1880–1899

Differences in construction material are readily apparent in this period: All buildings from group 2 were made of brick, as compared to most group 4 houses that were built from cheaper weatherboard (Figures 5.25 and 5.26). Accordingly, group 4 obviously constructed a significantly smaller proportion of their houses in the most decorative of all bonds, Flemish bond, compared to group 1, who built 50% of their houses in this period using that feature (Figure 5.27). Interestingly, another feature that clearly relates to group 1 is a significantly higher propor-

The Semiotics of Social Identity

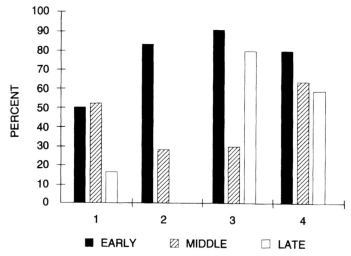

Figure 5.24. The distribution of symmetry according to class.

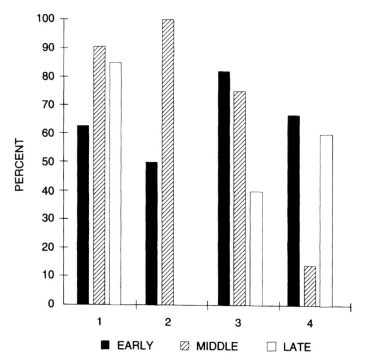

Figure 5.25. The distribution of brick according to class.

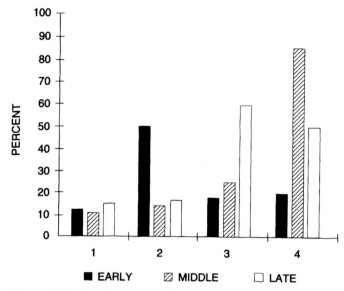

Figure 5.26. The distribution of weatherboard according to class.

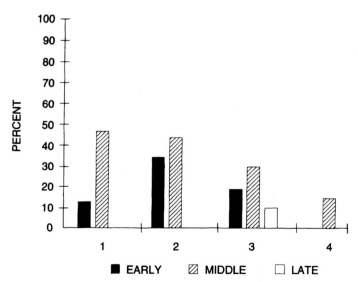

Figure 5.27. The distribution of Flemish bond according to class.

The Semiotics of Social Identity

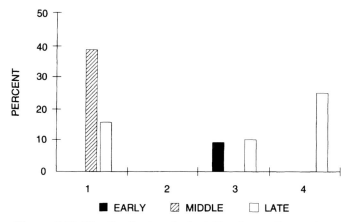

Figure 5.28. The distribution of colonial bond according to class.

tionate use of colonial bond, compared to groups 3 and 4 (Figure 5.28). The difference in frequency of this feature between groups 1 and 4 is significant at the 5% level, and between groups 1 and 3 is highly significant at the 1% level. Group 1 is also distinguished from group 4 in their use of classical design elements: 27% of structures built by group 1 employ these motifs, in contrast to no group 4 structures (Figure 5.29).

Bestowing a formal name on a property is also significant in terms of social class in the 1880s and 1890s (see Figure 5.23). Once again, a significant proportion of both groups 1 and 2 gave names to their houses, as compared to group 4.

The only element that characterizes group 4 structures in this

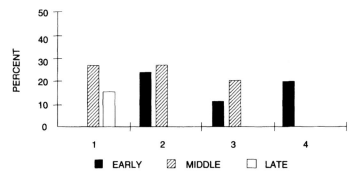

Figure 5.29. The distribution of classical design influences according to class.

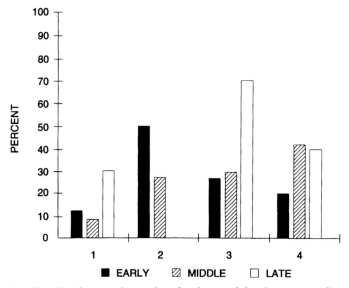

Figure 5.30. The distribution of stop-chamfered verandah columns according to class.

period are timber stop-chamfered verandah columns (Figure 5.30). The use of this feature in over 42% of structures clearly differentiates group 4 from group 1, who only employed it in 9.5% of structures. This difference is significant at the 5% level.

Late Period: 1900–1930

Asymmetry becomes a defining characteristic in this period between either end of the social spectrum: groups 1 and 4 (Figure 5.31). Almost 85% of group 1 built structures are asymmetrical in this period, compared to only 20% of group 4 structures, a difference that is significant at the 5% level. The reverse is also true, but at a less significant level (10%): 60% of group 4 structures were symmetrical, compared to only 15% of group 1 buildings (see Figure 5.24).

Apart from symmetry, only one other element characterizes group 4 structures in this period. Turned timber finials occur on 40% of the structures built by members of group 4, compared to the absence of these finials from group 1 structures. This difference is significant at the 10% level (Figure 5.32).

Piers are another significant feature in this period (Figure 5.33). They structure a relationship between group 1 and group 4, and between

The Semiotics of Social Identity

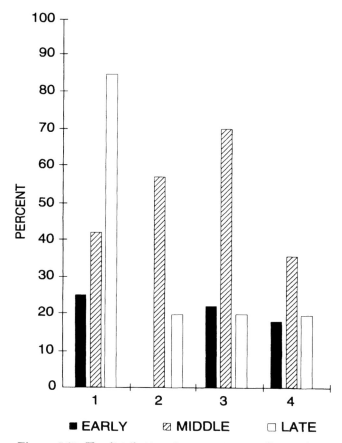

Figure 5.31. The distribution of asymmetry according to class.

group 3 and group 4. Groups 1 and 3 employed piers in 69% and 70% of their structures, respectively, as compared to the absence of this feature in group 4. In this period, group 3 structures also demonstrated an affinity with the public buildings of earlier periods through the use of scored ashlar brickwork on external wall surfaces (Figure 5.34). The difference in the use of this feature between 30% of group 3 structures and no group 1 structures is significant at the 10% level.

Group 1 buildings are separated from the structures of other groups by a range of other features in this period. Sidelights and stained glass distinguish group 1 and group 4 structures, with more than 90% of group 1 buildings having sidelights as part of their entry door decora-

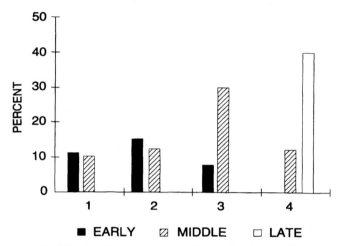

Figure 5.32. The distribution of turned timber finials according to class.

tion, in contrast to only 30% of group 4 structures (Figure 5.35). This difference is significant at the 5% level. Interestingly, although the incidence of stained glass in group 4 structures has increased dramatically to 60% in this period, it is still significantly different (at the 10% level) from the 100% use of this feature in group 1 structures (Figure 5.36). Bay windows also create this distinction, but at a highly significant level (1%). Sixty-one percent of group 1 structures were built with a bay window, however, only 7% of group 4 houses had this feature (Figure 5.37). Likewise, French doors occur in over 53% of group 1 buildings, in contrast to the absence of this feature from group 4 buildings (Figure 5.38). This difference is significant at the 0.05 level.

PARTIAL SOCIAL CONTEXT

Out of the total of 222 structures in the database, 37 were without at least one crucial aspect of their social context (either date of construction or identity of the original owner). In the early period the partial social context structures differed from group 1, 3, and 4 structures in making little use of brick as a construction material. They also differed from group 3 structures in a relatively low incidence of symmetry (50% of unknowns compared to 90.9% of group 3 buildings), and in never using piers and single-pitch verandah roofs. Compared to capital, par-

The Semiotics of Social Identity

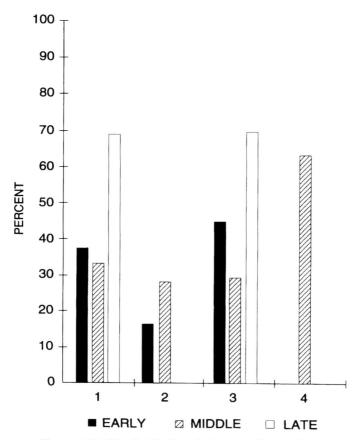

Figure 5.33. The distribution of piers according to class.

tial social context structures differ from pastoral houses in not formally naming their structures. Interestingly, they are also differentiated from both mercantile and pastoral structures in their marked preference for using English bond (100% of partial context buildings compared to no pastoral buildings and 4.7% of mercantile buildings). This last element would seem to suggest that the partial social context structures are from a separate social group in certain respects (given the multiple levels of meaning) to either mercantile or pastoral structures.

Unlike the figures for the 1840 to 1870s, the results for the middle period do not indicate any coherent groupings in the stylistic elements for partial social context structures, with a much greater range of varia-

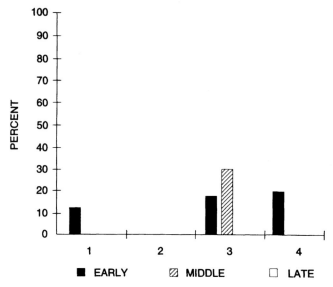

Figure 5.34. The distribution of scored ashlar brickwork according to class.

tion appearing. Like the early period, partial context structures are significantly associated with an absence of piers and single-pitch verandah roofs compared to structures of all other groups. Partial social context structures are also characterized by an absence of the use of colonial bond brickwork, compared to 38% use of this feature by group 1. Apart from being characterized by absence, partial context structures are

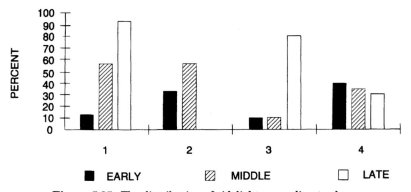

Figure 5.35. The distribution of sidelights according to class.

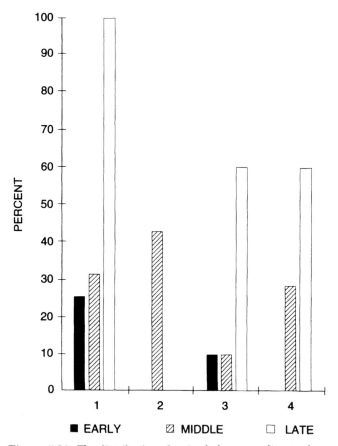

Figure 5.36. The distribution of stained glass according to class.

also significantly associated with low percentage occurrences of stained glass (11%), brick (52%), Flemish bond brickwork (5.8%), sidelights (26%), and turned timber finials (5.8%), compared to higher frequencies of these features in structures built by all other groups. At the other end of the spectrum are the features that occur with significantly greater frequency in partial social context structures: rendered scored brick (17.6% compared to the absence of this feature in group 1 structures) and symmetry (50%, in contrast to 30% in group 1 structures).

A similar patterning occurs according to capital. Partial social context structures have no piers and significantly fewer occurrences of

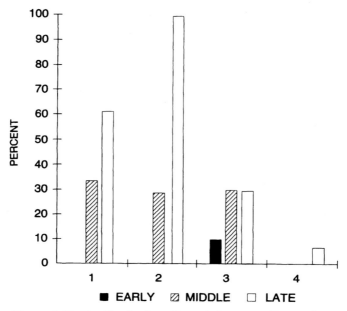

Figure 5.37. The distribution of bay windows according to class.

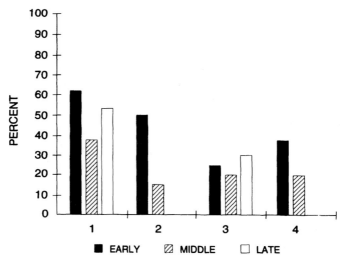

Figure 5.38. The distribution of French doors according to class.

formal names and sidelights (both compared to mercantile), stained glass (compared to mercantile and pastoral), and brick (compared to pastoral and public). Another significant difference occurs in relation to bay windows and cast-iron verandah decoration, which appear in 25% of partial context structures compared to no workers' buildings. French doors also distinguish partial context structures in this period: 62.5% compared to 10% of public buildings, 41.6% of mercantile buildings, and 37.5% of pastoral structures.

During the late period (1900–1930) structures of partial social context continue to avoid the use of single-pitch verandah roofs, compared to 40% of group 4 and 100% of group 2 structures. In contrast to the middle period, partial social context structures use no rendered and scored brickwork in the 1900s (compared to 15% use of this feature by group 3) and significantly fewer instances of stained glass (in contrast to group 1 and 3); hedges, sidelights, and brick (all compared to group 1); and symmetry (compared to group 3).

Compared to capital, partial context structures once again incorporate no single-pitch verandah roofs or colonial bond, in contrast to 25% of pastoral structures and 44% of mercantile structures that display these features. Relatively low frequencies of classical design elements and stained glass separate partial social context structures from both mercantile and pastoral buildings, respectively. In contrast, partial context structures include bullnose verandah roofs more often than mercantile structures, and use weatherboard more often than do pastoral structures. French doors are also significantly associated with partial context buildings in this period: 78%, as compared to none in workers' houses and public buildings. Partial context structures are distinctly separate from public buildings in a low percentage occurrence of formal names, brick, and label molds.

STYLE WITHOUT CONTEXT

If identity is both expressed and interpreted in style, then is it possible to make observations on the possible identity of the owners of structures for which there is no longer an established social context? In other words, where do those structures currently without associated social context fit within this analysis? What is their "style"?

Out of a total of 222 structures, 26 were completely devoid of any social context information at all. Because both the date and the person responsible for the construction of these buildings is unknown, they cannot be discussed in the same terms as the remainder of the database.

Neither is it possible to place them within broad time periods or to compare them in statistically meaningful terms, although it is possible, of course, to describe their style. The 26 structures entirely without any form of social context information possessed a range of features in common, as well as highly distinctive features that set them apart (Figure 5.39). The majority were designed to be asymmetrical (65%) and constructed of timber weatherboard (61.5%). Commensurably, very few were constructed of brick (19.2%) using decorative bonds or scored ashlar brickwork. Very few of the unknown structures possessed classical design elements, turned timber finials, fretted timber bargeboards, cast-iron verandah decoration (all appearing in only 7.6% of structures), or French doors (11.5%). A relatively high percentage of unknown structures were symmetrical, with bay windows and a view over town (all 30.7%), or possessed single-pitch verandah roofs (53.8%), stained glass (46.1%), or sidelights (34.6%).

Some structures exhibited highly individual stylistic features. The gable infill on 153 Mann St. is identical to that on Kilbucho, the mansion built by Russell Richardson from 1895 to 1896. The only unknown structure to possess an asymmetrical sidelight was 99 Rusden St.; 134 Barney St. and 77 Barney St. both included a round art nouveau window, which in 77 Barney St. was combined with highly decorative timber art-nouveau verandah decoration (see Figure 5.40). At 72 Beardy St. there were both a parapet and decorative corner quoins, and 155 Allingham St. had unusual timber corner quoins.

Given the patterns that have emerged from analyzing the style of structures with reasonably secure social context information, it may be possible to make some predictions for the identity of the people who caused the unknown social context structures to be built. These predictions are based on the physical features of architectural style and on how these are known to have articulated with particular social groups in the past (Table 5.2).

DISCUSSION

Although I began by recording 30 variables relating to architectural style, only 20 of these showed significant patterning according to social context. Some of these, symmetry; fretted bargeboards; classical design influences, such as pilasters, columns, and porticoes; medieval design elements, such as towers, label molds, and stained glass; construction material; decorative brick bonds; scored ashlar brickwork; roof pitch; projecting bay windows; and the use of cast-iron decoration, are all

The Semiotics of Social Identity 137

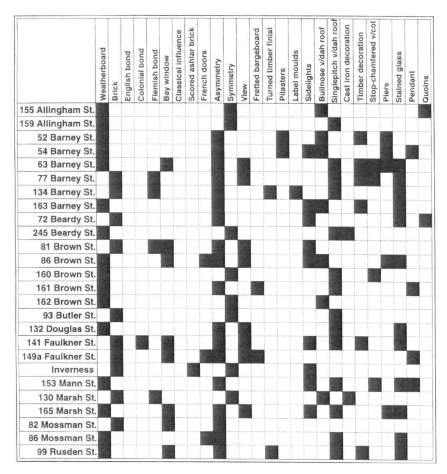

Figure 5.39. The style of the unknown social context structures.

dominant aspects of structures. Others were less prominent elements, such as entry piers, sidelights, turned timber finials, stop-chamfered verandah columns, and formal names. That all of these features should indicate that identity is being incorporated into the style of structures in Armidale suggests that membership in particular groups was established at various scales and that these elements can be viewed as indexes of a whole range of relative social positions.

I expected that there would generally be significant patterning in certain variables, which ultimately proved not to be significant. I found it surprising, for example, that a process of enclosure using increased

Figure 5.40. The timber verandah decoration on 77 Barney St..

fence height and screening hedges was not correlatable to any definition of social context (cf. Johnson 1991; 1993b; 1996). The cypress hedges, most of which were planted in the 1880s, are a recognizable aspect of many houses on South Hill (Figure 5.41), and effectively increase the height of the fence to enclose and render "private" property. In addition, the cypress hedges and many of the other dominant plantings in this area create visual links between mercantile houses and the ecclesiastical precinct in the center of town. The use of plantings to accentuate an impression of power in the land or to emphasize the apparent or actual extent and unity of an estate (Daniels 1988, 45) is a feature that is clearly evident in the avenues of exotic trees that line the entrance to all pastoral properties in the database (Figure 5.42). It is the species of these plantings and of those on South Hill that are as important as their placement: They are all exotic species (elm, birch, oak, poplar, cypress) with links to landed estates and visual images with a much older history of appropriation.

It was also surprising that often some, but not all, variants of a feature were significant. Colonial and Flemish bond, for example, did prove to be significant, but not stretcher or English bond. Likewise,

The Semiotics of Social Identity

Table 5.2. Predictions for the Social Context of Unknown Structures

Address	Date (?)	Main stylistic features	Group (?)	Capital (?)
155 Allingham St.	1880s	Symmetrical weatherboard, bullnose verandah roof and quoins	4	Worker
159 Allingham St.	1880s	Symmetrical weatherboard, single-pitch verandah roof	4	Worker
52 Barney St.	Early 1900s	Asymmetrical weatherboard, pilasters, bullnose verandah roof, piers	1 or 3	Mercantile
54 Barney St.	Early 1900s	Asymmetrical weatherboard, bullnose verandah roof, sidelights, pilasters, piers	1	Mercantile
63 Barney St.	1890s–1900s	Asymmetrical weatherboard, bay window, single-pitch verandah roof, stop-chamfered verandah columns, piers, stained glass	4	Worker
77 Barney St.	Early 1900s	Asymmetrical brick, Flemish bond, single-pitch verandah roof, stop-chamfered verandah columns, stained glass	1	Mercantile
134 Barney St.	1880s	Asymmetrical dichrome brick, Flemish bond, turned timber finial, label molds, single-pitch verandah roofs, stained glass	1 or 3	Mercantile
163 Barney St.		Asymetrical weatherboard, bullnose verandah roof, sidelights, stained glass	3 or 4	Mercantile
72 Beardy St.	1880s–1890s	Asymmetrical brick, sidelights, stained glass, quoins, parapet	1	Mercantile
245 Beardy St.		Symmetrical weatherboard, single-pitch verandah roof	4	Worker
81 Brown St.	Early 1900s	Asymmetrical brick, Flemish bond, bay window, sidelights	1	Mercantile
86 Brown St.	1880s–1890s	Asymmetrical weatherboard, bay window, French doors, bullnose verandah roof, sidelights, piers, stained glass	1 or 3	Mercantile
160 Brown St.		Symmetrical weatherboard, single-pitch verandah roof, stop-chamfered verandah columns	4	Worker

(continued)

140   **Chapter 5**

Table 5.2. (*Continued*)

Address	Date (?)	Main stylistic features	Group (?)	Capital (?)
161 Brown St.		Asymmetrical weatherboard, fretted bargeboard, single-pitch verandah roof	3	Mercantile
162 Brown St.		Symmetrical weatherboard, bullnose verandah roof	4	Worker
93 Butler St.		Symmetrical brick, single-pitch verandah roof	4	Worker
132 Douglas St.		Asymmetrical watherboard, single-pitch verandah roof, stained glass	3	Mercantile
141 Faulkner St.		Asymmetrical brick, colonial bond, bay window, sidelights, single-pitch verandah roof, stained glass	1 or 3	Mercantile
149a Faulkner St.		Asymmetrical brick, bay window, French doors, fretted bargeboard	2 or 3	Mercantile
Inverness (original cottage)	1890s	Symmetrical brick, scored ashlar, sidelights	3	Mercantile
153 Mann St.		Asymmetrical weatherboard, single-pitch verandah roof, sidelights, stop-chamfered verandah columns, stained glass	4	Worker
130 Marsh St.		Symmetrical brick, Flemish bond, bullnose verandah roof, cast-iron verandah decoration	1, 2 or 3	Mercantile
165 Marsh St.	1890s–1900s	Asymmetrical weatherboard, bay window, single-pitch verandah roof, sidelights, piers, stained glass	1	Mercantile
82 Mossman St.		Asymmetrical brick, bay window	1, 2, or 3	Mercantile
86 Mossman St.		Asymmetrical weatherboard, French doors, single-pitch verandah roof, stained glass	2 or 3	Mercantile
99 Rusden St.	Late 1890s–1900s	Asymmetrical weatherboard, bay window, turned timber finial, single-pitch verandah roof, stained glass	3 or 4	Mercantile

Sturry, Jessie St.
(1912)

Gladdiswoode, Mann St.
(1922)

Highbury, Faulkner St.
(c1902)

Figure 5.41. Cypress hedges, South Hill.

whereas single-pitch, corrugated-iron verandah roofs were significant, bullnose and concave roofs were not. The fine-grained scale of results also meant that it was the individual elements of particular architectural manners that were significant, rather than the manners themselves. Gothic, for instance, was typified by fretted bargeboards and turned timber finials; however, these elements were used differently by mercantilists and workers. Thus, it was not the totality of gothic that was used to signify identity, but the selective appropriation of its particular elements.

This turns the focus to the complexities of style as an indicator of individual and group identity: What might the use of these features signify? I will next address in more detail the construction of identity through the medium of architectural style. Because my analysis is

Figure 5.42. Avenues of exotic trees lining the approaches to pastoral properties in New England.

directed towards assessing the *potential* of style in Armidale's standing structures to encode information on various facets of personal and group identity, I will explore how these changes in stylistic components relate to the two principal forms of social context identified in Chapter 3: capital and social class.

Relations of Meaning and Relations of Membership | 6

If various forms of social identity are created through style, then any analysis of stylistic elements will describe some form of group mobilization through the use of particular stylistic elements or groups of elements. Style at this level is embedded in the first two of Stewart Clegg's (1989) circuits of power: mobilizing relations of meaning and relations of membership. Relations of meaning incorporate a group through shared concepts of identity; relations of membership establish the boundaries of the group and negotiate the processes of inclusion and exclusion.

CREATING SOCIAL IDENTITY

Some features are highly identifiable only with particular groups. In the 1880s and 1890s, for example, scored ashlar brickwork and label molds were closely linked to the appearance of public buildings; fretted bargeboards characterized mercantile capital structures, and symmetrical weatherboard houses with stained glass and single-pitch verandah roofs defined the workers. Likewise in the same period, Flemish and Colonial bond structures characterize group 1; weatherboard houses with stop-chamfered verandah columns identify group 4. This leads to a second observation—some groups of structures tend always to show distinct differences. The most obvious is that, in each period, public buildings are always significantly different from all other groups of structures. Although public buildings tend to be characterized by different features over time (classical features in the early and middle periods; scored ashlar brickwork in the middle period, and symmetry in the late period) they are always distinctly separate from private buildings.

Workers' houses tend to be clearly separable as well, sometimes through the total absence of features that render other groups of structures distinctive, and sometimes through their use of particular features. Workers' houses exhibit the most use of features in the 1880s and 1890s, mainly in elements that are components of the verandah, such as

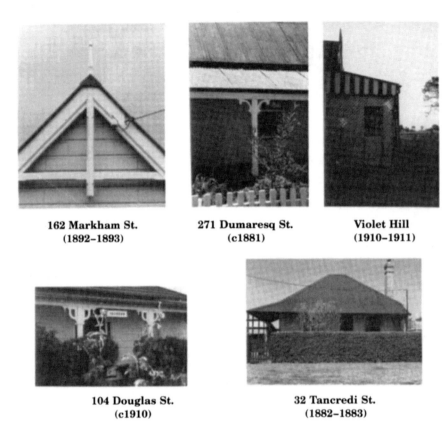

Figure 6.1. The style of working-class structures in the middle and late periods.

stop-chamfered verandah columns and single-pitch verandah roofs (Figure 6.1). The choice in some of these features appears strictly utilitarian, but the choice of others appears more decorative. Single-pitch verandah roofs, for instance, are hardly decorative, and represent the most functional form of roof, compared to the bullnose or concave alternatives. While this may simply represent the truism that workers' cottages were built without excess ornament, perhaps the significant choice here lies in terms of what the workers did *not* choose, rather than what they did. Both bullnose and concave verandah roofs were designed to be reminiscent of the canvas awnings of the Regency period, particularly the awnings of fashionable English seaside pavilions (Irving et al. 1985, 52; Stapleton 1983, 61). Perhaps in choosing an alterna-

Relations of Meaning and Membership

tive form, the workers were also deliberately distancing themselves from such upper-class associations.

Workers' houses remain distinctive in the early twentieth century, although not through use of the same features. In this period, the style of workers' houses is dominated by the use of turned timber finials (see Figure 6.1). As a mass-produced building element, turned timber finials were no doubt relatively cheap to purchase, but being a skyline element, they stood out from the rest of the structure. In all of the timber elements that became indexical of the workers in Armidale, there is a chain of emulation from mercantile, upper- and middle-class structures to the working class. The most frequent occurrence of single-pitch verandah roofs in the early period was in 36% and 37% of group 1 and 3 mercantile structures, respectively. By the time it had become an indexical marker of the workers in the middle period, it was still being used in 52% and 45% of structures from groups 1 and 3. Stop-chamfered verandah columns were used in 54% of group 3 structures in the early period and 30% of group 3 structures in the middle period. Likewise, turned timber finials were employed in 12% of group 1 buildings and 16% of group 2 buildings in the early period, and in 30% of group 3 structures in the middle period. The only examples of any of these features in pastoral buildings occurred solely in the early period, and in lower frequencies than in mercantile structures. This would seem to indicate that at the same time that the workers were creating a group identity for themselves from the range of stylistic elements available, they were also emulating the other groups in society. Moreover, they were not emulating a specific group, but all groups: The highest frequencies for the occurrence of all three features in the early period came from different social groups: single-pitch verandah roofs from group 1, stop-chamfered verandah columns from group 3, and turned timber finials from group 2.

The use of some features in common creates links between groups. Public buildings from the beginning are characterized by the use of classically inspired elements, such as porticoes, pediments, or Corinthian columns. A strong classical influence continues in public buildings in the middle period, but also begins to influence the components of mercantile buildings and the structures of group 1. Classically inspired stylistic elements are a conspicuous marker of the Georgian manner, and characterized most public buildings built in Australia in the nineteenth century, as well as in other British colonies, such as India. By linking themselves stylistically to these buildings, mercantile capitalists and members of group 1 were accomplishing two things. First, they were creating sets of associations between their relatively newfound wealth and the older, more pretentious claims of the Georgian, which was linked to an English country heritage (Cosgrove 1984, 216–217), and the divide between "town house" and "country house" (Irving et al. 1985, 49). In Australia, the concept of a Georgian country house was filtered to specifically symbolize the agricultural importance of the colony, particularly the wealth of the wool industry (Irving et al. 1985, 49). Second, by choosing classical design influences, mercantile capitalists and members of group 1 were linking themselves to the more general Victorian belief in the progress of Western nations towards ever higher levels of material prosperity as the British Empire continued to expand and acquire colonies (Apperly et al. 1989, 52; Freeland 1988, 93–97).

A movement towards growing similarity is evident between mercantilists and pastoralists in the increased association between these two groups after the early period. Mercantile buildings are often linked to pastoral buildings through the use of common features in the middle and late periods. Both incorporate bay windows and stained glass in their houses in the middle period, and both tend to build asymmetrical structures with dominant entry piers in the late period. This growing similarity may, to some extent, have been a result of the influence of individual "style setters," such as John Horbury Hunt. Hunt was an architect whose initial links with Armidale came through contact with the White family, wealthy and influential pastoralists who owned several properties surrounding Armidale. Although Hunt's first commission in Armidale was the Anglican Cathedral of St. Peter, built between 1871 and 1875, he later went on to design and supervise the construction of Booloominbah for Frederick White in 1888 and Trevenna for Elizabeth Wright, who was both neighbor and friend to the Whites (Mitchell 1995, 2). Hunt also designed the hospital buildings in Armidale, the St. Peter's Deanery, and St. John's Theological College.

Through the interconnections between Hunt and the Whites there are several stylistic similarities between the Gothic Revival manner of St. Peter's Cathedral and elements of Booloominbah, Trevenna, and the Deanery. All three are aggressively asymmetrical, with pointed window arches; Booloominbah and the Deanery both have stained-glass windows, and Booloominbah also incorporates gargoyles, buttresses, and a terracotta relief (Figure 6.2). Hunt's recurring use of Gothic Revival elements initially in ecclesiastical architecture, and later in private houses for wealthy pastoralists, created a chain of association between the imagery of the church and the position and influence of pastoral wealth, which could not only afford a unique building designed by an eminent architect, but also to import many of the internal finishings from England and America (Mitchell 1995, 24–25). This imagery was

Relations of Meaning and Membership 147

Pointed arches
St. Peter's Cathedral

Pointed arches
Booloominbah

Booloominbah
(1883–1888) c1920

Trevenna
(1890–1892)

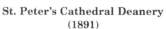
St. Peter's Cathedral Deanery
(1891)

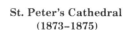
St. Peter's Cathedral
(1873–1875)

Figure 6.2. The Gothic revival manner of four of John Horbury Hunt's buildings: St Peter's Anglican Cathedral, Booloominbah, Trevenna, and the Deanery. (Photograph of Booloominbah c1920 courtesy UNE Heritage Centre collections.)

148   Chapter 6

soon to be appropriated by others, particularly by the dominant groups of mercantile and pastoral capital. The direction of emulation for this feature may have been associated with a symbolic transference of ecclesiastical imagery from the church to secular arenas, such as universities, schools, town halls, and family homes (cf. Clark 1988, 535). That the two groups were becoming consolidated into one at the time suggests that the appropriation of the previously dominant imagery of the church may have been linked to the transference of influence over aspects of daily life from the church to secular power.

Contrary to what is stated in the historical documents, mercantilists and pastoralists, in fact, have features in common more often than any other group, although the particular features in question change with time. Similarities in style between the two begin in the middle period and increase in the late period, although at no time could the two groups be deemed to be the same. In other words, at the same time as they are using features in common, so too are they also using distinctive features that mark them as separate groups (cf. Wiessner 1989). This may indicate both an increased awareness of their similar agendas, as well as a simultaneous subtle distancing in terms of status. Pastoralists were always more wealthy than mercantilists and, while choosing to live in the same area and perhaps pursue some of the same local goals, they also maintained links on a national and international scale that clearly separated them from their local associates. The fact that little intermarriage occurred between pastoralists and mercantilists tends to reinforce the notion of differential status between the two groups.

Some features show opposite trends in their use by different social groups. For example, asymmetry increases in use in the late period to mark pastoral and mercantile buildings, in opposition to the dominant symmetry of workers' houses in the preceding period. While this is probably in part a deliberate strategy employed by mercantilists and pastoralists to distance themselves from the workers, their increasing use of asymmetry is also in opposition to the symmetry of public buildings in the late period. That a trend observed in public buildings should exist side by side with the opposite trend in private mercantile and private pastoral buildings is curious. Clearly, the style of mercantile buildings no longer echoes the dominant themes of public buildings, but is demonstrating more affinity with the style of pastoral buildings as their respective agendas begin to converge. This raises the issue of the direction of emulation: Who imitates whom and when? Initially, emulation moves in two directions: from public buildings associated with the daily business of capital (banks, shops, hotels, and lodges) to mercantile buildings, and from public ecclesiastical buildings to pastoral struc-

Relations of Meaning and Membership 149

tures. From there, both pastoral and mercantile structures begin to grow more similar as the mercantilists emulate the pastoralists, and both begin to appropriate common associations.

The similarities and the differences that are evident between the styles of pastoral and mercantile capital illustrate a central facet to the working of style: stylistic comparison mirrors social comparison (Wiessner 1990, 107). In the early period, pastoral and mercantile capitalists were opposed to each other, each aligned to separate agendas and sources of wealth. The social comparison occurring at this time was part of a wider struggle between the two groups for control, and is reflected in the stylistic differences maintained between them. Each group was establishing their own realm of style in the face of the other. In the middle and late periods, when their respective agendas had begun to converge, social and stylistic comparison still occurred, but there was a greater degree of similarity than of difference. In all three periods, each group compared its ways of doing things with the other, and negotiated its relative identity accordingly. Initially negative comparisons occurred, but later positive comparisons emerged (cf. Wiessner 1990, 107).

The distinctive use of symmetry in the late period marks group 4 structures, in opposition to the asymmetry of group 1 buildings. In one interpretation, the rich might be using asymmetry to mark their aggressive individualism, while symmetry in workers' houses renders the workers homogenous. The two may also, of course, be complementary: As mass-produced elements come into building, symmetry may have become a distinctive marker of the economy inherent in using cheaper, modular designs while, in the process, asymmetry came to imply expense. The use of the latest "fashions" in the design of the buildings of dominant groups also telegraphs to the observer that the members of group 1 are able to tap into a much wider circle of influence. When in 1882 Frederick Robert White hired John Horbury Hunt to design his country house Booloominbah, he was not only hiring a proponent of the latest Queen Anne and Arts and Crafts influences, but also an architect trained in Boston, who "designed at the forefront of English and American styles" (Mitchell 1988, 8). At this scale, F. R. White became part of a national circle of wealth and prestige that could afford the latest innovations in architecture.

At another level, the use of symmetry by the workers may be a deliberate strategy to disguise their individuality, which may be expressed more in private than in the public exterior of their houses. In doing so they maintain a façade of obedience (Mullins 1993), while at the same time keeping their identities separate and obscure (Figure 6.3). This illusion of unity among the workers, and the stylistic distance that

261 Dumaresq St.
(1880–1882)

163 Jessie St.
(c1880–1881)

204 Barney St.
(1878–1882)

307 Beardy St.
(1893)

66 Ohio St.
(c1900)

32 Tancredi St.
(c1882–1883)

Figure 6.3. Symmetrical working-class houses in the middle and late periods.

is maintained between the construction of worker identity and that of the wealthier groups, illustrates a second central facet to the workings of style—that style is a mediator between the interests of the individual and the interests of the group (Wiessner 1989, 59). In many of her papers, Polly Wiessner (1989; 1990) concentrates on the tension between constructions of group and individual identity, and argues that·it may be one of the driving forces for social change. Individual identity may be created as unselfconsciously as group identity from the same common "way of doing," although, as Wiessner clearly indicates, there is also the potential for this construction to take place as recognizably deliberate. In this extension of her argument, Wiessner (1989, 59; 1990, 109) suggests that there are situations that may "switch on a strong sense of social group identity" (fear, intergroup competition, the need for cooperation to attain certain goals, imposed political control) and situations that may "switch on a strong sense of personal identity" (interindividual competition, options for individual enterprise, breakdown in the social order), and that the changing pattern of relationships between the two may be negotiated by the participants through style.

A need for cooperation to attain social, economic, or political goals may, in part, contribute to the emergence of stylistic similarities between pastoral and mercantile capital, and among the workers in the middle and late periods. On the other hand, the interindividual competition that is a fundamental constituent of capitalism, and the encouragement to individual enterprise that this entails, promotes the strong sense of personal identity that comes through so clearly in the distance maintained between owners and workers and in the individualism of many upper- and middle-class structures. It is important to note that these two workings of style—the construction of individual identity and the construction of group identity—are complementary rather than mutually exclusive, and often occur concurrently. While the stylistic features used by mercantile and pastoral capitalists, for example, may show a greater degree of commonality over time, they also continue to be used to uphold distinctions between the two groups.

It may not always be the case, of course, that significant use of a feature is part of conscious and symbolic choice. It may be more a choice made by necessity than stylishness. The occurrence of French doors in the database, for example, illustrates this point. In the early period, 83% of pastoral buildings were built to incorporate at least one set of French doors, compared to 33% of mercantile structures and no public buildings. In the middle period the pastoral emphasis changed, and both mercantile and workers' structures exhibited a significantly greater use of this feature. In the late period, however, pastoral buildings were once again identified with the use of this element. French doors were a feature that characterized the earliest forms of houses in Australia. Before houses had internal access halls, the verandah provided the main means of access to a horizontal series of rooms, each of which communicated onto the verandah via sets of French doors (Freeland 1988, 45). As the oldest buildings in New England, it is not surprising that pastoral structures from 1840 to 1879 exhibited significant use of this feature. Likewise, when 75% of workers' houses incorporate French doors in the middle period, this is also a utilitarian measure, reflecting the choice of those least able to afford more expensive or better-designed structures. The reappearance of French doors as a defining feature of pastoral houses in the late period, however, suggests something other than pragmatic choice and implies that there was an element of deliberate continuity in the use of this feature by pastoralists. I interpret this second trend as a deliberate appeal to an earlier connotation of status, when pastoral buildings were identified with French doors and the pastoralists themselves with indivisible power and prestige. Their appeal to status lay through continuity and took the form of a resistance to innovation. Continuity in the use of this feature reinforced the strength of established prestige but, by ignoring innovation, this choice also ran the risk of becoming entrenched conservatism.

In terms of class, group 1, which includes all of the most wealthy echelon of Armidale society, appears as always clearly distinguishable from other groups. Both pastoralists and mercantilists who belong to this group are set apart from the remainder of the population by virtue of the stylistic elements that dominate their structures. Formal names, classical associations, stained glass, piers, and asymmetry together define group 1 buildings and set them apart. As in the case of capital, in some periods these features also created links with other groups: In the middle period formal names link group 1 structures with group 2 structures, in the late period piers associate group 1 with group 3, and the use of scored ashlar brickwork links group 3 with dominant public buildings. At each of these times, groups 2 and 3 contain segments of the wealthier parts of the remaining population. In the 1880s and 1890s, members of group 2 are those who, although in debt, compete in assets and enterprises with the independently wealthy. In the late period, group 3 members include some of the successful and wealthy small enterprise operators, such as the popular builders George F. Nott and Mark Roberts.

Apart from symmetry, a second alternative choice in the style of group 4 distinguishes them from other groups in the middle and late periods. Stop-chamfered verandah columns in the middle period characterize almost half of group 4 structures, compared to less than 10% use of this feature by group 1. As a fairly non-descript design feature, it is difficult to understand why stop-chamfering should become identifiable with workers in the 1880s and 1890s. Partly, this may be because mass-produced building elements were becoming more accessible either through local production or through the cheaper transport costs offered by the railway. At another level, this example may also illustrate an alternative way in which stylistic choice operates. It is possible that choice over elements of style may operate as much *away* from particular features as in favor of them. In other words, the observable difference between the use of stop-chamfering by workers and others may be as much a function of the workers' deliberate choice to use this element as of their employers' deliberate choice to avoid it.

There is another aspect to the question of how style marks boundaries, which illustrates the point that both personal and social aspects of identity play a role in the creation of style (Wiessner 1989, 57). To what extent is individual variation discernable in style? As much as there are discernible features that bind people to a group identity, are there also features that distinguish them as individuals?

CREATING INDIVIDUAL IDENTITY

Isolated examples of individual style occur in all social contexts and across all time periods. Often this is more a function of a particular feature appearing in one location much earlier than in any other, but occasionally outstanding and unique examples occur that are not repeated. The house at Booroolong, for instance, a pastoral station established by Matthew Henry Marsh in the early 1840s, is the first recorded example of asymmetry in New England (Figure 6.4). Although this trait reappears in later structures, and actually comes to structure significantly the associations between mercantilists and pastoralists in the middle to late periods, its use in Booroolong is highly unusual because of its early occurrence.

In the 1880s, an increasingly individualistic component enters the architecture of private houses in Armidale, and several of these buildings incorporate features that occur in no other structure. Medieval associations influence the design of four private houses: Trelawney, Loombra, The Turrets, and Highbury, all in the same geographic location and built between 1880 and 1910. All four are located on South Hill and have projecting battlemented bay windows that dominate the skyline (Figure 6.5). Loombra combines the crenellated bays with wrought-iron finials, and Highbury has an unusual art nouveau portico, and both Loombra and The Turrets were designed by the same (unnamed) architect. Although these four structures cross cut both capital and social class (3 are mercantile, one pastoral; three are group 1, one is group 3), they show a uniformity of style that suggests a similar appropriation of the imagery associated with the gothic and its notions of medieval

Figure 6.4. The asymmetry of Booroolong.

chivalry. It was common in the late nineteenth century to restrict gothic elements to the skyline, to allow medieval taste to exist in tandem with modern comfort as a marker of the status of the gentleman (Girouard 1981, 162, 262). The changing image of the gentleman, in fact, was attractive to both those born into the ruling class (as an indication of inherited privilege) and those born outside it (as it enabled them to enter it without necessarily acquiring property) (Girouard 1981, 262).

Likewise, pseudomedieval design elements are apparent on other private structures from this period built by both members of the elite pastoral class and members of the middle mercantile class. Buttresses enhance Booloominbah, as well as Birida, built by grazier George Baker, and Palmerston, built by Albert Augustus Dangar, and link them stylistically to all of the dominant church buildings (Figure 6.6). Booloominbah also sports gargoyles, and both Booloominbah and Birida possess prominent towers, linking them to many public buildings, such as the Courthouse, as well as to a single mercantile dwelling, the Cotswold, built by the draper William Curtis in 1900 (Figure 6.7). Other medieval elements incorporated into private dwellings of this period are the heraldic shields left by builder Edmund Lonsdale as his trademark

Relations of Meaning and Membership

Highbury (c1902)

Trelawney (c1904)

Loombra (1880s)

The Turrets (c1884–1890)

Figure 6.5. The pseudomedieval skylines of Highbury, Trelawney, Loombra, and the Turrets.

(Figure 6.8) and the gothic label mold on 85 Rusden St. (Figure 6.9), also built by Lonsdale.

Booloominbah, in fact, is outstanding in most of its stylistic features. Along with Trevenna, it is one of the most highly individualistic buildings in Armidale, a status befitting its position as the largest country house constructed in Australia in the nineteenth century (Stapleton et al. 1993).

Some structures combine distinctive elements with features from clearly identifiable cultural backgrounds. Violet Hill, a relatively small-scale farming property west of Armidale, originally settled by Irish

Catholic Cathedral (1912)   Anglican Cathedral (1871–1878)   Presbyterian Church (1882)

Palmerston (1910)   Booloominbah (1882–1883)

Birida (1907–1908)   Booloominbah

Figure 6.6. Stylistic links using medieval design elements: buttresses on the major church buildings and on Palmerston, Birida, and Booloominbah, and gargoyles on Booloominbah. (Photograph of Palmerston courtesy of Ann Dangar.)

Relations of Meaning and Membership

Figure 6.7. Stylistic links through the use of prominent towers. (Photograph of the Cotswold courtesy UNE Heritage Centre collections.)

immigrant Richard Pearson, not only has unique timber ridge finials, but combines this with fretted shamrocks on the verandah columns (Figure 6.10). The present house was built in 1900 and is one of only seven in the database commissioned by a woman, in this case by Richard's descendant, Margaret Pearson.

The design of Violet Hill also illustrates a further facet to the expression of identity through style: the individuality to be found in subtle distinctions of style. At the opposite end of the spectrum from

Figure 6.8. Edmund Lonsdale's trademark shields and the gothic label mold on 85 Rusden St.

such grand and expressive statements of individuality as Booloominbah are the less overt expressions to be found in structures that subtly subvert tradition. Violet Hill is ostensibly symmetrical if approached from the front, its two gables giving the appearance of a balanced "U"-shaped structure (Figure 6.11). When viewed from the side however, Violet Hill is distinctly asymmetrical in plan, belying the formal impression of the façade. That Violet Hill could have been built to be symmetri-

Figure 6.9. The fretted shamrocks on the verandah columns of Violet Hill.

Relations of Meaning and Membership

Figure 6.10. The timber ridge finials on Violet Hill.

cal is without question; that it is built only to *appear* symmetrical, however, is a more interesting and individual choice. Two other structures are also not what they appear. Wyevale, the house that builder Mark Roberts built for himself and his family in 1917, is also subtly asymmetrical, as is Moore Park, the private residence of John Moore built in 1860. John Moore was a conspicuous member of the Armidale community. Although he was often deeply in debt, he was also a successful store owner, Freemason, Oddfellow, and mayor. That his residence, built at the height of the Georgian appreciation for symmetry and order, should be subtly asymmetrical, suggests both individuality and a willingness to subvert convention (Palkovitch 1988, 304). Mark Roberts, on the other hand, was a builder whose skill involved him in the construction of many prominent local buildings, such as Palmerston, Trevenna, and Violet Hill. Wyevale was the second of two houses that Roberts built for his family in Armidale: The first was a small brick cottage, also called Wyevale, located not far from the second larger home. When he came to build his second house, Roberts' fortunes and position as a prominent member of the community were well established, and gave him both the status suited to a larger private home and the power to be slightly unconventional. The asymmetrical symmetry of his second home demonstrated both his knowledge of the conventions and the power to be independent.

Figure 6.11. The symmetrical asymmetry of Violet Hill.

DISCUSSION

Most statistical significance appeared in relation to the type of capital concerned, rather than to membership in a social class, and although some features were patterned consistently according to both definitions of social context, some variables only occurred in relation to one of them. As social class is a relationship between the individual and the means of production, it is a relationship that exists at the level of the three fundamental divisions between people in a capitalist society:

- between the propertied and the propertyless
- between employers and employees
- between the leisured and the workers

Group at this scale is constructed at an extremely broad level, reflecting the crucial distinctions in the broad dichotomy of "owners" versus "nonowners" (see Wild 1978, 3). It is therefore not surprising that most of the observable differences in Armidale are a result of more community-scale relationships, that is, between local interpretations of what it means to be a particular type of capitalist. Although obviously these relationships are also a part of larger concerns, it was only the pastoralists in New England who, because of their wealth, were customarily members of groups at a larger than local scale. And once their agendas had begun to coincide with the agendas of local mercantilists to form a united elite, their outlook became more parochial and directed towards the local community.

The groups created by the deployment of various elements of style obviously vary through time and with the use of particular features. Initially I have questioned how particular stylistic features might function semiotically as markers of membership in various groups, and how this pattern might mark group boundaries at various scales. In this chapter, however, each stylistic element has been treated synchronously, rather than examining how their use changes over time. The questions that then arise concern how the construction of identity through style changes and how changing constructions of identity are renegotiated. Are boundaries subsequently broken down? By whom? How, then, does the symbolism of position change? In effect, what are the histories of stylistic social identity in Armidale and New England? To investigate these kinds of questions, it is necessary to examine how these styles exist in space. Groups are bounded in space as well as time, and the stylistic structuring of space is an integral part of the creation of identity. This conjunction—the construction of identity through style in space—leads directly to the construction of ideology and to Clegg's (1989) final two circuits of power: techniques of production and techniques of discipline.

Style in Space | 7

The previous chapters have investigated some of the sources of architectural style within the Armidale community. In terms of social context, both local-scale membership in a particular form of capital production, and larger-scale membership in a particular social class (as a relationship to the means of production), influence the stylistic construction of identity. These boundaries are not fixed, of course, but are symbolic of relative social position at particular points in time.

The issue of how these group boundaries relate to each other is a question of style in both time and space, and of how it may be possible for architectural style to structure space and, thus, the world of the people who inhabit this social landscape. As well as signifying positions of wealth, style may also index positions of poverty. Moreover, in the process, it may also signify the ways and means by which this difference is subverted, thus, creating new indexes of difference. When concepts of "stylishness" become appropriated into alternative social contexts, how are group boundaries maintained? What are the contexts in which these boundaries exist and change? How are boundaries between social groups sustained or broken down by changes in style?

THE CONTEXTS OF INTERPRETATION
FOR STYLE IN ARMIDALE

In any archaeological study, the contexts of interpretation for style cannot be analyzed in the same fashion as the contexts of production. It is not possible to know either who looked at these buildings or what they thought. It is only possible to approach this through the context of visibility, as suggested by Wobst (1977, 328–330, 334–335), that is, the place that an artifact occupies within the visible landscape and the possibilities for interaction with it that arise from this location. It *is* possible to suggest potential ways in which buildings may have been interpreted, given what we know about their purpose, their physical location, and their style. Analyzing style across space is one way of approaching some of the possibilities for how space can be structured

Chapter 7

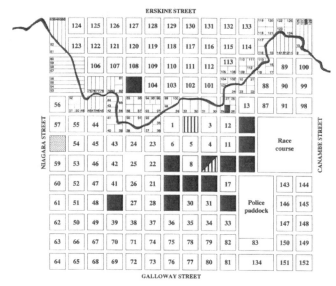

EARLY (1840-1879)

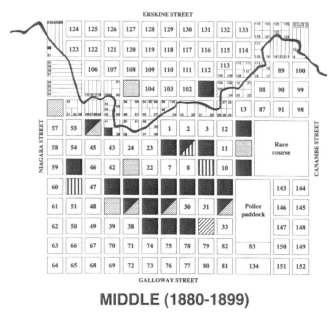

MIDDLE (1880-1899)

Figure 7.1. The changing location and nature of settlement in Armidale over time.

Style in Space 165

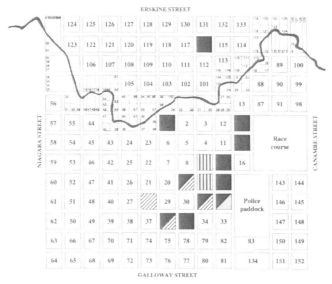

Figure 7.1. *(Continued)*

by class and capital and, in doing so, hints at how techniques of production and discipline might be mobilized.

Looking at the archaeological landscape of structures over time, several trends become apparent (Figure 7.1). At one level these are essentially a reflection of the historical trends described in chapter 3; however, at another, they illustrate the potential for historical trends to be rendered archaeologically visible through the persistence of the material structuring of the spaces that people create. An obvious mercantile focus is visible on the southern edge of Armidale, beginning in the 1860s and continuing until the 1920s. This area, "South Hill" or "South Armidale," occupies a visually dominant position in the landscape, which is clearly visible from most other parts of town. The high status of this area as a suburb in which to live was initially established as a result of steady mercantile focus, and compounded in the early twentieth century by several pastoralists moving there after retiring from outlying properties. Large and expensive structures have continued to dominate this area, which has contributed not only to the desirability of the neighborhood as a place in which to live over time, but also to the continuing care invested in the physical fabric of these structures. This has certainly extended into the present, when as a result of the 1991

Heritage Study, the entire area of South Hill was defined as a Conservation Zone or Heritage Precinct. As a corollary, over 27% of structures in my database are from this area.

A second mercantile focus existed in closer proximity to the center of town, on its eastern and southern outskirts. This is a less exclusive location than South Hill, but still contains grander houses than some other areas, such as West Armidale. West Armidale had been a focus for workers since the 1870s; however, they were not, of course, confined to this area and in the 1880s through 1900s also periodically built houses within high-status areas.

There is also a well defined "ecclesiastical precinct" in the center of town, surrounding the open area of Central Park (Figure 7.2). In the 1860s, the first church buildings to be located here were the Wesleyan Methodist church and an earlier Catholic church opposite the present Anglican Cathedral. The Anglican Cathedral was built in the 1870s, the Presbyterian church in 1882, and the Catholic cathedral in 1912. The spire of St. Mary and St. Joseph's Catholic Cathedral is a prominent

Figure 7.2. The ecclesiastical precinct in the center of town.

Style in Space 167

landmark from the north, west, and south. Central Park itself was dedicated in 1874 and its layout is still reminiscent of its nineteenth century planning.

Until the twentieth century, very little settlement can be seen north of the creek line that bisects Armidale. Although structures on North Hill would have had a similar vista to those on South Hill, few took advantage of this view. This trend may have a connection to the persistence of Aboriginal camps on the north side of the creek. An Anaiwan camp was recorded in the nineteenth century as "on the northern side of Dumaresq Creek opposite the town of Armidale" (Ferry 1994, 120), although its precise location is unknown. Variously, this camp may have been situated at Rugby League Park, immediately above the north bank of the creek (Graham Wilson, personal communication); on or near the summit of the hill, on the northern side of the hill (Davidson, & Kippen 1996, 8); or on the site of the Presbyterian manse (at the corner of Marsh St. and Kirkwood St.) (Personality Files HC, Memories of Mrs. Johnson Norris 1928). The camp may, of course, have been located at all of these sites at one time or another. Whether or not it was a persistent Aboriginal presence that dissuaded people from living here, North Hill seems to have been an area of relatively low status compared to South Hill, despite having relatively comparable geographic features and vistas. This divide continued well into the twentieth century, with residents of South Hill conspicuously disassociating themselves from residents of North Hill (Jennifer Johnstone, personal communication).

THE SPACE OF STYLE

The Space of Capital

There are a number of trends in the spatial distribution of particular features of style over time. The first and most obvious is that a high percentage of features (80%) appear first in houses located in South Hill. This would seem to suggest that this zone was indeed a high-status area, in which the inhabitants were always at the forefront of architectural "fashion." Notions of "stylishness" in many features would have flowed from the houses of people who inhabited South Hill and simultaneously established and reinforced their identities as leaders and "owners." Second, many elements initially appearing in employers' structures in this zone, moved both "out" and "down" to other geographic areas and workers' houses. French doors, single-pitch verandah roofs, piers, stop-chamfered verandah columns, stained glass, turned timber finials, and fretted bargeboards all originally appear in pastoral and mercantile houses located on South Hill, and from there all become incorporated in the middle period into workers' houses in other zones (west Armidale, east Armidale, and north Armidale). Some of these features (single-pitch verandah roofs, stop-chamfered verandah columns, turned timber finials, and French doors) subsequently become a significant index of membership in the working class.

This would seem to indicate at a superficial level that the workers were emulating the stylistic features of the pastoralists and mercantilists who were their employers. This may simply have been a function of better communications and transportation or of the establishment of local production, which caused these elements to be both more widely and cheaply available. Certainly all of the timber verandah decoration (finials, fretted bargeboards, and stop-chamfered verandah columns) would have become cheaper to purchase with the advent of mass production. There may also be a facet of deliberate appropriation in this movement, however, by which the workers consciously took on some of the connotations of middle-classness.

Often the movement of stylistic features is not always such a lineal and unidirectional progression. In the middle period, some features continued to be used within the same geographic zone (South Hill), but instead of remaining in the dominant mercantile and pastoral structures they became incorporated into the structures of workers who had moved into this area. Symmetry, asymmetry, stop-chamfered verandah columns, and piers all become incorporated into workers' houses located on South Hill, in close proximity to mercantile and pastoral structures that also possess these features. This suggests not only a deliberate colonization of middle-classness through the appropriation of stylistic elements, but also a more literal colonization of the high status area of South Hill. By appropriating both the appearance and location of middle-class houses, and of course the associations accorded to both of these, the workers were appropriating a system of meaning that previously had connoted high status, forcing the middle class to find new indicators of status and stylishness if they wished to remain separate. There was, of course, choice in this direction by the middle class themselves, whose identities were often competing with each other, as well as with the workers.

Interestingly, most of the movement of stylistic elements into workers' structures occured in the 1880s and 1890s, part of the period of working-class mobilization against employment and labor conditions. Some features, such as French doors or stained glass, were used by workers in that period only; others, such as turned timber finials and fretted bargeboards, continued to be incorporated into workers' structures in the late period.

The differences in style observed between mercantile and pastoral capital is extended through the construction and use of space by these two groups. Each structured their world in slightly different ways. By choosing to reside mostly on their properties, pastoralists were literally removed from the social and stylistic competition that may have occurred in town. The immediate result of this was that any stylishness of pastoral properties was less often available for emulation. When a retiring generation of graziers did move to Armidale, they maintained their separate status by residing only on South Hill. This both sustained and promoted the perception of this area as an exclusive coterie of status.

The Space of Class

Many of the same trends are apparent when people are categorized by class instead of capital. South Hill still appears as an exclusive suburb in which most stylistic elements originate. Because of greater subtlety in categorizing people by class (people may be grouped as 1, 2, 3, or 4 and still have fallen within the single group "mercantile") South Hill also appears as a less exclusive suburb when its inhabitants are divided according to their relation to the means of production. In this area, members from groups 1, 2, and 3 are often among the first to possess a particular feature, such as asymmetry, symmetry, stained glass, or brick. However this list of style "firsts" often includes members from group 4 as well: brick, single pitch verandah roofs, asymmetry, and cast iron are all included within group 4 houses in South Hill in the early period. There are thus less obvious correlations between status and style when people are divided according to class.

Some features continue to be incorporated into group 4 houses throughout all three periods. Symmetry, for example, is part of group 4 structures in West Armidale in the early period and on South Hill in the middle and late periods. This group seldom uses asymmetry except in the early period, in contrast to groups 1, 2, and 3, which employ it throughout. A discontinuity in symmetry is clearly evident for groups 1 and 2, suggesting that greater individual expression in style becomes a part of the identities of the upper echelons after 1890. There are two different trends being illustrated in the use of symmetry versus asymmetry across time in Armidale, which take on contrasting interpretations according to their spatial correlates.

Much has been made of the relationship between symmetry as an element of the Georgian manner and the standardization created by capitalist production (see, for example, Anderson and Moore 1988; Johnson 1996, 207–208; Leone 1984, 26–27; McGuire 1991, 107). The deliberate uniformity of Georgian symmetry was part of new ways of ordering the world and creating new notions of individualism and control (see Leone 1984, 26–27; Leone and Potter 1988, 373–374), but its semblance of sameness was also used to deny inequality. As a façade, symmetrical architecture suggests similarity and conformity, rather than individualism or eclecticism, and confers the same characteristics on people. Asymmetrical architecture, on the other hand, suggests the opposite, and can be identified with creating a distinctive and dissimilar identity.

For Armidale, the distinctive use of symmetry by the workers may indicate one of two things, although, of course, it may incorporate elements of both. It may suggest that the working class saw themselves as a unified group of people, if not the same then at least similar, with relatively common histories and goals. Seen from within the working class living in west Armidale, the use of symmetry may have affirmed contact with their roots, with a tradition of symmetrical working-class houses. Given that the workers in Armidale were employed in a range of different industries, however, and came from a wide variety of cultural backgrounds (Irish, English, Scottish, Chinese), there is no ostensible reason to suppose that their relation to the means of production, which they certainly held in common, gave them a feeling of common identity or purpose. The alternative interpretation rests on the assumption that symmetry is an adequate mask; while it may *suggest* conformity and uniformity, it may not literally embody these ideas. The use of symmetry then is a ruse to protect difference at other levels of cultural expression, such as privately inside the house or personally by membership in various organizations or societies. African Americans may have used this strategy in Annapolis, when they chose to live behind symmetrical Georgian façades and to circumvent racism through giving the appearance of assimilation (Mullins 1993). This may not, however, have been designed to hide difference at anything other than a superficial level.

While symmetry may have linked workers together in a common public face, it may also have been used as a device to suggest individuality according to where it occurred within the geography of Armidale. Once placed within the context of the predominant asymmetrical houses of the middle and upper classes on South Hill, the symmetry of workers' houses gave them a distinctive identity. It not only distinguished them from their neighbors, but may also have provided a physical and enduring reminder to the owners who employed them that the

Style in Space 171

workers were both visible and individual. By situating a pattern of architecture with strong links to the working class within a high-status area dominated by the upper and middle classes, the workers were both reinforcing their identities as members of a particular group and creating an identity that was distinctive compared to the identities of those around them, while at the same time ensuring that this "statement" was situated so that the middle and upper classes had no choice but to interact with it.

It would seem from these trends that perceptions of stylishness stem from the stylistic elements incorporated into dominant structures, both public and private. As an example, there is a strong association between the use of stained glass and the appearance of public buildings. The earliest stained glass occurs in the windows of two public buildings: the Courthouse and the Wesleyan church, both built in the early 1860s. In the next decade, stained glass continued to be used in public buildings, such as St. Peter's Anglican Cathedral, built in the 1870s; St. Paul's Presbyterian, built in 1882, the Uniting Church, built in 1893; and the Catholic Cathedral, built in 1912. The earliest use of stained glass in private houses is Comeytrowe, built for James Tysoe in 1868, and in the pastoral structure Micklegate, built by one of Charles Marsh's sons in the late 1870s. After this, there is a proliferation of stained glass in both doors and windows in private houses built in the 1880s. These span the entire range of the social spectrum, from large and dominant pastoral (Saumarez) and mercantile (Bona Vista, Mongoola) structures, to public buildings (Trim and Co stores) and workers' houses (136 Allingham St., 67 Beardy St., 80 Beardy St.). Stylishness, in terms of the use of stained glass, moves from the domain of public buildings to private houses built by group 1, and from there to the private houses of other groups.

A different sequence is observable for the movement of cast-iron verandah decoration over time. Initially this feature appears in private buildings built by mercantile capitalists and moves to both public mercantile buildings and the private houses of pastoralists. The earliest positively dated cast iron appears in the 1870s on private structures such as Peter Speare's Denmark House, John Moore's 111 Brown St., Police Magistrate James Buchanan's Westholme, and the Railway Hotel in West Armidale. In the 1880s it continues to be used in private mercantile structures such as Charles Wilson's Loombra (118 Mann St.), J. S. Chard's Mongoola (3 Reginald Ave.), James Miller's Kapunda, J. D. Bradley's Bona Vista, and Angela Spasshatt's Tregara (131 Brown St.), but from there moves to a variety of public structures such as the Imperial Hotel and the Lands Office, as well as to the private pastoral

172   Chapter 7

structure Saumarez. Saumarez, in fact, is an exception, as cast iron is only infrequently incorporated into pastoral structures. In terms of this feature of style, mercantile capitalists were clearly the innovators, and the direction of emulation moved from the private mercantile houses of groups 1 and 2 to the domain of public buildings, and from there to the structures of other groups. The movement of cast iron raises the issue of the movement of stylishness into the marketplace and the effect this has upon the direction of emulation. Much of the early cast iron was imported into Armidale from other cities in New South Wales, such as Maitland and Morpeth, although local production of a similar product began at least as early as 1872 with the establishment of Goddard's Foundry at Uralla, 25 km south of Armidale. It may be that once local investment in the capital infrastructure to produce cast iron takes place, there is an interest for the capitalist to make it an item of stylishness beyond the wealthy. In this case then, the earliest cast iron is not local, and emulation is partly in the form of local production. Unfortunately, without knowing more of the specifics surrounding the local production of cast iron, it is impossible to speculate further on the means of production for this feature of style.

Style without Space

Several of the structures included in this study are no longer standing, having been demolished to make way for "improvements" in the landscape. There are several repercussions that flow from this process, not the least of which is that the style of these structures is no longer a physical marker of the individuals and groups that created their identity through it. Neither space nor subsequent constructions of identity are constrained by the style of these buildings. The discussion so far has centered on the implications arising from the creation of style and its addition in the landscape, but what are the implications of its removal?

Nine structures were recorded from photographic sources, located in and around Armidale and spanning a range of social groups and types of capital (Figure 7.3). In terms of style, these buildings possess a range of features, and at least one of them (Kapunda built in 1889–1894 by James Miller, whose money came from successful gold mine speculation) is highly individual (Figure 7.4). Two immediate observations become apparent: Most of the buildings were located in or very near to the center of town and most of them were built by members of group 2. The removal of these structures from the central part of town is symptomatic of a long process of altering this section of the city. As the initial settlement focus for Armidale, this area once contained many private

Style in Space 173

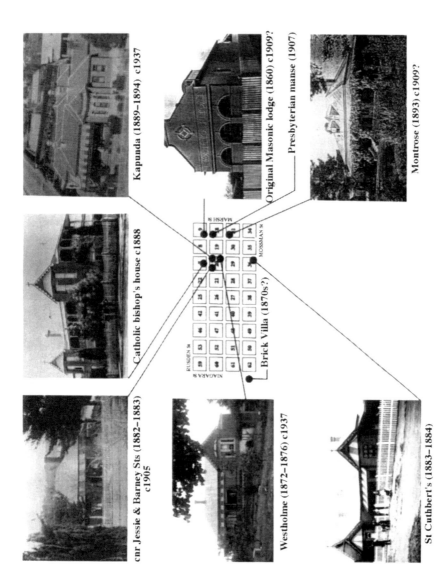

Figure 7.3. The style and location of the non-extant structures. (Photographs of Masonic lodge, Presbyterian Manse, and Montrose from Milner 1923; all others courtesy UNE Heritage Centre collections.)

Figure 7.4. Four views of Kapunda (courtesy UNE Heritage Centre collections).

houses, which have been gradually removed as the town has expanded. This has both deemphasized this area as a geographic source for stylishness, and reinforced the location of stylishness in other areas (South Hill) as preeminent. Furthermore, by gradually demolishing the private houses that were once located in or near the center of town, the separation of public buildings and "work" from private buildings and "home," is given three-dimensional substance. This destruction of style, and of the connotations of stylishness, has also effaced the identities of those who built and lived in these buildings. Given that most of these were members of group 2, there is a particular type of exclusion going on here. As part of this process, stylishness as arising from the wealth and position held by members of group 2 is denied and is instead located firmly with groups 1 and 3.

THE POWER OF STYLE

The use of architectural style to express both individual and group identity does more than simply bound groups in space and time, but also relates groups to each other in a way that is physical and persistent, such that, in the continual process of seeing and being seen (interpretation), these structures also reinforce more subtle aspects of capitalism and the relationship of groups to the means of production. This aspect of style has only been hinted at in the preceding discussion and is part of the second half of Stewart Clegg's observation that there are four interlocking and mutually reinforcing circuits of power operating in society: mobilizing relations of meaning and membership and mobilizing techniques of production and discipline.

Techniques of Production

The rigid street grid imposed by Galloway in 1849 was the first attempt to improve the productivity of Armidale and its inhabitants. By regulating both the present and future appearance of the town, Galloway was doing more than simply conforming to a worldview that equated order with moral worth, he was also enacting one of the basic tenets of capitalism—rendering space a controllable commodity. A grid street system not only made communication more rational and efficient, but was also an excellent scheme for the parceling and selling of property (Kostoff 1991, 11). Through the practicality of connecting two points in a straight line, transport was also rendered more ordered and efficient and, together with controllable space and rational communications, created a concept of relative rather than absolute space and of the community benefits of capitalism (cf. Harvey 1989, 29).

Other innovations also aided the mobilization of techniques of production. The introduction of gaslight and its subsequent replacement by the electricity power grid both claimed to be of benefit to society, but in effect extended the length of the working day. Introduced in Armidale in 1885, the Armidale Gas Company began by servicing the public buildings of the town, but was soon extended to other areas and to private subscribers. The Armidale Gas Company, while providing a service for individuals, was nevertheless a privately owned company run by several "leading capitalists" in the community, headed by John Moore and John Bliss. Gaslight was not replaced by electricity until 1922, when the Council opened the City of Armidale Electric Supply Company Ltd. (Gilbert 1982, 127–128).

Techniques of Discipline

In terms of the city landscape, a clear hierarchy is evident in the physical location of private houses, neatly and effectively separating the workers from the owners and employers. The same geographic spheres dominate when structures are compared in terms of how they articulate with the city landscape. By being located on both North and South Hills, mercantile and pastoral houses are situated in positions that command views of the town, in direct contrast to locations of the workers' buildings, which are located on the lower and colder areas beside the creek. The dominant position of mercantile and pastoral structures also contrasts with the location of public buildings, which are likewise not built to take advantage of a view, although in the case of the two cathedrals in particular, the public buildings often *are* the view. It was quite common in the nineteenth century for the spires and towers of ecclesiastical buildings to be designed for their "landscape qualities" (Apperly et al. 1989, 81), which were often aligned with city streets so as to be visible from all directions (Hareven 1982, 13) (Figure 7.5). The clock tower on the courthouse was constructed to be another landmark: Initially built in 1878 with a bell tower, it was replaced in 1898 by a clock face on the apex of the tower. The construction of views for the landscape qualities of clock towers was a means by which a public and universal version of time could be introduced to the community, rather than allowing everyone access to their own definition of time (Kulik 1988, 399).

In the 1880s and 1890s, this relationship between status and location became statistically significant. Fifty percent of the pastoral houses

Figure 7.5. The Catholic cathedral viewed from the outskirts of town.

Style in Space 177

built in and around Armidale, and 20% of the mercantile houses possess views over the town, while no public buildings and no workers' cottages possess a view. In terms of class, this translates to 70% of group 1 structures versus no group 4 structures. The private houses of the rich thus literally overlooked all spheres in the lives of the working class: their homes, their places of work, and the public buildings where they interacted socially. Ironically, this led to the possibility of working-class houses *becoming* the view for the middle and upper classes, a situation that was circumscribed by encouraging West Armidale to be a working-class suburb.

In at least one instance, this surveillance was overt. In 1873, Barnett Aaron Moses' house was not only one of the first to be built on the north side of the creek, but also was one of only a handful to be built there in the nineteenth century. Although, as the largest manufacturer in Armidale, Moses was wealthy enough to have afforded a site on South Hill, this location made sense for him because it directly overlooked his largest tannery. Ten years after his house was built, Moses purchased the block of land opposite his tannery and began the process of subdividing and selling it to his employees and encouraging them to build houses there. Although the ostensible intent of this process was no doubt to give his workers some degree of self-sufficiency, it had three main repercussions. Moses' corporate paternalism not only made the workers dependent upon his goodwill, but it also made them dependent on the capitalist system through their mortgages to the Armidale and New England Building Society. Second, it tied his employees firmly to their place of labor, reducing the amount of time they needed to travel to and from work, thus rendering the factory more efficient. It also located Moses and his family in a physically paternal position, overlooking the business and the *"busy-ness"* of the employees. The welfare capitalism practiced by Moses was designed to avert or diffuse employee discontent by providing amenities and fostering workers' loyalty to, and identification with, the employer (Hareven 1982, 39). It was a strategy that Moses continued to use overtly when he transported his employees *en masse* in an appropriately decorated cart to vote for his favored political candidate at election time.

This surveillance of the workers was part of a tendency by the ruling groups to invent new traditions of community to counter or contain the antagonisms of class (Harvey 1989, 31) through accepting responsibility for some of the social problems of the workers, such as health, education, or housing. Social order in this situation was envisioned as one where social positions were stable, with a paternalistic, authoritarian figure at the top and dependent, childlike plebeians look-

Figure 7.6. The image of corporate paternalism—B. A. Moses surrounded by his employees (courtesy UNE Heritage Centre collections).

ing to the capitalist for work, protection, and moral guidance (Slotkin 1985, 147):

> In such a society, the absolute dependence of ... worker on capitalist would be tempered and offset by paternalism, and class relations represented by an image of familial bonds ... rather than by images of conflict. (Slotkin 1985, 147)

This symbolic structuring of space in Armidale is clearly visible in an 1884 map of the city, which not only depicts the structured relationship between owners and workers, but also the rising sense of prosperity and control attached to the mercantile dominance of the city (Figure 7.7). The practice of cartography and its role in the history of property rights is closely connected to the practice of landscape painting, with its attendant techniques for representing spatial relations and particular ways in which to view the social landscape as "the way it is," rather than as a human construction (Cosgrove 1984, 190; Harley 1988, 297). This principle of the picturesque both invites people to exercise individual control over space by "composing landscapes through the selection of those elements which go to make up a pleasing picture of nature and

Style in Space 179

Figure 7.7. The 1884 map of Armidale from the *Illustrated Sydney News*, July 5th, 1884 (courtesy UNE Heritage Centre collections).

excluding those which do not," and suggests associations between landscape and historical or geographical references, and further through these to moral and political ideas (Cosgrove 1984, 204). In the visual hierarchy of Armidale, the neat grid system of the streets is a model of public order, with the moral imperatives of the two cathedrals located in the symbolic center of the map, surrounded by the progressive and "stylish" orders of mercantile architecture and enterprise.

It is not merely the case that this map reflects the social structuring of space within Armidale at a frozen moment in time. Rather, the territory of the map is part of the *same* construction as the material structuring of space within Armidale, and both are implicated in the process by which power is deployed. In this way, the material structuring of space comes to have a similar texture of value as the map, with the same associations to landscape painting, control over space, and moral and political ideas. In other words, in the same way as the map of Armidale is constructed from, and used to represent, particular formations of social action, so too is space. This is closely linked to the issue of persistence and how previous constructions of space come to be interpreted within subsequent contexts of meaning. The material structuring of space within Armidale itself comes to be seen as a physical and enduring manifestation of particular configurations of social relations, becoming symbolic to later observers and incorporated into later contexts of meaning.

Where this occurs—in other words, where sets of material remains persist into subsequent contexts—the material expression of ideology in itself becomes a "frieze"; the physical motif of a previous configuration of social relations that extends into and becomes part of the "present." Such a frieze makes an ideologically determined structure persist beyond the social relations that produced it, and in such a visible way that it continues to be interacted with, and thus acquire meaning within, later contexts of interpretation. This is particularly relevant when considering style in architecture and the negotiation of social identity, when the semiotic markers of relative social position persist into later contexts, and thus become symbolic of particular groupings of people in the past. It is possible that, as the frieze of a previous social landscape, those architectural features both provide a benchmark for subsequent constructions of stylishness and a reminder of previous social boundaries that have since been subverted and renegotiated. It is at this point that the issue of the construction of ideology becomes germane, as the structuring of space as a landscape and a map in itself is closely implicated in the process by which certain constructions of reality come to be legitimated and perpetuated over and above other constructions. The spatial structuring of style in Armidale was an accessory to the construction of identity under capitalism, and in doing so alludes to the construction of ideology. The street grid, the power grid, and the visual hierarchy of space within Armidale all contributed to, and helped perpetuate, the ideology of capitalism that existed in this place at that time and that also, of course, relates to the ideology that exists today. There are several issues of ideology that can be examined in relation to the data: These are both multilayered and mutually reinforcing, and highlight some of the public and private constructions of identity that existed in the past and how they have also come to structure identity in the present.

Styles of Ideology | 8

Style so far has been viewed as a physical expression of notions of relative identity through which groups are both incorporated and differentiated. There is another level to studying style, however, which attempts to understand how a constellation of groups might come to exist in those particular patterns and not others, and what those particular expressions of social identity might convey about the participant's construction of the world and the relative positioning of people within it. It is time to move beyond pattern recognition and focus upon the processes of pattern generation (Conkey 1990, 15). It is time to talk about ideology.

Ideology is constructed from people's perceptions of themselves and of others. Within capitalism, membership in a group (or groups) is created within the tensions of an unequal society and ideology is thus a process that brings individuals and groups into certain power relations, providing both social identity and knowledge about the world. Through ideology, which works to both include and exclude by suggesting standard sets of values against which everything can be measured, groups and individuals signify and respond to common arrays of values and beliefs. To briefly reiterate, from chapter 2, my definition of ideology is:

> false or deceptive beliefs and presuppositions implicit in ordinary ways of thinking, speaking or behaving in the world, which arise from the structure of society as a whole and the relations of the group to that structure and which serve to reproduce that world by concealing contradiction and by perpetuating an unequal pattern of existing material relationships between and among groups.
>
> Because it is concerned with concealment, ideology necessarily serves particular interests and thus refers to the specific ways in which signs, meanings and values help to incorporate and reproduce dominance as a social power and to manufacture consensus, while at the same time concealing the antagonisms resident at this point. Ideology may exist at more than one scale within the same society, or within the same individual: as unsophisticated ideology or implicit 'common sense,' which is shared most widely and as sophisticated ideology; or as a more or less coherent system of explicit beliefs about the world which favors the interests or expresses the feelings of a more specific group in society, without the members necessarily being conscious of their belonging to that group.

In terms of relating to day-to-day experiences, it is equally possible for ideology to refer to the specific ways in which signs, meanings, and

182   Chapter 8

values help to reproduce a dominant social power, or *any* significant conjunction between discourse and power (Eagleton 1991, 221). If ideology exists at sophisticated and unsophisticated levels simultaneously, then it is both an emergent property of groups of people who by shared experience hold similar things to be "true," and a formulation of such "truths" into a system of beliefs that some groups of people desire or insist that others (should) believe.

How might identity, as constructed in the past in Armidale, have influenced the construction of ideology? And how have the signs, meanings, and values of style helped to either reproduce a dominant social power or to incorporate groups involved in an alternative conjunction between discourse and power?

IDEOLOGY FROM ARTIFACTS

To attempt to answer such questions, it is first necessary to ask how patterning in archaeological artifacts might possibly be indicative of the construction of ideology. Ideological expressions of social asymmetry within capitalism operate either through reinforcing difference between groups or by denying that difference. One of the most obvious conclusions that can be drawn from any study is the extent to which material artifacts reflect similarities or differences between segments of a population, irrespective of the possible social strategies and ideological commentary perceived to lie behind this degree of variability. Once an emphasis or deemphasis on inequality is perceived, it can be understood as being created in various ways. In other words, there seems to be an initial movement towards either the denial or affirmation of inequality, which then becomes operationalized through other ideological strategies. For example, the expression of social differences between groups may be emphasized equally well through a strategy of naturalization (the social Darwinism of these people being "naturally" lesser than us), legitimation (tradition upholds this expression of difference), or universalization (these differences have always been so).

Archaeologically at least, it is possible to link ideological strategies with material remains by questioning the degree to which either similarities or differences are stressed between segments of the population. The main ideological strategies discussed in chapter 2 were (Eagleton 1991, 45–59; Thompson 1984, 137):

1. *Unification* as the emphasis on similarity so as to create a sense of community

Styles of Ideology

2. *Rationalization* and *legitimation* as the emphasis on difference, but appealing to traditional, rational, or charismatic grounds to legitimate it
3. *Dissimulation* as the emphasis on similarity through the masking of the relations of domination and through the denial of the act of masking itself
4. *Universalization* and *naturalization*, which would seem to be able to either deny or emphasize difference, depending on the historical context in question

Similarity or Difference? Strategies and Scale

Several possibilities for the existence of ideology emerge from the data. They indicate that both a fundamental class conflict (between producers and appropriators of surplus) and a subsumed class conflict (between appropriators and specific individuals who provide political, economic, and cultural conditions for fundamental class processes to exist, that is, landlords, moneylenders, and merchants) are taking place (Saitta 1994). In other words, between capitalists and workers, and between one group of capitalists and another.

Capitalists and Workers

The first and most obvious observation to be drawn from the Armidale case study is that, while statistically significant associations between social context and style did appear from the data, these were not at a very fine-grained level. Most of the differences occurred between groups on a very broad scale, most particularly between workers and owners. In many elements of style there are clear differences between the owners and the workers, both in terms of those features that the owners possess but the workers do not, and conversely, in terms of those which the workers use, but the owners do not. Having said this, there are a number of ideological strategies apparent in the patterning of the material remains.

The direction of emulation from public buildings to private buildings of the middle and upper classes is simultaneously an appropriation of dominant visual imagery and an ideological strategy to legitimate power. Through emulating the classical appearance of the public buildings associated with the daily business of capital—the banks and building societies—the mercantilists were appropriating a set of associations linking the practice of capitalism (making money) with the ostensible democracy and equality of ancient Greece and Rome. Likewise, although the Anglican church had long been regarded as supporting the privileged upper class (Connell and Irving 1992, 106), through appropriating the ecclesiastical imagery of the church, the pastoralists were not only making a statement of their fitness to lead society, but in doing so, were also assuming the mantle of moral guidance formerly held by the church (Figure 8.1). This was a crucial strategy in light of the gradual erosion to pastoral authority that had resulted from the earlier battles with rival mercantile capitalism. Although the pastoralists had lost their previously unassailable position, by reinforcing their links with ecclesiastical power, they were asserting their moral superiority, thus legitimating their right to govern in the one arena in which their authority remained unchallenged—as the arbiters of virtue and correctness.

Each of these strategies became ideological in that each used legitimation and rationalization to establish the "right" of the upper and middle classes to govern others. Through appropriating particular, dominant types of visual imagery, the ruling groups were appealing to tradition and to associations established in the past to legitimate their dominant position. Furthermore, by linking themselves stylistically with structures that persisted and continued to dominate the landscape, these associations were periodically reinforced. As the members of other groups continued to interact with the original structures that fixed these meanings to the landscape—as they attended church or conducted business in banks or building societies—the similarities continued to be emphasized.

There was an element of the strategy of universalization in this as well, in that by linking themselves to the older societies of Greece and Rome, the mercantile capitalists were also presenting their specific values and interests as part of a common human "truth." Through the medium of architecture, the centrality of standing structures was emphasized as a universal human value, distinguishing those who owned from those who did not. In this fashion, it may have been possible to construe the propertyless working class (both European and Aboriginal) as "lesser" beings, and to legitimate the appropriation of wealth displayed in the standing structures of the middle and upper classes. Furthermore, as elements of upper- and middle-class stylishness came to be emulated in the structures of other groups, an impression of leadership by the wealthy was accentuated. As a strategy, this incorporated the wealthy as dominant, and reinforced a perception of stylishness as being created through access to wealth.

The use of stylistic features in common among members of the working class suggests that there may have been an element of commu-

Styles of Ideology

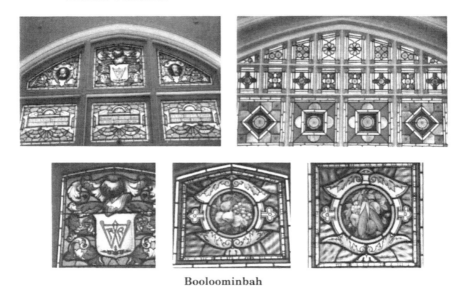

Figure 8.1. The use of stained glass in pastoral houses and church buildings.

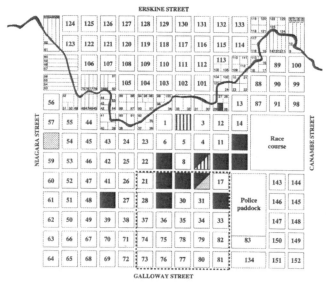
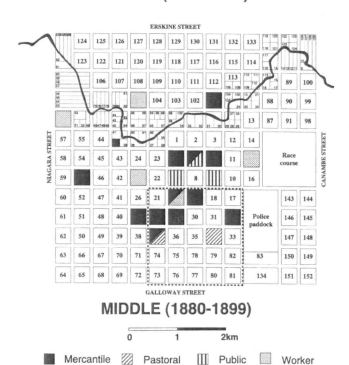

Figure 8.2. The movement of symmetrical working-class houses into South Hill, an area of higher status.

Styles of Ideology

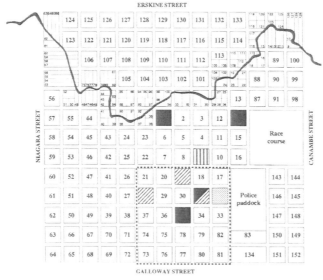

LATE (1900-1930)

Figure 8.2. (*Continued*)

nity surrounding the workers in Armidale. Through the use of distinctive elements, such as single-pitch verandah roofs, turned timber finials, stop-chamfered verandah columns, and weatherboard, the workers were creating a unique identity for themselves that set them apart in their own right from the owners. The question of whether all of these elements were employed through deliberate choice by members of the working class, or whether some may have been an incidental result of the relative inexpense of mass-produced building elements, is largely irrelevant in this light. Even if it were the owners who were in a sense the ones ensuring that workers continued to live in structures such as symmetrical weatherboard houses (through the economies of scale inherent in mass-producing such inexpensive structures), the subsequent location of this stylistic choice in areas of higher status ensured that it still came to be regarded as an index of the working class (Figure 8.2).

At some level then, it indicated an appeal to working-class tradition and common roots, and thus encouraged a perception of community amongst the workers. This too, of course, is an ideological strategy. Through unification, the workers were creating a sense of coherence and local identity among themselves, which both hid their real conditions of existence from themselves and lent a veneer of coherence to what was still an internally differentiated group. The perception of equality lent by this strategy denied that there may still have been disenfranchised members within this group, such as women. Unification, as a possible ideological strategy employed by the workers, is an example of sophisticated ideology—it expresses beliefs about the world that favor the interests of a specific group in society. It is not necessarily true, of course, that the workers must have been conscious of these beliefs, simply that they shared in them.

A sense of community fostered among the workers may have served a dual purpose, however. As well as providing a common tradition around which the working class could construct their own identity, it may also have provided a new direction for working-class discontent. By focusing attention inwards towards the communal maintenance of group identity, instead of outwards towards the differences between that identity and the identity of the owning groups, dissatisfaction may have been channeled in new directions. It is certainly the case that while many of the distinctive elements in the character of West Armidale, such as the hotels or the public schools, were demanded by members of the working class, a sense of community was also reinforced by the owners. One of the main dominating features in West Armidale is the provision of public space in the form of Lambert Park, dedicated in 1889, 15 years after the creation of Central Park. While Central Park was a reserve linking the plantings of the gardens of South Hill with the structures of the town center, Lambert Park was early established a sport ground, particularly for cricket. One of the dominant impressions of Lambert Park is as a village green, complete with original picket fence (c1900) and plantings (Figure 8.3). As Connell and Irving (1992, 106) have argued, the emphasis on organized sports played a large part in creating a sense of identity among workers, and by situating Lambert Park in West Armidale, the mercantile capitalists may have been contributing to and reinforcing a sense of community.

Creating a sense of community held in common through the emulation of stylistic traits by the workers may have had other ideological shadings as well. The appropriation of emblems of stylishness may have served to hide the true conditions of the workers' existence from themselves. By believing that better things were possible, and by making this materialize through emulating stylishness, the conditions of labor were masked. Those who could afford to appropriate stylishness could express beliefs that improvement was possible, while those who could not, at least could believe that it might be so. In this sense, then, ideology was a set of beliefs fostered by the workers amongst themselves, not something which originated in a ruling class conspiracy. These beliefs also gave the workers power, of course, in that the embodi-

Figure 8.3. Lambert Park in West Armidale.

ment of these ideas through style my have reaffirmed a sense of the capability of the working class to succeed and prosper.

Capitalists and Capitalists

Stylistic differences between mercantilists and pastoralists in the early period suggest that these groups were also constructing different identities for themselves, and thus subscribing to different sophisticated ideologies. The dominant sophisticated ideology held by the pastoralists in the colony was linked to the notion of moral ascendancy, and originated in an artificial contrast between the moral and virtuous gentry and the depraved and immoral convict workforce. Mercantile capitalism, by contrast, supported a notion of progress through individual enterprise, regardless of inherited social position. Appropriation of ecclesiastical imagery by pastoralists would suggest that they did indeed subscribe to a view of themselves as morally superior, or at the very least closely aligned to the function and position of the church. The mercantile focus upon classical features, on the other hand, suggests a separate source of origin for their position: The appeals to classical antiquity, embodied in the dominant style of public buildings and private mercantile structures, echo a belief in the ideals of progress through enterprise, and the individual freedom and democracy idealized in ancient Rome. This is a secular position more closely related to the democratic ideals of liberty and individualism grounded in the past. There is a clear division here between the sacred imagery emulated by the pastoralists and the secular imagery emulated by the mercantilists, which supports the contention that each subscribed to a different sophisticated ideology and may have been involved in a struggle with each other to legitimate their respective positions.

From historical sources, it was clear that pastoralists and mercantilists were becoming more, rather than less, convergent over time; this process of reconciliation was manifested in a convergence of style. From the 1880s onwards, pastoral and mercantile structures exhibited a range of stylistic features in common, such as asymmetry, formal names, bay windows, and piers, and were located in a common suburb, South Hill. As well as becoming more similar to each other, pastoral and mercantile structures were also becoming more distinct from workers' houses over time. Most distinctive among these features was the use of asymmetry in middle- and upper-class houses, culminating in highly individual structures such as Booloominbah, Trevenna, Birida, the Cotswold, or The Turrets. There is also a convergence between mercantile and pastoral capital in features of style possessing distinctive associations with ruling groups, notably the crenellated bay windows on Loombra, Trelawney, The Turrets, and Highbury (see Figure 6.5). As an element linked explicitly to notions of chivalry and respectability, these particular features were symbolic of both authority and tradition, and thus part of the legitimation of wealth and prestige, as well as the construction of social position that occurred through assuming the rule (and rules) of the "gentleman."

Adopting the manners and accouterments of the gentleman as part of a broader understanding of chivalry and respectability was nowhere more apparent than in F. R. White's design for the central stained glass window in his country house, Booloominbah. As a celebration of the life of General Charles Gordon, it was also a celebration of his death in battle at Khartoum and of the cult of hero worship that grew up around his death (Girouard 1981, 229; Mitchell 1988, 28–29). Celebrated as the quintessential British hero, Gordon was eulogized for combining "the attributes of Sir Lancelot, of Bayard, of Cromwell ... as unselfish as Sidney, of courage dauntless as Wolfe ... Doubtful indeed it is if anywhere in the past we shall find figure of knight or soldier equal to him" (quoted in Girouard 1981, 229). Gordon's death became a symbol of the struggle of the British Empire against its enemies, and Gordon himself became a martyr for the cause of British colonialism and the drawing of

Styles of Ideology   191

a "red British line through Africa" (Burleigh 1899, 295). Commissioned by Frederick White in 1901, the Gordon window had everything: gothic arch; stained glass; and most importantly, General Gordon himself, center stage, enshrined in a very medieval art form as a modern saint.

As such, it was a brilliant amalgam of symbolic imagery. The spirit of self-sacrifice for the good of others, which the legend of Gordon's death embodied, was one of the essential tenets of the code of the chivalrous gentleman; his duty was to protect from oppression those who were unable to protect themselves (chiefly women and the working classes). Created partly in an atmosphere that questioned the right of the upper classes to rule solely by virtue of their ownership of property, the gentlemanly moral code produced a new model for training the elite: "The aim of the revival of the chivalric tradition was to produce a ruling class which *deserved* to rule because it possessed the moral qualities necessary to rulers. Gentlemen were to run the country because they were morally superior." (Girouard 1981, 260–261, emphasis added). This is not far from the earlier pastoral ideology based on an inherent (and inherited) moral superiority, with one crucial difference. Having weathered the challenges to pastoral authority posed by the mercantile middle class, the pastoralists could no longer assume a right to rule, but instead had to prove that they were worthy of doing so. The ideological construction of the gentleman, and the strategy of legitimation that this employed, both reinforced the long-held pastoral notion of moral superiority and clothed it in a new guise: In the Gordon window, the ruling-class appeal to the authoritative position rightfully accorded to a gentleman, and the pastoralist appeals to the tradition and moral superiority of sacred church imagery, were fused irrevocably (Figure 8.4). As such, it is perhaps one of the most effective artifacts of ideology in Armidale.

This would suggest that the ruling groups were constructing a mutual identity for themselves, thus, possibly subscribing to a similar form of sophisticated ideology. The use of distinctive and distinguishing features by the ruling groups enshrines stark material difference as an indicator of relative group identity. In other words, the ruling groups were setting themselves apart from the workers by emphasizing a set of absolute differences, not only in the size and style of their structures, but also by accentuating their ability to be stylish.

This marked distinction was also a facet of the spatial organization of Armidale. By the ruling groups choosing to locate themselves in the visually dominant position of South Hill, the visual hierarchy of Armidale became at once an expression of, and a buttress for, the organization of the social system. The distinction created by contrasting a high-status suburb with the lower-status areas it overlooked and in a sense dominated, created and contributed to an impression of differential wealth, position, and influence. The tangibly dominant nature of mate-

Figure 8.4. The Gordon window, Booloominbah (courtesy UNE Archives collection A583-P1346).

Styles of Ideology

rial structures and the spaces people created rendered social relations it terms of physical distance and position, and through persistence implied that the ordering of the social system was itself immutable and enduring. Just as the workers were "beneath" the position of their employers, so too were they "beneath" the position of their employers' houses. This uses naturalization as an ideological strategy to delete the social agency that allows those with capital to make more capital. With such a strategy, the resulting social product is presented as "natural," and as enduring as the houses of South Hill. Naturalization as an ideological strategy involving standing structures is only possible if those structures persist. The persistence of spatial arrangements from the past, as symbols of the relationships between previous groups, strengthens each new generation of relationships. Through persistence, the social order of the present can be linked to an order of the past and manifested as enduring and unchangeable.

Scale

The strategies of unification, legitimation, rationalization, and naturalization refer to particular ways in which ideology operates, without commenting on the scale at which ideology might exist. Unsophisticated and sophisticated ideology are complementary aspects of ideology that exist at different scales: Either as widely held common sense, or as beliefs that favor particular groups. The use of legitimation, rationalization, and naturalization strategies by the middle and upper classes, and of unification among the workers, suggests that this is ideology at a sophisticated level. In other words, each of these contains beliefs about the world that favors the interests, or expresses the feelings of, specific groups in society, rather than society as a whole.

The relationship between sophisticated and unsophisticated ideology is in part a relationship between levels that make sense of each other, rather than scales *per se*. The strategies of individual groups exist within a broader construction of identity that incorporates them all—capitalism. Capitalism, as I see it, is an unsophisticated ideology that is used to bind and incorporate many sophisticated ideologies. Sophisticated ideology is constructed within the bounds of unsophisticated ideology, and the latter helps to make sense of the former, as it gives it both outline and form. Ideology exists at a variety of scales, sometimes it is concerned with manufacturing similarity between groups, sometimes with difference. Sometimes ideology is concerned with diverting resistance, and perhaps in other contexts is even about accepting and lauding difference as another means of diversion. The ideological forms that existed in the past bear a relationship to the patterns that exist in the present: The past informs the present as much as the present

194 Chapter 8

informs the past. It is certainly the case that in Armidale the ideological patterns of the past are incorporated into the perceptions of the present, such that Armidale's notion of heritage and its public identity are closely linked to the precedents of the nineteenth and early twentieth centuries.

IDEOLOGY AND PUBLIC IDENTITY

The relationship between ideology and public identity is at once obvious and subtle. In Armidale, a public version of identity was constructed within the ideological patterns of the past, but is reproduced in later contexts because it also proceeds from an ideology of the present (Gero 1989, 103). There are three concurrent strands being spun together here: the creation of identity in the past from the particular contexts of production that existed then; the recreation of identity through time in contexts that include the friezes of previous social configurations; and the continual reappropriation of pieces or aspects of those pasts as germane to the construction of identity in the present. All of these strands are important in terms of how people have constructed, and continue to construct, their own identities, and subsequently identities for the places in which they live, a process that is at least partly rooted in the particular mix of capitalisms and ideologies that prevailed. Identity in all of these strands includes both private and public versions; the identity of dominant groups, as well as their relationships to other groups, constructs at a larger scale the public version of identity that is embodied in the presentation of Armidale to outsiders.

The public image of the town in the late nineteenth and early twentieth centuries, in particular, was a construction of identity at the larger scale that closely reflected the mercantile/pastoral struggle for control over Armidale and its outcome. It is worth considering in more detail just what facets of group identity informed the construction of a public identity for Armidale, as this construct not only played on a general English resemblance, but also borrowed heavily from pastoral wealth and prestige as a means of reinforcement.

Armidale—Cathedral City: Public Identity and the Construction of "Landscape"

The Nineteenth Century

In the twentieth century, the identity of Armidale as a community is well established, with strong emotive links to ecclesiasticism, education, and cultural refinement. There is a strong history to this image,

Styles of Ideology 195

which has been carefully cultivated for more than 100 years. In many ways this is not surprising, as the choice of Armidale for the seat of both the Anglican and Roman Catholic bishops was the deciding factor in the incorporation of Armidale as a city. It is also what distinguished Armidale's Anglican and Roman Catholic chapels as cathedrals, rather than as mere churches. By 1881 Armidale was already referred to as a cathedral city, with definite and conscious links between religion and education being used to promote it as a cathedral town with a country estate setting and elite schools. As part of this cultivation, accounts of Armidale's history often emphasize a movement away from initial impressions of disorder and unruliness towards images of rural tranquility that stress success, achievement, and order (see, for example, Ferry 1994; Gilbert 1982). Emphasis is often placed upon the increasing control over space, nature, and particularly behavior, which can be disentangled from successive changes in Armidale's appearance and social codes and that is presented ubiquitously as "development." Early descriptions, such as that provided by Surveyor John James Galloway in 1849 of "the low debauchery of the place which seduces [my employees] into great irregularities" (quoted in Ferry 1994, 252), are often contrasted to later pastoral scenes:

> In the springtime ... it [Armidale] is very beautiful; the fruit trees such as you see in Old England are in full blossom, the earth covered with brilliant grass, the paddocks waving with corn, and the open bush redolent of the bloom of the wattle or the acacia; no wonder bishops, pastors and officials have found in Armidale a chosen seat, and rest satisfied. (*Town and Country Journal* May 2, 1874, cited in Gilbert 1982, 260)

What was often found worth describing in detailed accounts were the sources of wealth that existed within Armidale and images of its investment in the physical structure of the town: "it is a pleasing task to write about a place like Armidale. Its exceeding picturesqueness, the combination of art with nature in the scenery, the formation of streets, the private residences and gardens, the public buildings, churches and schools, all go to make up a very agreeable picture" (*Town and Country Journal* May 7, 1874, cited in Gilbert 1982, 260). In the same vein, but 11 years later, Armidale was described as:

> eminently respectable—in her bishops, in her cathedrals, in her churches, in her schools, in her many government officials, in her merchants, in her one clock that sweetly chimes the fleeting hours.... Walking through the streets of Armidale ... one somehow soon begins to feel that he is in a place which is not as other places are. The streets are cleaner: ... there are a number of very superior private residences, and a park. There is evidence of a large and well-to-do population, not the least of which is the number of elegantly dressed beauties who may be seen promenading the streets or gaining a more vigorous exercise on the lawn tennis ground. (*Town and Country Journal* November 17, 1883, cited in Gilbert 1982, 265)

196   Chapter 8

These word images are reinforced by strong visual links to particular built features of the Armidale landscape, particularly the Anglican and Roman Catholic cathedrals, the two Anglican private schools, and the private houses associated with wealth and privilege. Associations between climate, religion, education, and "significant" buildings were periodically reinforced:

> There is an opulent station owning class and the manual worker between whom is a great social gulf. Of course there is a fair proportion of a well-to-do middle class ... [which] brings into existence a number of private schools which seem to depend largely on class distinction. Of course an excellent climate also assists these schools [and] ... There is probably more competition from private interests than in any other portion of the State. (Submission by Inspector McDowell for the establishment of a high school at Armidale, May 1918, cited in Gilbert 1982 180)

These images are all essentially urban images, referring directly to the material and moral spheres firmly encompassed by the mercantile capitalists. In many cases there is an absence of images similarly representing the pastoral interests within the community, although, as the center for a squatting district, Armidale was initially founded as a direct result of those interests. Although a social divide between pastoral and mercantile capital was apparently ameliorated by the early 1890s (Ferry 1994, 251, 323), pastoralists still often only resided in the town after their retirement or on a temporary annual basis. Given that Armidale's public identity stressed tradition and permanence, there is a great irony in these images of stability owing their genesis to an undoubtedly wealthy, but largely absent or transient, group of pastoral capitalists. It was also ironic that, although a "sense of belonging associated with the Armidale community" developed in and after 1891, and partly wedded earlier sectarian disagreement between pastoral and urban capital (Ferry 1994, 251), in the late nineteenth century a new rift emerged. This still targeted the detrimental effects of transience on the Armidale community, albeit by a different group of people. Although both graziers and merchants were now merged in property-owning solidarity and classed themselves together as locals, a continuing divide between locals and transients subsequently focused in the early 1890s upon disputes between local graziers and transitory, union-organized shearers, and beginning in the mid-twentieth century, upon a dichotomy between "townies" and university students.

The Twentieth Century

The urban mythology of "Armidale: the cathedral city" has been under construction for over 100 years and is encapsulated in the present labels still attached to the place: "a cathedral city of education and the arts" (Barker 1980) or "A city of culture and learning" (Armidale City Council 1993). The public identity of Armidale in the twentieth century, however, is no longer limited to the pages of Sydney newspapers, but has become part of a more general process of heritage awareness that imbues our perception of the past. The heritage conservation movement simultaneously defines and captures a public appreciation for a past, and at the same time directs it in particular ways. As a cultural production, it mediates in-group/out-group distinctions, and is used to create identity at the same time as it is purported to merely reflect it. The public identity of Armidale is constructed from the material remains of its past; that is, from the persistence of structures and their spatial arrangement, and from the direction of emulation and links between groups. The creation of a public identity, of course, extends to the public presentation of that identity. This is not simply the creation of a texture of dominant values, but also of how this texture comes to be legitimated for other subordinate groups and how it is presented or "sold" to outsiders (visitors and tourists), and thus reinforced.

In part it is the content of particular stories attached to particular places that defines how the city will be interpreted. In Armidale, the stories attached to sites invariably center around "pioneering" men, both pastoralists and mercantilists from the upper and middle classes. By stories, I mean accounts of the person who caused a structure to be built or who was otherwise involved with it: thus Henry Mallam is the identity attached to 94 Rusden St., but so too is John Richardson, the mercantilist who rented the house in the 1870s. Typically, the issue of whether structures have enduring stories attached to them is weighted heavily in favor of the ruling groups at the expense of the working class. In a statistical analysis, structures from the early period are characterized by stories pinpointing mercantile and pastoral capitalists from groups 1 and 2 as the identities attached to sites. Although there are no statistically significant results from the middle period, in the late period the same pattern is evident. Mercantile capitalists, pastoral capitalists, and members of group 1 are overwhelmingly associated with structures, while workers are not. There is a clear bias here in favor of dominant identities and thus dominant structures, which is both a direct consequence of the social patterning that has existed in the past and a reinforcement of the current heritage tendency to perpetuate this patterning in the present.

This structuring of place by the dominant sections of the community is also reflected in the street names allocated in the nineteenth and twentieth centuries. The original street names given by Galloway in 1848 exclusively celebrated pastoralists as central to the formation of

Armidale: Dangar St. after Henry Dangar; Dumaresq St. after William and Henry Dumaresq; Marsh St. after Matthew Henry Marsh; Rusden St. after T. J. Rusden of Europambla, and Faulkner St. after John Falconer of Falconer Plains. Although Beardy St. ostensibly seems an exception to this, it was named after two stockmen, collectively called the Beardies because of their facial hair, who were instrumental as guides for many of the early pastoralists.

Subsequent street names both extended this pastoral emphasis and layered it with mercantile overtones. Taylor St. was named after W. T. Taylor of Terrible Vale; Mott St. after Charles Mott of Springmount; White Ave. after Harold White; and Hargrave St. after Richard Hargrave of Hillgrove. Early mercantilists were celebrated in the naming of Markham St. after auctioneer George Markham; Mossman St. after Archibald Mosman (the misspelling is unexplained); Allingham St. after storekeeper and first mayor George Allingham; Galloway St. after surveyor John James Galloway; and Kirkwood St. after Robert Kirkwood, who established the first steam-powered flour mill. In the twentieth century, Tysoe Crescent, Trim St., Moore St., and Richardson Ave. are all named after members of the mercantile elite. By choosing to name streets after such figures, the same pattern evident in the preservation of stories about structures is evident in the naming of streets—the past is structured to reflect the lives and position of the financially powerful.

It is unknown to what extent this texture of dominant values was accepted by the working class and other disenfranchised groups in Armidale. Unlike in nineteenth century Stockholm, where subversive versions of major street names were nurtured and disseminated amongst non-elite groups (see Orser 1995, 142–144), there is no evidence that similar practices occurred in Armidale.

There is another level to the issue of how a place is interpreted in the present, which stems from the conception of the past as a commodity, one result being that there are many ways in which a buying public can assess the past. Cultural heritage, or the past as accessible through artifacts, is only one means of commodifying the past, but one that is not often acknowledged as such. Relics cannot be sold in isolation (or rather they can, but to less effect: what constitutes the effectiveness of a story about the past will be discussed later), and therefore interpretation of some sort is a necessary medium between a buying public and a salable past. Lowenthal (1985, 238), in fact, argues that relics in isolation are not an autonomous guide: they "light up the past only when we already know they belong to it." Thus an awareness of something as being "history" is contingent first upon an awareness of it as being "historical":

Styles of Ideology

"Memory and history pin-point only certain things as relics; the rest of what lies around us seems simply present, suggesting nothing past" (Lowenthal 1985, 238). A farmer's appreciation of nineteenth century farm equipment is bound to be different than that of an archaeologist's.

This tendency to elide history with being historical is particularly apparent when applied to standing structures, and is part of the process by which indexical markers of groups come to be symbolic in later contexts of interpretation. As a sign no longer having any direct resemblance or connection to the object it once marked, these previous coteries of status still possess meaning to observers among whom there is a convention that it stands for another thing (Noble and Davidson 1996, 68–69). Structures (and their style) become symbols in the present with meaning in the present, and interpretation, in effect, becomes an outline of the historicalness of a certain object or place, as part of the process of then commodifying it as history. What this entails, however, is not only choosing which parts of the story are best able to be interpreted, but also which parts are "good," in terms of which are most salable. In essence, effective interpretation depends on a good story, and to be truly good (in a capitalist sense) it has to be salable. By salable I do not mean that this is always determined by strict cost–benefit analyses, in fact, it may be more intuitive than analyzed. It may be that salability is simply based on what has been proven to work in other cases; that is, what sorts of experiences consistently draw the public to a place. As with all products, however, not all versions of the past are deemed to be equally desirable, and thus various qualities in some versions of the past will render these more appealing (to both insiders and outsiders) in the present.

I will return to the repercussions inherent in the symbolic meanings of past structures and in selling the heritage industry after briefly examining the place of those meanings and the industry within Armidale.

Producing Armidale in the Present

Since the 1991 Heritage Study, the Armidale City Council has been implementing the recommendations of the final report through a program of historic building preservation and interpretation (Figure 8.5). This has taken on a number of forms, from the recognition of successful and sympathetic renovations through the Heritage Award scheme, to the official recognition of a limited range of important buildings by attaching custom-made commemorative plaques, to the implementation of a Heritage Walk and Heritage Drive covering a selection of relevant sights and structures. The latter are designed to be complementary and together cover over 80 "landmark" structures (Figures 8.6

Figure 8.5. Heralding the value of Armidale.

and 8.7), the choice of which emphasizes the bias towards the dominant section of the community.

Structures such as houses occupy a particular place in the construction of public identity and ideology, both figuratively and literally (Yentsch 1988). As physical and enduring elements of the landscape, buildings both encode a range of past social meanings symbolic of past social structures, and tie this literally to the construction of space in the present by associating the identity of the person who built or controlled it and their position within the community with the physical fabric of the house. The Heritage Walk and the Heritage Drive are prime examples of the chain of connection between identity, place, and ideology, and of the way in which public identity both derives from and feeds this process.

The Heritage Walk is confined geographically to the center of town and to South Hill. The Heritage Drive, while encompassing a greater number of structures, remains concentrated within the same area. Both focus heavily on public buildings and a selection of private houses, with some reference to the identities of both builders and owners. All of the identities associated with structures relate to families and individuals who dominated the community, for example: George Baker (pastoral capital; group 1), the McKinlay family (mercantile capital; group 1), Charles Wilson (mercantile; group 2), Joseph Slade (mercantile; group 1), Henry Solomon (mercantile; group 3), Barnett Aaron

Styles of Ideology 201

Moses (mercantile; group 1), George Morse (pastoral; group 1), Henry Mallam (mercantile; group 2), William Curtis (mercantile; group 1), Frederick White (pastoral; group 1), and George Nott (mercantile; group 3). It is notable that most members of this list are associated with the later period of Armidale's growth (1880s–1900s), and that earlier members of the community, such as John Moore, James Salmon, and John Trim, all of whom could be associated with extant structures, are missing entirely. By collapsing time and space in such a way, the Heritage Walk and Drive effectively telescope the history of Armidale into a narrower window associated with the peak time of expansion and prosperity.

In line with such an emphasis, the workers are not represented within either of these schemes. Only the Heritage Drive encompasses sections of West Armidale within its boundaries, although none of these structures are tied explicitly to working class identity. For example, 307 Beardy St. is described as "typical of West Armidale timber residences built at the turn of the century," without any reference to the role of such weatherboard structures to be symbolic of the working class. Likewise, the West Armidale primary school is described in two sentences that do not reference the increasing sense of dissatisfaction and solidarity among the inhabitants of working-class West Armidale, which led them to agitate for separate educational facilities accessible to them: "West Armidale School commenced in 1890 as an infants' school and was rebuilt and renamed as the Drummond Memorial School in 1966. The school was named in honor of David Henry Drummond, Country Party MLA for the Northern Tablelands and Armidale from 1920–1949" (Heritage Drive pamphlet). By removing the connotations of its original name, which both denote its location in a working-class suburb and celebrate its origins as a result of working-class mobilization in the nineteenth century, the school becomes disassociated from any connection with the workers, and instead becomes associated explicitly with a member of the middle class.

The structures that the Heritage Drive and Walk incorporate and revere as the physical fabric of heritage are constructed well within the dominant values of Armidale's public identity. As a result, the visual dominance of South Hill is taken for granted, and the preservation of its houses reified as the natural result of the heritage process. The workers have no place within this scheme, and West Armidale becomes merely an area to travel through in order to get to somewhere else. This is the face that Armidale presents to outsiders: combined mercantile and pastoral wealth and its attendant leisure, focusing on the boom years of the 1880s and 1890s, leaving an impression of wealth and

202   **Chapter 8**

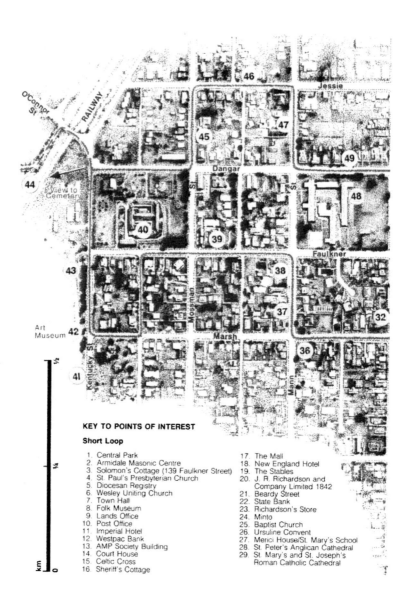

Figure 8.6. The Armidale Heritage Walk.

Styles of Ideology

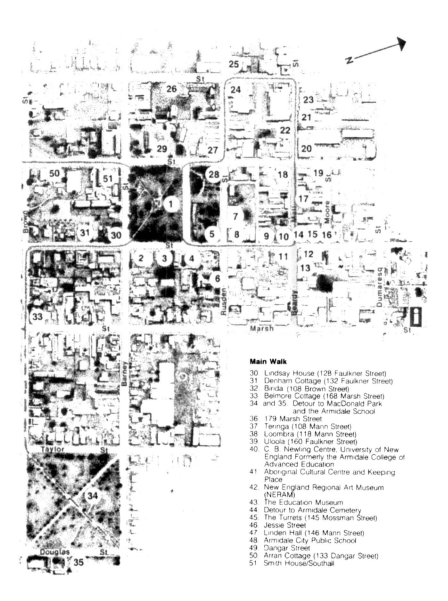

Figure 8.6. (*Continued*)

204 **Chapter 8**

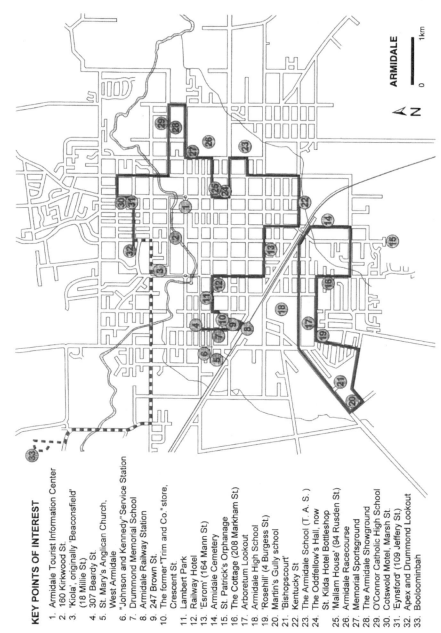

Figure 8.7. The Armidale Heritage Drive.

KEY POINTS OF INTEREST

1. Armidale Tourist Information Center
2. 160 Kirkwood St.
3. 'Kiola', originally 'Beaconsfield' (18 Millie St.)
4. 307 Beardy St.
5. St. Mary's Anglican Church, West Armidale
6. "Johnson and Kennedy" Service Station
7. Drummond Memorial School
8. Armidale Railway Station
9. 247 Brown St.
10. The former "Trim and Co." store, Crescent St.
11. Lambert Park
12. Railway Hotel
13. 'Esrom' (164 Mann St)
14. Armidale Cemetery
15. St. Patrick's Orphanage
16. The Cottage (208 Markham St)
17. Arboretum Lookout
18. Armidale High School
19. 'Rosehill' (4 Burgess St)
20. Martin's Gully school
21. 'Bishopscourt'
22. Kentucky St
23. The Armidale School (T. A. S.)
24. The Oddfellow's Hall, now St. Kilda Hotel Bottleshop
25. 'Mallam House' (94 Rusden St)
26. Armidale Racecourse
27. Memorial Sportsground
28. The Armidale Showground
29. O'Connor Catholic High School
30. Cotswold Motel, Marsh St.
31. 'Eynsford' (109 Jeffery St.)
32. Apex and Drummond Lookout
33. Booloominbah

Styles of Ideology

prestige without any of the overtones of "work" or "employees." The workers are deliberately made to be invisible and this invisibility legitimates the appropriation of the wealth that labor produces.

There are two crucial repercussions following from the way that the past in Armidale is recreated as meaningful through the heritage industry in the present: the propagation of an ideologically loaded version of the past as an effective story, which the issue of salability necessarily entails; and closely related to this, the way in which the combination of the persistence of structures and directions of emulation lead to a recognition of symbolic meaning not just *from* the past, but also in the present.

THE PAST AS PRODUCT

The argument that in our capitalist society the past has become just another product that has been commodified is not new (see, for example, Shanks and Tilley 1987; Tilley 1989). It implies that the past is a salable commodity, with a consequent value dependent upon its salability and upon its capacity to symbolize previous configurations of social relations (see also MacCannell 1976, 19–20). Like all products, the public wants certain qualities from the past: Value then becomes an issue of what constitutes a "good" story or what ingredients must be present to attract and entertain a viewing public. How then do you define "good"? This is not meant in a moral sense, but in terms of engagement value, in an ability to engage an audience. This can be achieved by either entertaining them, an approach often criticized as largely passive, therefore, fostering a consumer, rather than a producer, mentality (see Handsman and Leone 1989; Tilley 1989), or by teaching them, which is often seen as more active and self-reflexive (see, for example, Leone 1995; Leone et al. 1987; Potter 1992). Though more critical, this last is not necessarily more successful (see Potter 1995).

Purveyors of a past represented by material remains not only expect certain qualities from artifacts, but also certain specific experiences to be contained by those material objects, which will enhance their appreciation of a generalized past. Lowenthal (1985, 52–62) argues that there are three general attributes that give the past value: antiquity, continuity, and termination. Antiquity is the ability of age to convey a number of characteristics, such as a demonstrable lineage or heritage, a "beginning," or a nostalgic purity and innocence. Antiquity is also conveyed by remoteness: "sheer age lends romance ... the older past has a status that later periods cannot match." (Lowenthal 1985, 53).

Continuity implies that the past is appreciated because it has led to the present, particularly so if there are demonstrable "living pasts" bound up with the present. Termination provides a sense of completion: The past can be appreciated because it is over, so there is thus a sense of stability or permanence that may be lacking in the present. These attributes are partly escapism, the persuasion that the visitor is *in* the past, but they are also partly a sense that the past is alive in the present. Each of these attributes, of course, is only conceivable because of the persistence of at least some material aspects of the past into the present. Persistence is thus the first quality that must exist for the other attributes of the appreciation of age to be able to give value to the past.

Artifactual material—"relics" or "heritage"—is a particular avenue for accessing the past, and although only one among many, is an important one, as people may not simply want a historical past, but also a material one. As the basis for many constructions of the past, relics interact with the four general attributes—persistence, antiquity, continuity, and termination—to provide a guide to the sorts of qualities that people might wish to experience. First, there is a need to recognize that artifacts actually stem from, or link with, the past. Thus that artifacts should look "old" (Shanks 1992, 101), either through patinas of age (discoloration, lichen, weathering, etc.) or through anachronism (it should look "old fashioned," or at least curious enough to convey a sense of age) (Lowenthal 1985 241). Second, there is a desire for origins (the oldest date), and demonstrable lineages or pedigrees (histories). Third, detail provides amplification of the residues of the past, but more so at the level of familiarity with everyday things. If people desire to be "put" in the past, then the past they desire is not always grand, extraordinary, or precious: "... rich and grand finds to not really belong to anyone, their human significance is less than the incidental." (Shanks 1992, 59). There is also the consideration that the value of a relic may be based on more formal aesthetic qualities, which can incorporate any or all of these particular qualities. Taking this further, Shanks (1992, 108) argues that the power of heritage lies particularly in how each of these aspects are significant today. Their value is not so much present in isolation, but in signification—"things meaning *for* what we are now." (1992, 108, italics in original). This is the crucial point that I will return to in the next section.

If commodification of the past works on this basis, then these are the distinct qualities of the past that render it most salable to a public audience: authenticity (see MacCannell 1975, 105), the look of age, the demonstration of origins, contextual detail, and aesthetic pleasure. This is public history and public archaeology: It is popular, not academic.

Styles of Ideology 207

The criteria of a popular past are different to those of an academic past: "Heritage is not about the attractive presentation of a past as it is understood by archaeology ... The meaning is what the past can do for the present.... Above all it is accessible to people other than those acquainted with the academic value system of archaeology." (Shanks 1992, 108). Popular pasts are more emotive than rational, and they demand some form of emotional interaction. A boring and unsalable past is one in which there is nothing for the visitor: "... having bought the past intellectually or cognitively, [there needs to be something] to buy, thus expressing and possessing conviction through individual, voluntary action" (Leone 1981, 11).

What will become classed as heritage, to be interpreted at a place, will therefore be a result of two things: what is identifiable and what people will best identify with (i.e., a good, detailed, emotive story that allows them to place themselves readily and effectively in the past). "Identify" here is meant in two senses: You can either identify with something because you do it yourself, that is, it is comfortable and familiar, and therefore its existence in the past allows you to draw comparisons between "them" and "us"; or because you do *not* do it yourself, therefore the links that are made with the past are ones of contrast, rather than comparison. Often these forms of identification and thus self-definition are complementary, and an effective interpretation will probably be one that employs both senses of the word to convey its message.

This has obvious implications for the way in which a salable identity for Armidale can be constructed. If what can be interpreted most successfully (or sold most effectively) are those features that are most evocative, and if all too often the material evidence that is most evocative is the large scale or durable features, in other words, the artifacts of the powerful, what does this mean for the identity of the workers? If effective interpretation rests most successfully upon a good story, and if the types of material remains that will realize that story are more likely to be the artifacts of one dominant class in society only, how difficult then is it going to be to write a story about the powerless groups in society? If it is possible, will it be salable? If it is possible, but not salable, then which view of the past is most likely to be disseminated?

In Armidale, the structures that are most often celebrated as heritage, and thus interpreted to a viewing public, are those associated with the middle and upper classes, and with a leisured lifestyle only made possible by wealth. Heritage focuses on stylishness. This enshrines particular directions of emulation in style, from public buildings to mercantile buildings, from ecclesiastical structures to pastoral houses, and from both mercantile and pastoral buildings to subordinate groups. The dominance of South Hill as an area of high status is not challenged, but reified in the classification of this area as the Conservation Zone. Although workers' structures exist within this area, they were not recorded by the Heritage Study team, and the workers' houses in West Armidale are mostly scenic background in the drive to somewhere else. Even when they are deliberately incorporated into the circuit, their structures come without the enduring stories that are commonly attached to private mercantile and pastoral structures.

This comes to the heart of the problem surrounding the presentation of public identity. It might be argued that a public identity for a place such as Armidale cannot provide a means to construct a convincing story of the identities of the workers, although of course one of the stories about the workers is that there is little material evidence for them. The small sample size in this study is not simply a result of poor data collection methods, but a result of the impermanence of workers' structures. They are neither particularly durable, not accorded sufficient importance to warrant conservation. This particular interrelationship, between the survival of structures as a result of the degrees of significance accorded by a professional heritage consultant (in this case, an architect) and the survival of particular dominant textures of identity, is both dependent and mutually reinforcing. A structure is more likely to be celebrated as heritage if it is already part of the dominant identity pattern; after all, much of the research done by a heritage consultant rests upon interviewing the present inhabitants for insights into what they already hold to be valuable. Conversely, by touching only briefly on the spheres of subordinate groups (here, of the workers' cottages), the identity of the workers is neither incorporated into the construction of the present, nor their structures preserved to be reinterpreted in the future. Thus, the dominant pattern remains dominant and is, in fact, enshrined through legislation as the determining identity for Armidale.

It is not necessarily the case that this narrative of the past is accepted uncritically by those who stand outside the dominant pattern, for example, by workers or Aborigines. Richard Johnson (in Larrain 1994, 163) has argued that public versions of identity and the enormous variety of ways of life found in a place are two moments of an identity circuit that feed upon each other. All groups in society participate in the reading and reception of public versions of identity, and these need not be necessarily passive or uncritical. This process of reading and reception is part of the way of life of members of all groups, and in turn contributes to the reproduction of society, and thus to public versions

Styles of Ideology 209

of identity. That the workers' identity remains unincorporated suggests that either there is currently little appreciation for a demonstrable "living past" bound up with nostalgic notions of the working class, or that their position is not sufficiently remote, anachronistic, or opulent to convey a sense of distance or romance.

The commodification of heritage at once constructs, and is constructed from, a capitalist notion of value. For the architects from Perumal Murphy, "value," in terms of what should and should not constitute "heritage" in Armidale, is defined according to the value already attached to the labels; in other words, according to the value that particular elements of style are accorded as a result of the continuing process of moving from index to symbol. It is not surprising, then, that only those structures with high status (i.e., those buildings constructed by the upper and middle classes, particularly on South Hill) are deemed to have value. Classification of these buildings in terms of their architecture is thus used to give value, not to seek it. This process is both pervasive and persuasive, and extends to the incorporation of these notions of value into the presentation of public identity and in heritage reinforcing a capitalist notion of value. Real estate agents in Armidale commonly use the age of a structure or its associations to sell it as heritage, appealing to both nostalgia and constructions of stylishness to entice buyers: "a glimpse of gracious living from days gone by," "one of the best examples of Federation residential architecture in Armidale," "Armidale's second oldest home," or the "charm and character of yesteryear" (Figure 8.8).

STYLE (AND MEANING) FROM THE PAST IN THE PRESENT: THE IDEALOGY OF HERITAGE

Style, as a choice between options of form, is not just selected from the range of new choices available in the present, but also from the range of old options that have existed in the past. Both old and new form a repertoire of shared concepts that can be drawn on and incorporated into the present. In many ways, the choice between old options is directed in a similar way to the process of establishing a good story about the past—through the various attributes of old styles that come to have meaning in the present. The style of many recent buildings in Armidale mirrors aspects of older styles, as particular elements become incorporated into later ideas of "stylish" architecture, such as turned timber finials, stained glass, French doors, decorative gable collar ties, classical design influences, and cast iron (Figure 8.9). This is closely

Figure 8.8. A selection of real estate advertisements selling the value of heritage in Armidale.

Styles of Ideology

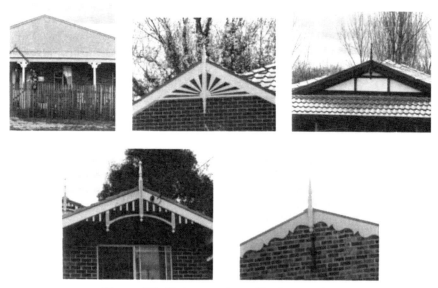

Figure 8.9. Modern versions of heritage style.

linked to the concept of heritage, and builds on the notions of antiquity, continuity, termination, and persistence as they relate to the creation of the past as product.

I have already discussed the ways in which past patterns of social identity structure what is thought to be stylish. The direction of emulation in previous discussions, however, has always treated elements as synchronous and centered around the way in which features are emulated across class and space in any given period. Emulation, however, can also take place across time, although it does not do so in precisely the same fashion. Figure 8.9 illustrates a range of elements that are thought to be sufficiently stylish to structure present contexts of interpretation; however, it also illustrates an apparent paradox in the direction of emulation. While classical emblems, cast iron, stained glass, and French doors are symbols distinctive of nineteenth century upper- and middle-class structures, turned timber finials, an almost ubiquitous element of present-day notions of heritage architecture, were once indexical of the working class. In the case of these elements, emulation has occurred in the opposite direction: *from* the working class *to* the middle class.

This would suggest that heritage as a source of contemporary choices for style is not necessarily viewed in the present as symbolic of the class relations that existed in the past. Instead, another process is operating. Through commodification, the past is created as a product that is separate from the present. It is "buyable" because it is objectifiable and apart. The persistence of various elements of style creates a repertoire of previous choices available to be mined in the present for new symbols to emulate.

In this process, persistence is recognized, not as structuring space and symbolic behavior in the present (contrary to the position adopted by archaeologists), but as the material referent of belonging to a past that is distant and opaque. Persistence interacts with the remoteness of antiquity, with the connections of continuity, and with the detachment of termination to represent this past and to form a repertoire. Emulation across time is thus not class-based *per se*, although class is, of course, related. Old notions of stylishness and the social description that occurred to introduce these elements in the first place derive from class, but the elements themselves come to acquire value as old, rather than as symbolic of a particular class. That is, appropriating these symbols through commodification of the past creates them as symbols of age (old/enduring/persisting), rather than of class. Thus, turned timber finials are valued as old, rather than as working class. This returns to the idea that not all versions of the past are equally desirable, and that the qualities in some versions of the past will render them more desirable than others. If the repertoire is not very productive, that is, if the conditions of labor were sufficiently miserable and oppressive, then presumably there is little, if anything, from the past to emulate.

Emulating the repertoire is a particular definition of heritage. Heritage preserves style elements *in situ* and thus protects the repertoire, but the repertoire itself, and the past social patterns that created it, also structure what is thought to be heritage in any given place. This circuit is embedded in the present and relies upon the commodification of the past. There are two consequences that follow from this circuit: Creating the past as an object creates artifacts as universally old, and in doing so constructs an ideology of heritage.

Objectifying the past renders it remote and removes the associations that connect it explicitly with the situation in the present. Heritage as an ideological strategy thus denies the antecedents to present circumstances, and masks the historicity of class inequality. By removing the connotations of class from the structures and elements that persist, heritage obscures the dynamics of the class process and renders things ubiquitously old. This is a strategy of dissimulation—denying that the class situation now may be a result of the dynamics of capitalist formation in previous decades. Where a commodified past thus becomes a source of stylishness in the present, the accident of the persistence of the existence of labor (the persistence of working-class structures and elements) is masked by the ideology of heritage.

THE MATERIAL CONSTRAINTS
TO STUDYING IDEOLOGY

The study of ideology is an area of research that has long been acknowledged as part of archaeology in various capacities. The changing extent and ways in which archaeology has acknowledged ideology as an area for productive research is part of the way that archaeology itself has changed as a discipline. This is no simple or unidirectional process, of course, but is part of wider changes in the social sciences, politics, and society. Although Thomas (1990, 67) has claimed ideology as a notion that has been central to the development of a post-processual archaeology (and to a certain extent by claiming ideology as the central subject matter of a research project it is almost inevitable that the research will be labeled post-processual), it has surfaced in various guises in processual and other literature.

The main problem many archaeologists appear to have with the notion of ideology is that it is a concept not directly amenable to archaeological analysis (see, for example, Binford 1989; Hawkes 1954). While variability between groups is directly expressed by material artifacts and is therefore easier to infer, the possible ideological strategies behind this are at least one step removed from the initial analysis, and therefore from the possibility of conjecture. In this study I have attempted to isolate the possible ideological strategies by which capitalism and its unequal relations are constructed, although some strategies proved more amenable to archaeological analysis than others. Legitimation and rationalization, as strategies that appeal to historical precedents— no matter how spurious—were archaeologically visible in the use of elements associated with older traditions and in the associations that these created. By creating links with past societies, some of the particular qualities of present social structures were presented as universal. Unification was likewise visible in the similarity created by the use of symmetry among workers. Naturalization may have been manifested through the physical use of space and the solidity provided by enduring physical spaces and structures.

This issue returns to the constraints inherent in studying ideology through material artifacts, particularly in historical archaeology. Because archaeological studies of ideology are concerned with illustrating the historicity of present circumstances, rather than reifying an ideological notion of values as permanent and fixed, it is not possible to know, without a minimum of social context information, what particular artifacts may have meant to those who created and used them. Without knowing who William Paca was and to what group he saw himself as belonging, it is not possible to speculate on the ideological reasons behind his choices of style. This constraint is inherent in studies with a behavioral basis grounded in identification via comparison (see Wiessner 1989, 58), since people can only be defined as comparable within their own peculiar historical and social contexts. Without at least knowing something of the cultural and symbolic structures that define people as comparable (Wiessner 1989, 58), there is no way of approaching the particular constructions of identity that mediate style and ideology.

Claiming to identify ideological strategies also logically depends upon at least a minimum knowledge of social context obtainable from other classes of data. To a certain extent, separating ideological constructions of identity into distinct strategies is an artificial process: Just as context is complex and multilayered, so too are the strategies by which ideology is deployed. Although I have represented ideology here in terms of four strategies, there are considerable degrees of overlap between them. Naturalization, for example, relies on appeals to the past as much as do legitimation and rationalization; and unification, legitimation, and rationalization all stress similarity at some level. Furthermore, naturalization, legitimation, and rationalization all depend upon the phenomenon of persistence as a prerequisite for establishing lineage or tradition. This is an important link for archaeological studies of ideology: Persistence defines what archaeologists study and, thus, as a discipline, archaeology is well situated to comment on the dynamics of ideology.

DISCUSSION

This study has several important repercussions for the archaeological study of ideology within the domain of standing structures. Of these, one of the seemingly more obvious, yet previously unconsidered, is that it is entirely possible for more than one sophisticated ideology to exist within one society. The issue that is germane here, is that in New England, in the early and middle periods at least, there was more than a single type of capitalism that was prevalent, and more than a single group of capitalists seeking control. The pastoral capitalists in New England and the mercantile capitalists in Armidale, for example, were

Styles of Ideology

embroiled in an initial struggle for control of the direction of the colony, although always centered within different domains. The rural pastoralists always controlled the dominant form of wealth (wool), but the urban mercantilists controlled the town. Their ideologies were necessarily separate and opposed, but because each was involved in the process by which separate domains of wealth legitimated their position, each was also a part of the broader process of domination.

This observation has another implication. The trajectories followed by both mercantile and pastoral capitalists were initially clearly separate as each took on different realms of associations to legitimate their position. As a result, it became possible for the middle class to influence a notion of stylishness as much as did the elite upper class. Gothic manner was largely a function of middle-class taste (see, for example, Campbell 1987, 33) in both England and Australia, and illustrates the potential for the emerging bourgeoisie to become the "tastemakers" for society as much as the upper class. In Armidale this was no doubt aided by the fact that the pastoralists were most often situated away from the town, and thus their constructions of stylishness were literally hidden from view.

It is no accident that most archaeological discussions of architectural style focus upon the place of dominant ideologies and elites. Focusing on the medium of style in architecture to access ideology effects a particular type of social closure. In short, rich people dominate the landscape, posing a recurring set of problems for archaeological (re)constructions of ideology. As Miller (1987, 163) has argued, by choosing a particularly dominant area of cultural production, such as standing structures, there is a danger of reifying a particular conception of power:

> The class which is defined in relation to buildings ... is not the same as that defined by another division such as profession. Although dominant as far as building styles and the press are concerned, this same social segment may be less influential in the areas of trade unions and popular culture.

In Armidale it was possible to isolate examples of architectural difference employed by the workers: They chose to use particular elements in a way that the upper classes did not, and thus maintained some semblance of separate and alternative identity. Certain elements were indexical of what it meant to be working class, but it was often the placement of these elements, rather than their form, which rendered them distinctive and implicated them in resistance. Orser (1996, 178) has noted this point:

> Historical archaeologists can often attribute particular artifacts and thereby conscious action to a member of the elite, while only being able to relate groups of artifacts to groups of non-elites. We may know the names of the

Boott Mills workers from census rolls, but the way the owners housed them under the strictures of corporate paternalism makes it forever impossible (except in the rarest of cases) to correlate excavated artifacts with specific individuals.

The wider comparative approach taken in this case study made it possible to correlate specific artifacts with specific members of the working class. In Armidale, the workers certainly possessed power as individual potency or capacity, even though they did not possess it in the control of social settings or in the organization of the settings themselves (Wolf 1990, 586). As a result, it became possible to comment on the creation of working-class ideology and on the ideological interplay taking place between this group and other groups. While such a data-intensive approach is not necessarily always possible, it does begin to illustrate some of the complexities attendant upon studying ideology as a social process. At worst, studying the material remains of a single individual or group makes it difficult to comment on the wider web of connections that together generate ideology, and at best only provides a part of the answer.

Investments of Meaning | 9

> *Successful accounts of ideology must combine two attributes. The first, emphasized by Mannheim, is a hermeneutic subtlety which sees both that it is necessary to understand ideology before criticizing it and also adopts a self-reflexive attitude towards its own premises. The second, stressed in most strands of the Marxist tradition, is to preserve the concept's critical potential by linking it with analyses of control and domination, thereby extricating it from the labyrinth of relativism associated with the hermeneutic circle.*
>
> —MCLELLAN (1986), p. 83

The notion that the spatial distribution of stylistic elements is not random, but is instead related to the patterning of specific groups, and thus to the way society is organized, is not a new concept (see, for example, Hill 1970; 1972; Longacre 1970; 1972). Linking this variability to issues of social power and to the construction of ideology, however, is a direction becoming increasingly common to archaeological analysis, particularly within historical archaeology. This is one of the main strengths of archaeology, and one of the few contributions it can make to the analysis of ideology, that is, contributing to the understanding of the material character of the production of a social order.

I began with a discussion of William Paca's garden and it seems appropriate to end with it as well. When Mark Leone (1984, 26) commented that "ideology ... may very likely be found amid all those items archaeologists have for so long lumped under labels like ... style," he pointed in a direction that many historical archaeologists would later travel, one along which style became a preferred avenue through which to access ideology. By choosing to analyze William Paca's garden in a way that emphasized the eighteenth century Anapolitan's attempts to control nature and time, Leone focused attention on a different range of questions. Rather than simply asking "Why that garden in that pattern?" Leone was inquiring into the relationships behind both garden and pattern, as well as William Paca's place in the world. Paca's identity as an individual and a member of a ruling group was fashioned in a particular way for particular reasons, and was continually created in the patterning of relationships between his group and other groups. Thus, Charles Orser (1996, 167) is correct in commenting that "the only way that subalterns can ever be said to speak at Paca's garden is through the voice of Paca himself, in his visual attempt to negate them. He had to make them invisible through his visibility."

The attempts by Leone and others (see, for example, Hall 1992; Johnson 1991; 1992; McGuire 1988; Orser 1988a; Potter 1992; Shackel 1993) to articulate the complex patterning of ideology, power, and everyday life, illustrates a serious engagement with the nature of archaeology that is often lost sight of in the rhetoric surrounding the processual/ postprocessual debate. In other words (and words not mine) "while we can never know *the* meaning of an artifact, we can make some interpretive moves towards an understanding of what it might have meant" (Conkey 1993, 114). Knowing what the artifacts of rich and poor in Armidale in the past might have meant is by no means either a straightforward or impartial exercise. There are reasons for choosing particular topics and particular ways of approaching them. In undertaking this study, I have attempted to tie the discussion of ideology to a particular, explicit definition, and to widen it beyond the artifacts of a single, elite individual. In doing so, I have focused on persistence and the emulation of symbols through time in considering the dynamics of ideology.

In my archaeological approach to ideology, the assignment of meaning is implicated in the construction of social identity. Both ideology and identity are fluid categories, which respond to the various social and political coordinates of their interpreters; much of this study is thus concerned with the ways in which meaning is created and recreated in context. "Meaning" is not an intrinsic property of the artifact *per se*, but is produced in the interaction between people and the things themselves (Davidson 1997, 125). It is an interpretive category that becomes attached to objects as much through their continual use by people as through the initial act of creation, when a style is made or used for the first time. And it is through questioning the productive context, in which certain constructions of social identity come to have significance for people's understanding of "the world" and to attain legitimacy, that ideology might be reached.

Style and ideology have thus formed two complementary levels to my analysis. Initially, I questioned how particular stylistic features might function semiotically as markers of membership in various groups, how this pattern might mark group boundaries at various scales at different times, and how particular stylistic features or groups of features come to be symbolic of relative social position. Just as important is the issue of how these boundaries were subsequently broken down, by whom, and how the symbolism of position then changed. Ideology, as the second level of analysis, depends upon this knowledge of the social mosaic. Such a study is fundamentally concerned with the mutability of social identity and with how style both relates to and expresses its negotiation. It attempts to test links between archaeologically identifiable social patterning and perceived networks of social power, and to link this, in turn, with ideology. In pursuing this second level of study, my broad aim has been to assess the strengths, as well as the limitations, of the concept of ideology as a research tool for archaeologists attempting to understand past human behavior. Among these are several issues concerning the material constraints to studying ideology, as well as at what level distinction between groups, between social strategies, and between ideologies is archaeologically retrievable from style in architecture. Although there are several problems inherent in this kind of study, it does lead to some observations on the ideological ensemble.

CONTEXT AND IDENTITY

In terms of social context, I found that both local-scale membership in a particular form of capital production and larger-scale membership in a particular social class (as related to the means of production), influence the stylistic construction of identity. Individuals and groups construct identities for themselves that relate them to other individuals and groups, and thus that structure the world. The patterning of groups in Armidale indicated that elements of both a fundamental class conflict and a subsumed class conflict were taking place (Saitta 1994). This meant that the "ruling class" was not a singular entity in Armidale, and that it was possible to distinguish groups within it, divided by the interests attached to domestic and world divisions of labor (McMichael 1984, 249). It also meant that the workers were clearly distinguishable from the owners, and not always by virtue of their structures being less visible or decorative. Some elements were used assertively by members of the working class to contribute to a characteristic working-class identity, at times when working-class resistance to capitalism was on the rise.

It is undoubtedly the case that in Armidale the rich people dominated the landscape, and that through the continual process of constructing identity, the stylistic elements of the dominant buildings continually changed. In contrast, the elements that came to be indexical of the workers, the cheaper, mass-produced, timber-building elements, were not selected in the same fashion, but were open to little choice. Having said this, despite the fact that the workers were not dominant

220   Chapter 9

in terms of their architecture, resistance to domination still took place. Although the features of the workers' houses in themselves were indexical, it was their placement on South Hill in an area of high status, and thus the subsequent manner of their use, which was symbolic. In this way, although the style of the workers' cottages in West Armidale was unremarkable and unprepossessing, once these structures were located on South Hill, they became both distinctive and stylish.

STYLISHNESS

The use of style in the past in Armidale was part of a semiotic process. Various features came to be indexical of certain groups, in that they functioned as markers of membership, as well as of those groups themselves. Style by virtue of this arbitrary and conventional association was subsequently symbolic of the set of relations between groups. In Peirce's (1985[1931]) terms, there was thus a progression from index to symbol over time, as the original conditions for meaning changed. In any particular period, those features that symbolized the status difference were deemed by those who had them as "stylish," and their migration across boundaries reinforced a perception of stylishness as coming from particular groups. It is not possible to know exactly what particular elements meant to those for whom they were indexical at the time: Any attempt at this kind of "inside" meaning is impossible in a purely archaeological study. It is possible, however, to know which elements might have been regarded as meaningful and to assess this through analyzing the sets of relationships mediated by style in the past.

DIRECTIONS OF EMULATION

In one respect, style is as subjective a term as culture or ritual. In everyday language usage there is a hierarchy of meaning for such terms, depending upon the values placed upon interpretation (Noble and Davidson 1996, 83). Style at a value-neutral level is simply a choice among options of form, but at a more romantic level is the difference between style-setters and the rest. Rather than use the term style as a value-laden description of the upper class, I have instead referred to stylishness, which is ultimately (and intimately) concerned with the direction of emulation. The incorporation of upper-, middle-, and working-class houses into the database has allowed me to trace the progressive emulation of stylistic attributes by other classes. In Armidale in the past, the direction of emulation moved from public structures to the private buildings of dominant groups, and from there both out and down to the private houses of the middle classes and the workers. There were thus a number of social groups negotiating their identity within this landscape. The wealthy were always style innovators, and used this in a very individual way to establish and reinforce their dominant position. In emulating this, the less wealthy were describing their own rising sense of place in the world. Both the wealthier segments of the middle class (either those who, although in debt, competed in assets and enterprises with the independently wealthy, or the successful and wealthy small enterprise operators) and the working class emulated various features of upper-class stylishness.

There are several implications following from these results. First, the indexicality of style is a prime component of the construction of personal and group identity, but stylishness is primarily generated by choice among the wealthy. Ideology serves to limit this variation, and new variation occurs in the working class by emulation. Style only becomes stylish when it is adopted by another party, but once style is emulated, there is a consequent need for new variation in the wealthy groups to maintain group boundaries through stylishness. In the potentially mobile class systems that exist within a capitalist society, the creation of new, elitist stylistic forms are a significant component of the mediation of access to power (cf. Appadurai 1986, 31ff). In Armidale, members of the upper and middle classes who wished to maintain stylistic distinctions between themselves and others were forced to seek new styles by the behavior of those who emulated them. This gives some insight into the power structures of the time. The style innovators did not have the power to prevent members of other groups from emulating their styles, and were compelled by the behavior of those "below" them to continually seek new styles. The impetus for stylistic change over time in Armidale thus came from two directions: from intergroup competition between wealthy capitalist classes, and as a reaction to middle- and lower-class emulation of previously exclusive styles. As a result, the creation of new stylistic forms originated not only from stylistic choice among the wealthy, but also from the behavior of the other groups who emulated them.

Second, the assumption that there is some form of direct relationship between wealth levels and architectural decoration informs many archaeological treatments of style. For instance, Louise Bavin (1989), in an Australian case study of the architecture of Collingwood and Kew, working-class and an upper-class suburbs of Melbourne, respectively, makes a number of direct correlations between the amount of wealth that a person holds and the ability to attain certain ends because of it. The notion that style is implicated in the process by which identity is constructed, and thus in the process of the construction of ideology, would suggest, however, that there is not such a direct correlation; power lies as much in the ability to deny difference as to flaunt it (cf. McGuire 1988). Bavin (1989, 20) regards the elaboration on a building as dependent upon both the period of its construction and changing architectural fashions, and notes that residents of upper-class suburbs are much more likely to have sufficient surplus wealth to purchase decorative accessories. The Armidale case study would suggest that it's not necessarily the *ability* to decorate that may be at issue, but what the stylistic features that constitute "decoration" may or may not signify. Essentially, Bavin and others appear to view decoration as an unnecessary cost, but it may not always be unnecessary in terms of ideology. The directions of emulation for style in the architecture of Armidale, the selective process of incorporation, and the resultant continually changing notions of indexical representation, suggest that wealth is not necessarily an equation whereby more wealth equals more things, but that the wealthy had access to a concept of stylishness.

DOMINANT IDEOLOGY

It is within the social mosaic that ideology is constructed, partly as strategies to legitimate social position and partly as motives for action. In the past in Armidale, the mercantile and pastoral ruling groups were legitimating their right to rule through appropriating the imagery associated with other, less questionable, contexts of power, with the traditions that stemmed from the church and from the societies of ancient Greece and Rome. Their will to justify, of course, was directed as much, if not more, towards the opposing ruling group as towards the workers whom they employed.

This has obvious repercussions in the debate by many historical archaeologists over the dominant ideology thesis. All too often capitalism is seen as a monolithic and directed entity, and seldom has attention been directed towards explicating the varieties of capitalism that might exist within a single historical situation. This study is unique because it has directed attention towards different types of capitalism, which, although based on the same attitudes to appropriation of private property, were nonetheless distinct and in many ways conflicting. This raises the possibility of more than one dominating ideology existing in

Investments of Meaning

the same social context, and illustrates the continually emergent nature of ideology. Ideology is a highly dynamic process and is continually changing in response to its engagement in the world and the patterning of the relationships between given groups (Therborn 1980, 77–78). It is both complex and complicated, and any attempt to freeze (frieze) it will only be a partial explanation. The very nature of ideology is that it is continually changing and is not a fixed property of either a group or a time, and archaeology must come to terms with this. Any contextual approach demands the same attention to the intricacies of ideology as to history or social context, while at the same time resisting a tendency to metaphorize and reify ideology as an organism in itself. Ideology is *only* articulated and made sense of through its continual reading and reception by people, and only expressed materially within the varieties of ways of life of the people who live it.

SCALES OF IDEOLOGY

When ideology is viewed on a more subtle scale, a different understanding of the term "dominant" emerges. The ideologies of pastoral and mercantile capitalism that existed in Armidale and New England were sophisticated ideologies, which in their turn were incorporated by the unsophisticated ideology of capitalism that bound and directed them both. In this sense then, capitalism in effect becomes a dominant ideology, although it is neither monolithic, nor unchanging, nor propagated by a single group. Rather than an artificial dichotomy between dominant and subordinate, the patterning of ideology is the mosaic produced by conflicting scales of sophisticated ideology encompassed by a more embedded and taken-for-granted unsophisticated ideology (Figure 9.1) (see also Meltzer 1981). As an extension of this, it is entirely possible that successful ideology is the construction of identity at different scales, such that dissent at one level becomes consent at another.

There is a further point to be made here about scale. When Plamenatz (1970) conceived of the distinction between sophisticated and unsophisticated ideology, he was thinking in terms of only one society: white Western and European. When a truly other "Other" is introduced, unsophisticated ideologies may differ as radically as sophisticated ideologies and, when colonialist societies come into contact with indigenous societies, unsophisticated ideology may become sophisticated ideology. Columbus and the Indians may eventually have come to share an ideology of capitalism, although for their part, the Indians may not have elected to share in it. They were forced to share in it just as slaves were,

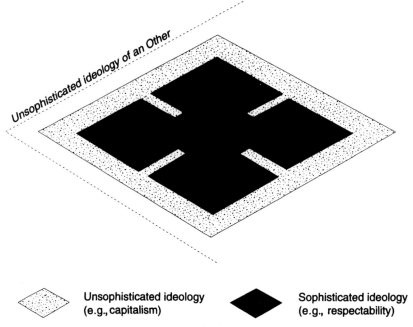

Figure 9.1. Scales of ideology.

but because they were only participating in part, capitalism did not help them to make sense of their world. Rather, they interpreted capitalism in terms of their own sense of the world, and capitalism became a sophisticated ideology for them that was mutable.

PERSISTENCE

Recognizing the move from index to symbol is only possible if past indexes of social identity persist into subsequent contexts of interpretation. William Paca's garden, as an index of wealth and power, no doubt possesses all of the properties and roles that Leone argues for, but one of its key features is that it *persists* as a source of identity and ideology. Persistence is the key to the movement of style from index to symbol, as both groups and indexical uses of style change. This leads to emulation across time, instead of merely between contemporary social groups. In this way, the past becomes a source of wealth and of stylishness, which is in large part valuable because it is persistent.

Investments of Meaning 225

Paca's garden does not just represent the persistence of style, of course, but also the construction of space. This can also function indexically and is linked inextricably to issues of power. In Armidale, as in Paca's garden, the structuration and marking of space is indexical of power. Over time, the constructions of space that persist become symbolic of those relations of power, and hence active constituents of asymmetrical relations of power. Each previous configuration of social relations that endures into subsequent contexts is a symbol that informs and is reinterpreted in the present.

This returns directly to archaeological discussions of style. Polly Wiessner (1989, 58–59) has argued that one of the most crucial aspects to style is the social and symbolic role of the artifact:

> changes in patterns of stylistic variation through time and over space can be generated both by a changing social landscape and by [the] changing roles of an artifact that make it more or less subject to stylistic and social comparison.

The stylistic features that became indexical of certain groups both across space and over time were generated by the constantly changing social landscape of Armidale. This landscape is, of course, still changing, and parts of it at least are embedded in the landscapes of the past. This, too, has led to stylistic variation: With the commodification of the past and the consequent rise of heritage as an industry to manage this, past notions of style, however stylish they may have been in the past, have become stylish in the present.

THE COMMODIFICATION OF HERITAGE

Creating persistence as a marker of age, and the past as a source of wealth, can only take place if the past itself is objectified through heritage and commodified by capitalism. Heritage is the process by which we give value to the past, but is itself based on the capitalist experience of assessing value through money relationships and exchanges of equivalence. This alliance creates the past as an object. It must possess certain qualities in order for it to be salable, and it is likely that those qualities will be most readily found in the dominant and enduring aspects of the past. While this implies that a good story is most likely to be constructed from the artifacts of the wealthy, there is a second process operating through the commodification of heritage. Creating the past as a reservoir of value simultaneously values things because they are old (because they have persisted), and removes the connotations of class from such artifacts. The features that were once indexical of the working class come to have value in the present because they are old, and are incorporated into present structures beside other features that were once indexical of the wealthy. This quite effectively masks the previous existence of the conditions of labor and creates a new ideology of heritage.

A HISTORICAL ARCHAEOLOGY OF IDEOLOGY

Ideology is more than something that only existed in the past, and to deny that it exists in the present is only another ideological strategy. One of the most common archaeological approaches to the study of ideology within capitalism and capitalist societies is through Marxian contributions. Ideology is a concept that is critical of relationships of inequality between groups, and within historical archaeology is often specifically directed towards unequal relations within capitalist social formations. It is one opinion that historical archaeology has almost always been about capitalism (see, for example, Little 1994; Orser 1988b; Potter 1994, 35), and since ideology has been recognized as an integral part of capitalist society since Marx, historical archaeology provides an excellent context in which to attempt to isolate ideological variables and link them to the development of particular social structures. This would seem to imply, however, that the recognition of ideology is relatively unproblematic, particularly within our own society. As Leone and others have pointed out, one of the main features of those beliefs and behaviors we call ideology is the disguise of its own history.

Archaeologists interested in the recent origins and forms of ideology therefore face a unique problem: The recent past is not so "other" that it does not inform or extend into the range of our living experience. For Leone and Potter (1988, 372) our problem is:

> how to find significant meanings in yesterdays that look so much like today ... not only does the similarity between the present and the recent past complicate the recovery of meaning; so too does the fact that many aspects of that past are alive in our contemporary world.... the ideology we study as scholars [of the recent past] is the same ideology we deal with as members of society.

What is the intellectual investment in my particular answer? (cf. Preucel 1991; Yoffee and Sherratt 1993). It is possible that viewing style as an expression of individual identity takes on particular meanings under capitalism. Wiessner (1989, 59; 1990, 109) has argued for a position that regards style as an indicator of the balance between an individual and the group:

Investments of Meaning

> Situations which switch on a strong sense of social group identity include fear, intergroup competition and the need for co-operation to attain social, political or economic goals, or imposed political control. Those that switch on a strong sense of personal identity would include inter-individual competition, options for individual enterprise and breakdown in the social order. (Wiessner 1989, 59)

The construction of the individual, however, has been isolated as one of the central processes of capitalism; so much so that the very notion of "the individual" has been characterized as ideological. For Leone and others, the transition to and between various forms of capitalism is reducible to the process by which an individual is created as a wage laborer, through control over individual behavior in terms of time (time discipline), space (commodification), work (work discipline), and social position (socializing rules of behavior). Capitalism, while ostensibly characterized by the trading of equivalent individuals in a free marketplace, instead relies on a notion of the individual as at once separate and inseparable from other individuals. There is basic agreement between studies on the segmenting nature of capitalism, creating such separations. Barnett and Silverman (1979) argue that, as a basis, all of these fragmentations reflect the same fundamental separation that capitalism creates between substance (a person's internal essence) and performance (his or her ability to perform). They argue that this separation is basic to Marx's concept of alienation in the sense that it is a

> break between an individual and his or her life activity ... Idealogically, [this] break ... is expressed in the idea of individual substance not affected by or affecting contractual performance. The loss of control over the material world is also expressed by the separation of substance and performance. (Barnett and Silverman 1979, 80)

Barnett and Silverman then link the two components of this fundamental break to the forms of domination possible under capitalism. They argue that the ideological domination of individuals requires the prior ideological creation of antecedent, autonomous selves. The individual can be represented both as a *substance*: "the real individual individual," a creation that legitimizes personal domination (in the sense that the person can be defined as less than an individual in the performance sense, i.e., as incomplete or defective) or *abstractly*: "the individual as faceless, equivalent to all other individuals," a creation that legitimizes abstract domination (or control from an external, scientific perspective) (Barnett and Silverman 1979, 62–63, 69). While control in terms of personal domination characterizes the "incomplete" person, that is, someone whose essence is inadequate (for example, the criminal who must be incarcerated, or the child who must be controlled),

228   Chapter 9

abstracted domination expresses ideological equality and ostensibly characterizes equivalent selves freely agreeing to contractual arrangements (performance) in a "free" marketplace (Barnett and Silverman 1979, 64).

Style as an indicator of the balance between an individual and society may also be an indicator of an individual's resistance to the tendency under capitalism to render all individuals faceless and equivalent. To take this still further, the notion of style as being able to characterize the individual at all might itself be regarded as ideological—especially if coupled with the recent postprocessualist agenda for uncovering the "individual actor" in the past. The heavy emphasis placed by postprocessualists on the active role of ideology and symbols in shaping the past has been related to a common effort on their part to disengage themselves from the ecological materialism of the "new archaeology" (Kohl 1985, 109). Handsman and Leone (1989, 134), however, have suggested that the tortuously self-critical examination of aims and methods of the new archaeology personalizes failure and is itself a reflection of the ideology of individualism. Postprocessualism (as I see it) is the search for the individual in the past, and for the individual (archaeologist) in the present, and may be just as ideologically laden. Cross-cultural generalizations represent the individual for the group's sake—at this scale for humanity's sake—but contextual archaeology reifies the individual for no other reason than his or her own sake. This may be part of the answer to Handsman and Leone's (1989, 134) rhetorical question: "What are the class origins and histories of this newest ideology of individualism? No one knows yet. How is it legitimized in our society?"

In making any of these connections I am not suggesting that ideology be taken as the mechanism that causes style; it is not necessarily an explanatory theory to account for this phenomenon. Rather, ideology plays a part in the construction of identity, which is itself influenced by many other factors and is mediated by style. It is neither a simple nor automatic elision to argue that style encodes ideology. As Morphy (1991, 145) has argued for another kind of artifact, in analyzing any artifact as a code "the individual sign can only be understood as part of a system, ... the operation of the system depends on pragmatic factors, and ... the meaning of the sign—the relation between signifier and signified—is not in any ultimate sense fixed for all time but is something that has to be continually re-created." This recreation extends, of course, into the present and becomes part of the perception of the past.

The historical ideologies that existed in Armidale in the nineteenth and early twentieth centuries created a public perception of the town that idolized the physical symbols of wealth and power (the churches,

Investments of Meaning

schools, and private mansions) at the center of the value of the place. This string of associations continued to inform the public construction of identity for Armidale until the heritage movement gained ascendancy, and literally enshrined these symbolic representations of identity in style as the *only* conduits of meaning and value. When the time came to record structures, these were the principal and obvious choices, and even searching the primary documents isolated few alternative examples of workers' structures. Although I have tried not to reify the already ideologically loaded perception of the city, this study nonetheless has a number of ideological repercussions.

Leone (1982, 750) has argued elsewhere that archaeologists, as members of a capitalist society, need to consider the degree to which archaeology creates the past in its own image. I regard this as a particular concern for a study such as this, which creates such a strong framework for ideology, although I am more comfortable in ascribing ideology to the recent historic (Western) past than to any prehistoric societies. This framework is also a part of the secularization of ideology— deliberately removing it from the ritual sphere and linking it to everyday life. Both of these tendencies may grant ideology a strength all out of proportion to its function.

Yet, no matter how critical an approach a study takes towards ideology and the structure of capitalism, there is the pervasive power of capitalist metaphors with which to contend. Even in the midst of critique, buildings can be spoken of as "possessing" a view; strategies as being "employed"; the presentation of identity as how one group might "sell" this identity to another; people as "valuable" and "productive" members of society; and style as the "business" of choosing among options. The terms "interest" and "investment" (both meaning involvement or stake) are obviously borrowed from property and financial terminology, and as Raymond Williams (1976, 143–144) argues are "saturated with the experience of a society based on money relationships."

Unique in the methods of this project is a consideration of the relationships between style and conflicting forms of capitalism, and between style and the standing structures of a variety of social classes. This approach is of particular value because it makes it possible not only to discover how style is used by different social groups to transmit different kinds of information and to negotiate different aspects of social identity, but also to use information relating to each social group to complement, qualify, and clarify that expressed by all other social groups. Thus, while this study extends Leone's approach to the analysis of standing structures and the ideology of capitalism, it also addresses the legitimate criticisms of Leone's work put forward by Hodder, which explicitly target the partial nature of studies that focus on a single individual.

The human behavior that generates style is embedded in the relationships between individuals and groups, and the ongoing social comparison these relationships entail. Ideology, as constructed by this social comparison, is thus only able to be understood within the patterning of these relationships. In widening the study of ideology beyond the sphere of a single wealthy individual, this study has made it possible to comment on some of the ways in which the world is ordered for and by others.

An important point to recognize here is that analyzing the artifacts created or used solely by members of one class will give only a partial view of that class. Considering the material manifestations of the relationships between members of different classes actually presents a fuller view of all classes under study, including the upper classes. By analyzing the range of relationships that are negotiated by and through style, it becomes possible not only to look at how the upper classes saw themselves, but also to identify their responses to the pressures placed upon them by other classes.

While I agree with Ian Hodder (1993, 68), that "inequality," the basic assumption of this study, is a value-laden term, which itself can be described as ideological, I also believe it necessary to avoid McLellan's labyrinth of relativism. As archaeologists and social scientists, we must certainly have some concern for not merely replicating the present, but we can only gain by recognizing the relationship between the present and the past.

Appendix: List of Structures

Date refers to the date of initial construction, as well as subsequent dates for known alterations (given in bold). Where dates conflict, references have been provided at the end of the table.

Owner refers to the person responsible for the construction of the building. In the case of public buildings, this category does not always apply.

Addresses in bold italic (e.g., ***55 Allingham St.***) indicate that the structure is without accompanying social context information.

Addresses in bold (e.g., **78 Barney St.**) indicate that the structure was not included in the 1991 Armidale Heritage Study database.

Structure	Date	Owner	Comments	Alterations	Sect	Allot
Extant Public Buildings						
AMP society (135–137 Beardy St.)	1886/**1929** 1929 (HW)		Fully rendered Georgian revival			
Courthouse	1860/**1870/ 1878/1897**		Builder: Edmund Lonsdale 1878: pediment and bell turret 1897: clock tower replaced bell turret			
Richardsons	1904/**1930s**					
Imperial Hotel	1889–1890	John Kickham (publican)				
Railway Hotel	1878					
Oddfellows Hall (101 Marsh St.)	1868 (HD)/ 1870s		Oddfellows established 1865 Land donated by James Tysoe			
St. Kilda Hotel	1865?/**c1900**					
Post office	1880/ **1897** (balc)/ **1916** (arc)/ **1929/1938**					
Telegraph office (164 Beardy St.)	1884–1885		Former CBA bank			
State Bank	1887–1889		Former Australian Joint Stock Bank			

Appendix

233

Former police lockup (247 Railway Pde)	1886–1893	Association with West Armidale police station and railway
Trim's store (3 Crescent St.)	1881–1882	
Masonic lodge	1860/**1889**/ 1925 1900/**1920** [1924 (HW)]	Masons established 1850 Builder: George Nott Original structure 1860 Present façade 1925
Lands Office	1886–1887	Originally with slate roof and chimney pots
Folk Museum	1859?/1863/ **1897**	1859?/1863: School of arts?
Former sheriff's cottage/lockup (Faulkner/Moore St. corner)	1877–1878	Converted in 1906 from lockup to residence
Town hall	1882–1883/ **1990**	£4,200 Renovated Art Deco interior 1990
Johnstone Memorial hall	1912?	Presbyterian Ecclesiastical Gothic
St. Paul's Presbyterian	1882–1883	Ecclesiastical Gothic
Wesleyan church/hall (former Methodist church)	1864	

Structure	Date	Owner	Comments	Alterations	Sect	Allot
Uniting church	1893		Replaced 1864 structure as church			
Catholic complex St. Mary/St. Joseph Catholic Cathedral	1912		Architects: Sheen and Hennessy (Sydney) Builder: George Nott			
St. Anne's building	c1920					
Former St. Ursula's College (facing Barney St.)	*1890–1915* 1889 [HW] 1888 (Kn)		Jubilee wing added 1907			
Ursuline Convent See private buildings						
Anglican complex St. Peter's Anglican Cathedral	1871–1878/ **1938**		Architect: John Horbury Hunt Clergy, choir vestries, chapter house: 1910 Tower built (1928?) 1938			
St. Peter's church hall (corner Rusden/ Faulkner Sts.)	1875					
St. Peter's Anglican Deanery	1891		Architect: John Horbury Hunt			
St. Mary's Anglican (286 Rusden St.)	1896		Architect: William Henderson Lee Builder: George Nott			

Railway Station	1882–1883	Builder: Edmund Lonsdale				
Stationmasters house	1882–1883					
Girrahween (Smith House) 88 Barney St.	1889/**1928**	Originally NE Ladies' College built by John Bliss Victorian Classical Revival 1928: second story verandah				

Extant Private Buildings

136 Allingham St.	c1880	John Harper (carpenter/builder)			25	9
Rosewood Cottage 144 Allingham St.	1880s [1882] (CT)	H. J. P. Moore (speculative builder)	Georgian Rated at £35 in 1882–1883 Sold to Albert Lane (draper): 1883	Replacement verandah	26	10
155 Allingham St.	Unknown				28	18
159 Allingham St.	Unknown				28	19
52 Barney St.	Unknown		Similar to 54 Barney St.		17	15
54 Barney St.	Unknown		Similar to 52 Barney St.		17	16
63 Barney St.	Unknown				16	8
77 Barney St.	Unknown				16	2

Structure	Date	Owner	Comments	Alterations	Sect	Allot
78 Barney St.	c1886 (owner) 1884–1887 (TS)	John Moore? (large retailer)		Gabled section added 1920s	18	11
79 Barney St.	1884				16	1
80 Barney St.	1880/**1888** (owner)	??	Onwed by Lawrence George Mallam until 1902		18	12
Warrawee 82 Barney St.	c1886	John A. McDonald (solicitor)	Builder: Thomas Chester Cook	Replacement verandah	18	13
Southhall 98 Barney St.	1886 (Gilbert 1982)	George Wigan (doctor)	Architect: Albert Bond Builder: Harper Bros. (Armidale) (Gilbert pp. 94–95)	Replacement verandah	19	11/12?
134 Barney St.	Unknown		Still paddock by 1884		21	16
163 Barney St.	Unknown				25	5
ASCA House 166 Barney St.	c1880	Bernard Herzog (cordial manufacturer)	Victorian Gothic Assoc. with 136 Markham St.		42	11
205 Barney St.	1878–1882	William Proctor (solicitor)	Owned in 1882 by Miss Proctor		52	21
63 Beardy St.	1875–1885	Charles Wilson (stock and station agent)			14	8
67 Beardy St.	1885–1886	Franklin Jackes (large retailer)	Bought Charles Howe: 1886		14	6
72 Beardy St.	Unknown				15	8

80 Beardy St.	1884–1894	Patrick Rafferty (senior sergeant of police)		15	9/10
88–90 Beardy St.	1911 (date on parapet)	?? (horse trainer)	University House called Kendall by 1950/52	11	8
245 Beardy St.	Unknown			CA	39
Victoria Cottage 261 Beardy St.	c1880 c1881–1882 (TS)	Andrew Cunningham (photographer)	Sold to Richard Palmer 1882; to Enoch Jones 1882; eventually to Alice and Joseph McKinlay 1889	CA	40 (Allot 14)
273 Beardy St.	c1915 1898–1915	Patrick Ryan (mail contractor)	Once attached to a cordial factory	44	8
275 Beardy St.	c1890–1895? c1889 (TS)	Andrew Cunningham (photographer)	Mortgage by Cunningham 1889 (£325) + £400 1889 + £300 1890	44	7?
307 Beardy St.	c1905			55	1
Bona Vista	1884–1886/ **1911**	J. D. Bradley (inspector of schools)	Bought by C. F. Tindal (pastorlist) 1910 Wing added 1911		
81 Brown St.	Unknown			17	9
Trelawney 84 Brown St.	c1904	Josias Moffatt (small farmer/mining speculator)	Bought *Yarrowyck* in 1900	32	13

Structure	Date	Owner	Comments	Alterations	Sect	Allot
Danbury House **86 Brown St.**	Unknown				32	14
Wiluna 89 Brown St.	c1920				17	7
Rothley 90 Brown St.	1890	Edmund Lonsdale (builder)		Heavily renovated	32	16
93 Brown St.	1928	(Christopher?) Allingham (grazier)			17	5
Iroka **94 Brown St.**	1883–1889	Henry Elliott (builder)	Pair with 98 Builder: Edmund Lonsdale/Henry Elliott. Sold to Henry Pitkin 1889		32	17
96 Brown St.	1891–1894	Henry Pitkin (bricklayer)			32	18, part of 17
98 Brown St.	1890s/183–1889 (TS)	Henry Elliott (builder)	Pair with 94 Builder: Edmund Lonsdale/Henry Elliott. Sold to Walter Pitkin 1889. Sold to Isabella and Louisa McKinlay 1895		32	18, part of 19
100 Brown St.	1900	Walter Pitkin	Morgage: 1895–1906		32	19
102 Brown St.	1903–1907				32	20

Birida 108 Brown St.	1907–1908 1984 (HW)	George Baker (grazier)	Architect: Ranclaud (Tamworth) Builder: George Nott			31	9
111 Brown St.	1874 (JF)	John Moore (large retailer)				18	4
Tregera 131 Brown St.	c1886	Angela Spasshatt (widow of Dr. Spasshatt)	Like 247 Railway Parade			19	2
134 Brown St.	1883–1884 [c1860] (NT)	John Moore (large retailer)				29	11
138 Brown St.	c1866/**early 1880s**	James Salmon (large retailer)	Partner of Moore and Richardson	Bays part of renovations in early 1880s		29	13
145 Brown St.	1889–1891	Patrick McKinlay (mineowner)				20	3
152 Brown St.	1881–1883	William Cook (spec builder and bricklayer)	Sold to Cornelius Fitzgerald (tobacconist) 1886			28	14
154 Brown St.	1881–1883	William Cook (spec builder and bricklayer)	Sold to Samuel Irwin (gaol warder) 1883			28	15
160 Brown St.	Unknown		Pair with 162			28	18
161 Brown St.	Unknown					21	5
162 Brown St.	Unknown		Pair with 160			28	18
166 Brown St.	c1915		Block subdivided in 1910			27	11

Structure	Date	Owner	Comments	Alterations	Sect	Allot
176 Brown St.	1892–1987?	Henry McShane	Mortgage (£200) in these years, but already house on block owned by H. McShane in 1878	Mortgage possibly for extensions?	27	14
180 Brown St.	1890?	Charles Wilkins?			27	15/16
182 Brown St.	1890	Charles Wilkins	Mortgage for S27/16 and part of 15 in 1889 (£300)		27	16
186 Brown St.	1879–1884	Seabrook and Brown (spec builders)	Spec built workers cottage		27	17/18
193 Brown St.	1883–1884	Joseph Cooper (miller)			27	2?
195 Brown St.	1883–1884	Joseph Cooper (miller)			26	2?
Arello 196 Brown St.	c1915				40	11
198 Brown St.	c1915		Pair with 196		40	11
204–206 Brown St.	1878–1889	William Cook (spec builder and bricklayer)	Sold to Wiliam Harris (Bank of NSW manager) 1880		40	
93 Butler St.	Unknown				CA	41
99 Butler St.	c1918–1922		Built on side of Armidale Brewery; well original to brewery		CA	41
163 Butler St.	c1905				40	19?

Merici House 124 Dangar St.	1900 (GW)	Cornelius Fitzgerald (tobacconist)		7	9
	[1882] (HW)	Founded by Ursuline nuns (HW)	Can't be 1882, in 1889 lot still owned by TB Fitzgerald		
Arran House 133 Dangar St.	1865 [1862] (NT)	S. P. Spasshatt (doctor)	... typical of those built for the middle class in the 1860s" Sold to John Bliss 1865/6/7?	19	15
Mavorna 160 Dangar St.	1887–1889	Alexander Richardson (large retailer)	Formerly Hilton School Described Armidale Express 4/12/08, p. 8 Joined to 162 late 1910s by Alethea Collis Tendall Former university residence	29	9
Kilbucho 161 Dangar St.	1895–1896	Russell Richardson (large retailer)	Builder: George Nott Architect: William Henderson Lee	35	16
162 Dangar St.	1882–1883 (RB)	Alexander Richardson (large retailer)	Twin of 164	29	9
164 Dangar St.	1882–1883 (RB)	Alexander Richardson (large retailer)	Twin of 162	29	8/9
168 Dangar St.	1887–1890	Alexander Richardson (large retailer)	Mrs Adam White's school 1890s Former university residence *Patterson*	29	8

Structure	Date	Owner	Comments	Alterations	Sect	Allot
170 Dangar St.	1886–1890	Alexander Richardson (large retailer)			29	7
174 Dangar St.	1886–1890	Alexander Richardson (large retailer)			29	6
176 Dangar St.	*1890–1915/* [c1900] (NT) 1886–1890?		Former university residence *Lawson*		29	6
Tintagel 194 Dangar St.	c1930				36	5/6
108 Donelly St.	c1915				101	11
132 Donelly St.	1893–1906	William Cyril Higginbotham (large retailer)	Builder?: Danielson		102	14
98 Douglas St. (Formerly *Miona*)	c1910		Georgian style Builder: Dyke and Bliss		14	11
Stanley 100 Douglas St.	c1910		Georgian style Builder: Dyke and Bliss		14	11
Ingress 104 Douglas St.	c1910		Georgian style Builder: Dyke and Bliss		14	10
Luther 106 Douglas St.	c1910		Georgian style Builder: Dyke and Bliss		14	9

Beverly **108 Douglas St.**	c1910		Georgian style Builder: Dyke and Bliss		14	2
132 Douglas St.	Unknown				16	10
93 Dumaresq St. (Woodshed Antiques)	1860s/1867– 1869 (TS)	William McIlveen (innkeeper)	Colonial Georgian	Initially a private home, later converted to a hotel?	CA	28
255 Dumaresq St.	1883–1902/ c1882–1883 (RB)	Robert Morrison (bootmaker)	House cose £100		56	5
261 Dumaresq St.	1880–1882 (TS) c1882	William R. Mathew	Part of Moses' subdivision. Cost £100. Sold to George Walker 1882, then Joseph McKeon 1895		56	4
263 Dumaresq St.	c1870s 1880– 1883/2nd mortgage 1883–1886 (TS)	George Howarth	Part of Moses' subdivision		56	4
Woodville 271 Dumaresq St.	c1881 c1870 (NT) 1880–1882 (TS)	John Morrison	Part of Moses' subdivision		56	1–2
Lindsay House 128 Faulkner St.	1920–1921 (Gilbert 1882) (1880s–HW)	Walter Harris (doctor)	Part of UNE, 88 Barney St.		19	9

Structure	Date	Owner	Comments	Alterations	Sect	Allot
Denham Cottage 132 Faulkner St.	1913 (Late 19th century–HW)	Catherine Marsh Blomfield (grazier)	Townhouse		19	8
136 Faulkner St.	c1866	Frank Newton (newspaper proprietor)			19	7
Laurel Cottage 139 Faulkner St.	c1872 (NT) c1860 (GHM, p. 27) 1863 (HW)	Edward Grover (builder) (HW) Bought by Henry B. Solomons in 1880s?	Georgian Occupied by Moses before Beaconsfield (Kiola)	Shutters and doors are replacements	9	16
141 Faulkner St.	Unknown		Dr. Ellen Kent Hughes' house		9	16
149 Faulkner St.	c1873	George Pitkin (plasterer)	Described as a boarding house 1878		18	15
149a Faulkner St.	Unknown				18	15
Wadenhoe 153 Faulkner	1902–1915				19	16
Uloola 160 Faulkner St.	c1908	Joseph Slade (married Charlotte Richardson)	Builder: W. B. Leck		35	6 + 7
Highbury 177 Faulkner St.	c1909–1911/ c1902 (owner)	Laurence? Mallam (doctor)	Builder: George Nott Formerly university vice-chancellor's residence		31	1
12 Great Northern Road	1878–1882	William Proctor	Owned in 1882 by Miss Proctor		52	21

79 Jeffery St.	c1900		Block bought 1890 by George Nott	115	3
95 jeffery St.	1893–1896 (TS)	Thomas J. Adams	Georgian	115	1
Ursuline Convent **Jessie St.**	1877 (Ferry; HW)/ **1882/1901– 1902/1922**	Peter Speare	Speare built it from money from Hillgrove and called it *Denmark House* Sold to Ursuline sisters in 1881. Extensions 1882 by Mr Elliott (Kn) Extensions by George Nott 1901–1902 Front verandah and bay windows added 1922	7	16
	c1860s (Kn)		Kniepp records it as originally built 1860s for Mr Bradley. Later occupied by Mrs Curry, then sold to Peter Speare in 1877		
152 Jessie St.	1882–1883 (RB) 1890–1891 (TS)	John Moore, Jr.	Mortgage by Moore is dated 1890–1899	21	8
163 Jessie St.	c1880–1881	John Hogan	Cost: £100	29	16

Structure	Date	Owner	Comments	Alterations	Sect	Allot
Sturry 170 Jessie St.	1912	Charles Blaxland (pastoralist)	Also owner *Wollun* (near Uralla)		28	8
Garthowen 174 Jessie St.	1884	Henry Hogarth (surveyor)			37	11
177 Jessie St.	1928	Joseph Scholes, Jr.			36	16
Soudan 3 Judith St.	1884					
27 Kennedy St.	1851–1853	William Bligh			CA	14
160 Kirkwood St.	1873–1874	Joseph Daly (died 1874)	Former farmhouse		CA	95
187 Kirkwood St.	c1880	Edwin Burgess (tanner)	Part of Moses' subdivision		105	1
Opawa 65 Mann St.	1896 [1908]	Samuel Herbert (Gov. architect) £300 mortgage	Inhabited by "a succession of pastoral families" 1911: sold to Alexander Mackay (grazier from Rockvale), £1000 1931: sold to D. H. Drummond		153?	
Teringa 108 Mann St.	1893–1894 [c1889] (NT)	George William Dight (grazier)	Architect: J Routledge Louat		34	10

Loombra 118 Mann St.	1880s	Charles Wilson (stock/ station agent)	Same architect as the Turrets Former university residence	34	14
128 Mann St.	1924	Curtis family?	Clara Bell Allingham living here by 1936	35	12
Strathlea **137 Mann St.**	1885–1900	George F. Nott		29	1
Linden Hall 146 Mann St.	1890 [c1880] (NT)		Former university residence	36	12
Gladdiswoode **150 Mann St.**	1922	Hannah Cooper (widow of Henry Cooper, Anglican bishop 190111916)		36	14
153 Mann St.	Unknown			28	5
Esrom **164 Mann St.**	1890/**1911** **(alterations/** **additions)**	George Philips Morse	Built after the Morses left Newholme (Abington → Newholme → Esrom) Additions designed by RN Hickson Former university residence	37	14? 16? 17? 18?
63 Markham St.	1893–1897	Frederick Stidworthy		105	18
87 Markham St.	c1892/**1920**	George Mallaby (manufacturer)	Verandah added 1920	Ca	88
123 Markham St.	c1920			25	19?

Structure	Date	Owner	Comments	Alterations	Sect	Allot
162 Markham St.	1892–1893	William Plant (carpenter)			40	8
Wyevale / Little Wyevale 208 Markham St.	c1882	Mark Roberts (builder)				
Hepplegate Off Markham St. south	1900	William Lewis (farmer)	Originally Bryn Herford, copied from a Welsh farmhouse			
Cotswold 34 Marsh St.	c1918 [1900–1910, owners]	William Curtis (draper)	Curtis had branches in Uralla and Hillgrove		116	6
45 Marsh St.	c1920				113	3?
49 Marsh St.	c1895				CA	105
130 Marsh St.	Unknown				9	7?8?
165 Marsh St.	Unknown				32	22
Belmore Cottage 168 Marsh St.	c1866	Spec built by John Barnes	Sold to John Moore in 1868—lived in it from 1880+ still there 1885 Later bought by Richardson (Gilbert, 82)		18	6
Newtown Terrace 175 Marsh St.	1863	Spec built by John Barnes? Joseph Scholes, Sr.	Block not bought until 1857 Sold to Alice M. McKinlay in 1884		32	24

179 Marsh St.	1891–1892	James P. McKinlay (died 1891)	Made money from Hillgrove gold	32	1
Comeytrowe 184 Marsh St.	1868	James Tysoe (carpenter/publican)	Builder Charles Brashier Has distinctive ruby glass sidelights and chimney mouldings	31	6
Kiola 18 Millie St.	1879–1800/ **1905–1915**	B. A. Moses	Moses left Armidale 1899	105	
89 Mossman St.	Unknown			82	14
The Turrets 145 Mossman St.	1884–1890 [1860s] (NT) Late 1880s (owner)	William Cyril Higginbotham, married Alice Richardson	WCH manager of Richardson's Builder: H. Lotham (or architect?)	36	2–3
Tralee 108b Niagara St.	c1910	Jeremiah O'Shea (engine driver)			
148 O'Dell St.	1884–1894		Owned by Alexia Urquart Trim 1921	52	19
66 Ohio St.	c1900		Allotment sold 1896. Inhabited by Elizabeth and Thomas William Grantham (carter) by 1917	57	11
68 Ohio St.	c1900		Identical to 66 Ohio St.	57	11
Mongoola 3 Reginald Ave.	1883	J. S. Chard (surveyor)		35	8, 9 + 10

Structure	Date	Owner	Comments	Alterations	Sect	Allot
69 Rusden St.	c1870 1876–1878 (TS)	Wiliam Bliss			15	3
76 Rusden St.	1889–1893	William Seabrook			16	17
78 Rusden St.	1889–1893	William Seabrook			16	17
84 Rusden St.	c1905				10	14
85 Rusden St.	c1890 1887–1894	Edward and Elizabeth Sharp	Gothic Builder: Edmund Lonsdale? Mortgage for £700		11	6
87–89 Rusden St.	c1890 1886–18??	Elizabeth Sharp?	Double house Gothic Built by Edmund Lonsdale? Lot bought by Sharp 1996		11	5
94 Rusden St.	1869–1870	Henry Mallam	Built for rental—first tenant Bishop Mahoney, also John Richardson (1872–1880s) Cost £1200 Builder: Charles Brashier		10	18
98 Rusden St.	c1900	W. R Groth (dentist)	Described "city improvements"		10	20

Appendix

99 Rusden St.	Unknown			11	3
Inverness, corner Rusden and Allingham St.	Unknown			24	5
277 Rusden St.	c1880s/1878–1880 (TS)	William Glover (carpenter)	Family home after 208 Markham St.	58	1
Wyevale 16 Short St.	1917	Mark Roberts (builder)			
32 Tancredi St.	Post 1880/1882–1883 (RB)	James Saunders	One of Moses' workers. Bought by JS and converted to Torrens in 1880; house built after that	56	14
7 Taylor St.	*pre-1890*		Possibly original farmhouse		
36 Taylor St.	c1915			132	17? 18?
145 Taylor St.	1882–1883? (RB)	J. Walsh	Block certainly subdivided, with three cottages by 1899	16	1
146 Taylor St.	1886–1894	James Miller		17	12
150 Taylor St.	c1920s		Shingle window hood recent	17	11
Moore Park	c1860/**1900**	John Moore	Includes a chapel		

Structure	Date	Owner	Comments	Alterations	Sect	Allot
Roseneath	1854	Thomas Lamb (town clerk)	GHM pp. 73–74 Sold to John Macneill Simpson 1866 Sold to Agnes Scott (grazier) 1877 to Marion McDonald (AS's grandchild) 1885			
Wood Park Cottage Off Old Inverell Rd.	1842 (NT)	Walter Pearson				
Violet Hill 32 Old Inverall Rd.	1910–1911	Margaret Pearson	Replacement of earlier house Farm originally established by Richard Pearson, Sr.			

Pastoral Properties

Structure	Date	Owner	Comments	Alterations	Sect	Allot
Booloominbah (main house)	1883–1888	F. R. White	Architect: John Horbury Hunt			
Lodge	1887					
Trevenna	1892	Elizabeth Wright	Architect: John Horbury Hunt			
Saumarez	1834	Colonel Henry Dumaresq (run)	Sold to Henry Arding Thomas (1856/7) Sold to F. R. White (1874)			
	1888/**1906**	F. J. White (main house)	Architect: W. Pender Builder: Henry Elliott Second story 1906			

Micklegate Bundarra Rd.	late 1870s	Son of Charles William Marsh	
Fairleigh New England Highway	c1910	Molly Baker and Frank White	Built by MB's father, George Baker, for his daughter and son-in-law
Palmerston	1840? 1910	Henry Dangar House, Albert Augustus Dangar	Architect: FC and AC Castleden, Newcastle Builder: William Palmer
Chevy Chase	1908–1911 1921 (NT)	Perrott	Builder: Mark Roberts
Booroolong	1843?	Matthew Henry Marsh (run)	
	1850?	House	Matthew Henry Marsh Sold to David Williams Williams' son
	1913	*Te dapa*	
Salisbury Court	1839	Edward Gostwyck Cory (run)	Sold to Robert Ramsay McKenzie 1837 Sold to Matthew Henry Marsh 1843
	1844	House	M. H. Marsh

Structure	Date	Owner	Comments	Alterations	Sect	Allot
Gostwyck	1833	Ed. Gostwyck Cory (run)	Sold to William Dangar 1835 Sold to Henry Dangar 1836? Henry Dangar built original house. Present house			
	1930	Nora Dangar (Gordon)				
	1921	Nora Dangar (Gordon)	All Saints' church			
	late 1800s?		Gardener's cottage			
Waterloo	1837	A. C. Innes	Mortgaged to Alexander Macleay Sold to Edward and Albert Norton 1859 Sold to A. A. Dangar 1907			
	House	1840s?				
Thalgarrah	c1879	House, A. E. Bigg				

Non-Extant Structures

Structure	Date	Owner	Comments	Alterations	Sect	Allot
Corner Faulkner and Barney St.	1907	Presbyterian Church	Manse	Demolished	18	14
Corner Dangar and Mossman St.	1883–1884	Anglican church	Bishop's house	Demolished	36	6–7
Corner Barney and Dangar St. *Kapunda*	1889–1894	James Miller	Later sold to Dr. Austin	Demolished	20	9

Corner Dangar and Brown St. *Westholme*	1872–1876	James Buchanan (police magistrate)	Later the Hilton School			20	6
Corner Brown and Faulkner St. *Montrose*	1893	Aaron Crossman	Later the Montrose Academy	Demolished		31	14
Corner Jessie and Barney St.	1882–1883?					20	14
Original Masonic Hall	1860			Rebuilt (see public buildings)		9	1
Barney St.	1869–1940	Catholic church	Bishop's house	Demolished		7	3?
Corner Miller St. and Bundarra Rd. *Brick Villa*	1870s? (there by 1884)	William Palmer (brickmaker)		Demolished			

Key to abbreviations: CT = Christine Thomas 1993; GHM = Gilbert et al. 1992; GW = Graham Wilson 1992; HD = Heritage Drive pamphlet; HW = Heritage Walk pamphlet; JF = John Ferry 1994; Kn = Pauline Kneipp 1982; NT = National Trust Register 1976; RB = rate book 1878–1882; TS = Title search, old system.

References

Abercrombie, N., S. Hill, and B. Turner, 1980, *The Dominant Ideology Thesis*. George Allen and Unwin, London.

Abercrombie, N., S. Hill, and B. Turner (eds.), 1992, *Dominant Ideologies*. Routledge, London.

Anderson, T., and R. Moore, 1988, Meaning and the Built Environment. A Symbolic Analysis of a Nineteenth Century Urban Site. In *The Recovery of Meaning. Historical Archaeology in the Eastern United States*, edited by M. P. Leone and P. Potter, Jr., pp. 379–406. Smithsonian Institution Press, Washington, D. C.

Appadurai, A., 1986, Introduction: Commodities and the Politics of Value. In *The Social Life of Things*, edited by A. Appadurai, pp. 3–63. Cambridge University Press, Cambridge.

Apperly, R., R. Irving, and P. Reynolds, 1989, *A Pictorial Guide to Identifying Australian Architecture. Styles and Terms from 1788 to the Present*. Angus and Robertson, Sydney.

Armidale City Council, 1993, *Annual Report and Community Directory*, Armidale City Council, Armidale.

Armidale City Council, nd., *Armidale Heritage Drive* (pamphlet), Armidale City Council, Armidale.

£255 Reward, *Armidale Express*, January 31, 1979. Armidale, p. 5.

B. A. Moses vs. William Saggus & James Green, *Armidale Express*, October 22, 1880. p. 6.

Local News, *Armidale Express*, June 17, 1881, p. 4.

Opening of Railway to Armidale, *Armidale Express*, February 2, 1883, p. 4.

Armidale Rate book, 1878–1881. Armidale City Council, Rusden St., Armidale

Atchison, J. F., 1977, European Exploration of New England. In *An Atlas of New England Volume 2—the Commentaries*, edited by D. A. M. Lea, J. Pigram, and L. M. Greenwood, pp. 137–151. Department of Geography, University of New England, Armidale.

Atkinson, A., 1987, The Creation of Armidale. *Armidale and District Historical Society Journal and Proceedings* 30:3–14.

Barker, T., 1980, *Armidale: A Cathedral City of Education and the Arts*. Cassells, Sydney.

Barnett, S., and M. G. Silverman, 1979, *Ideology and Everyday Life. Anthropology, Neomarxist Thought, and the Problem of Ideology and the Social Whole*. The University of Michigan Press, Michigan, Ann Arbor.

Bavin, L., 1989, Behind the Façade: the Expression of Status and Class in Material Culture. *The Australian Journal of Historical Archaeology* 7:16–22.

Beaudry, M., L. Cook, and S. Mrozowski, 1991, Artifacts and Active Voices: Material Culture as Social Discourse. In *The Archaeology of Inequality*, edited by R. H. McGuire and R. Paynter, pp. 150–191. Basil Blackwell, London.

Binford, L. R., 1962, Archaeology as Anthropology. *American Antiquity* 28(2):217–225.

Binford, L. R., 1989, Science to Seance, or Processual to 'Post-processual' Archaeology. In *Debating Archaeology*, edited by L. R. Binford, pp. 27–40. Academic Press, San Diego.

258 **References**

Blakey, M., 1987, Comments on Leone, Potter and Shackel "Towards a Critical Archaeology." *Current Anthropology* 28(3):292.

Blanton, R. E., 1994, *Houses and Households. A Comparative Study*. Plenum Press, New York.

Blomfield, G., 1981, *Baal Belbora: the End of the Dancing*. Apcol, Sydney.

Bocock, R., 1986, *Hegemony*. Ellis Howard, Chichester.

Bradley, R., 1987, Comments on Leone, Potter and Shackel "Towards a critical archaeology." *Current Anthropology* 28(3):293.

Buckley, K., and T. Wheelwright, 1992, *No Paradise for Workers. Capitalism and the Common People in Australia 1788–1914*. Oxford University Press, Melbourne.

Burleigh, Bennet, 1899, *Khartoum Campaign 1895 or the re-conquest of the Soudan*. George Bell & Sons, London.

Campbell, C., 1987, *The Romantic Ethic and the Spirit of Modern Consumerism*. Basil Blackwell, Oxford.

Chase, P., 1991, Symbols and Palaeolithic Artifacts: Style, Standardization, and the Imposition of Arbitrary Form. *Journal of Anthropological Archaeology* 10:193–214.

Chase, P. G., and H. L. Dibble, 1992, Scientific Archaeology and the Origins of Symbolism: a Reply to Bednarik. *Cambridge Archaeological Journal* 2:43–51.

Clark, C. E., 1988, Domestic Architecture as an Index to Social History: the Romantic Revival and the Cult of Domesticity in America 1840–1870. In *Material Life in America 1600–1860*, edited by R. B. St. George. Northeastern University Press, Boston.

Clark, M., 1971, *Sources of Australian History*. Oxford University Press, Oxford.

Clegg, S., 1989, *Frameworks of Power*. Sage Publications, London.

Conkey, M., 1990, Experimenting with Style in Archaeology: Some Historical and Theoretical Issues. In *The Uses of Style in Archaeology*, edited by M. Conkey and C. Hastorf, pp. 5–17. Cambridge University Press, Cambridge.

Conkey, M., 1993, Humans as Materialists and Symbolists: Image Making in the Upper Palaeolithic. In *The Origins of Humans and Humanness*, edited by D. Rasmussen, pp. 95–118. Jones and Bartlett, Boston.

Connell, R. W., and T. H. Irving, 1980, *Class Structure in Australian History*. Longman Cheshire, Melbourne.

Connell, R. W., and T. H. Irving, 1992, *Class Structure in Australian History. Poverty and Progress*. Longman Cheshire, Melbourne.

Cosgrove, D., 1984, *Social Formation and Symbolic Landscape*. Croom Helm, London.

Daniels, S., 1988, The Political Iconography of Woodland in Later Georgian England. In *The Iconography of Landscape. Essays on the Symbolic Representation, Design and Use of Past Environments*, edited by D. Cosgrove and S. Daniels, pp. 43–85. Cambridge University Press, Cambridge.

Davidoff, L., and C. Hall, 1987, *Family Fortunes. Men and Women of the English Middle Class, 1780–1850*. Routledge, London.

Davidson, I., 1989, Is Intensification a Condition of the Fisher-Gatherer-Hunter Way of Life? *Archaeology in Oceania* 24:75–78.

Davidson, I., 1995, Paintings, Power, Politics and the Past: Can There Ever Be an Ethnoarchaeology of Art? (Review of Morphy, 1991.) *Current Anthropology* 36(5):889–892.

Davidson, I., 1997, The Power of Pictures. In *Beyond Art: Pleistocene Image and Symbol*, edited by M. Conkey, O. Soffer, D. Stratmann, and N. G. Jablonski. Memoirs of the California Academy of Sciences, No. 23, pp. 125–129.

Davidson, I., and W. Noble, 1992, Why the first Colonisation of Australia is the Earliest Evidence of Modern Human Behaviour. *Archaeology in Oceania* 27:135–142.

Davidson, I., K. Kippen, and R. Fife, 1996, Supplementary Archaeological Investigations

References

of Portion 964, (Pikton Estate), Erskine Street, Armidale. Unpublished report prepared for R. F. Wright and Associates, Armidale.

Denholm, D., 1979, *The Colonial Australians*. Penguin, London.

Department of Lands, 1987, *Armidale Heritage Walk* (pamphlet). Department of Lands, Crown Lands Office, Armidale.

Duncan, R., 1951, *Armidale: Economic and Social Development 1839–1871*. New England University College, Armidale.

Durrans, B., 1987, Comments on Leone, Potter and Shackel "Towards a critical archaeology." *Current Anthropology* 28(3):293–294.

Eagleton, T., 1991, *Ideology. An Introduction*. Verso, London.

Earle, T., 1990, Style and Iconography as Legitimation in Complex Chiefdoms. In *The Uses of Style in Archaeology*, edited by M. Conkey and C. Hastorf, pp. 73–81. Cambridge University Press, Cambridge.

Easthope, A., and K. McGowan, 1992, Introduction, Section 1. Semiology. In *A Critical and Cultural Theory Reader*, edited by A. Easthope and K. McGowan, pp. 5–6. Allen and Unwin, Sydney.

Ferry, J., 1988, Henry and Grace Dangar and the Gostwyck Estate. *Armidale and District Historical Society Journal and Proceedings* 31:95–116.

Ferry, J., 1994, Colonial Armidale. A Study of People, Place and Power in the Formation of a Country Town. Ph.D. dissertation, University of New England, Armidale.

Feuer, L., 1975, *Ideology and the Ideologists*. Basil Blackwell, Oxford.

Fletcher, M., and G. R. Lock, 1991, *Digging Numbers. Elementary statistics for archaeologists*. Oxford University Committee for Archaeology, Oxford.

Freeland, J. M., 1988, *Architecture in Australia. A History*. Penguin, Melbourne.

Gero, J., 1987, Comments on Leone, Potter and Shackel "Towards a critical archaeology." *Current Anthropology* 28(3):294–295.

Gero, J., 1989, Producing Prehistory, Controlling the Past. In *Critical Traditions in Contemporary Archaeology. Essays in the Philosophy, History and Socio-politics of Archaeology*, edited by V. Pinsky and A. Wylie, pp. 96–103. Cambridge University Press, Cambridge.

Giddens, A., 1979, *Central Problems in Social Theory. Action, Structure and Contradiction in Social Analysis*. Macmillan Press, London.

Gilbert, L., 1982, *An Armidale Album. Glimpses of Armidale's History and Development in Word, Sketch and Photograph*. New England Regional Art Museum Association, Armidale.

Gilbert, L., D. Hope, and C. Mulquiney, 1992, *Images of Armidale*. Accommodation for the Confused Elderly, Armidale.

Girouard, M., 1981, *The Return to Camelot. Chivalry and the English Gentleman*. Yale University Press, New Haven.

Hall, M., 1992, Small Things and the Mobile, Conflictual Fusion of Power, Fear and Desire. In *The Art and Mystery of Historical Archaeology. Essays in Honor of James Deetz*, edited by A. Yentsch and M. Beaudry, pp. 373–400. CRC Press, Boca Raton.

Handsman, R. G., and M. P. Leone, 1989, Living History and Critical Archaeology in the Reconstruction of the Past. In *Critical Traditions in Contemporary Archaeology. Essays in the Philosophy, History and Socio-politics of Archaeology*, edited by V. Pinsky and A. Wylie, pp. 117–135. Cambridge University Press, Cambridge.

Hareven, T. K., 1982, *Family Time and Industrial Time*. Cambridge University Press, Cambridge.

Harley, J. B., 1988, Maps, Knowledge and Power. In *The Iconography of Landscape. Essays on the Symbolic Representation, Design and Use of Past Environments*, edited by D. Cosgrove and S. Daniels, pp. 277–312. Cambridge University Press, Cambridge.

260 References

Harvey, D., 1985, *Consciousness and the Urban Experience. Studies in the History and Theory of Capitalist Urbanization.* The Johns Hopkins University Press, Baltimore, Maryland.

Harvey, D., 1989, *The Urban Experience.* Basil Blackwell, Oxford.

Hawkes, C., 1954, Archaeological Theory and Method: Some Suggestions from the Old World. *American Anthropologist.* 56:155–168.

Hill, J., 1970, Prehistoric Social Organisation in the American Southwest. In *Reconstructing Prehistoric Pueblo Societies*, edited by W. A. Longacre, pp. 11–58. School of American Research, University of New Mexico Press, Albuquerque.

Hill, J., 1972, A Prehistoric Community in Eastern Arizona. In *Contemporary Archaeology. A Guide to Theory and Contributions*, edited by M. P. Leone, pp. 320–332. Southern Illinois University Press, Carbondale.

Hirst, P. Q., 1985, Constructed Space and the Subject. In *Power and Knowledge: Anthropological and Sociological Approaches*, edited by R. Fardon, pp. 171–192. Scottish Academic Press, Edinburgh.

Hodder, I., 1987, Comments on Leone, Potter and Shackel "Towards a critical archaeology." *Current Anthropology* 28(3):295–296.

Hodder, I., 1990, Style as Historical Quality. In *The Uses of Style in Archaeology*, edited by M. Conkey and C. Hastorf, pp. 44–51. Cambridge University Press, Cambridge.

Hodder, I., 1993, *Reading the Past. Current Approaches to Interpretation in Archaeology.* Second edition. Cambridge University Press, Cambridge.

Irving, R., R. Apperly, S. Baggs, S. Forge, M. Lewis, P. Murphy, D. Saunders, M. Stapleton, R. Sumner, J. Taylor, and P. Watts, 1985, *The History and Design of the Australian House.* Oxford University Press, Melbourne.

Johnson, M. H., 1989, Conceptions of Agency in Archaeological Interpretation. *Journal of Anthropological Archaeology* 8:189–211.

Johnson, M. H., 1991, Enclosure and Capitalism: the History of a Process. In *Processual and Postprocessual Archaeologies: Multiple Ways of Knowing the Past*, edited by R. W. Preucel, pp. 159–167. Center for Archaeological Investigations, Southern Illinois University Press, Carbondale.

Johnson, M. H., 1992, Meanings of Polite Architecture in Sixteenth-Century England. *Historical Archaeology* 26:45–56.

Johnson, M. H., 1993a, Notes towards an Archaeology of Capitalism. In *Interpretative Archaeology*, edited by C. Tilley, pp. 327–356. Berg Publishers, Oxford.

Johnson, M. H., 1993b, *Housing Culture. Traditional Architecture in an English Landscape.* Smithsonian Institution Press, Washington, D. C.

Johnson, M. H., 1996, *An Archaeology of Capitalism.* Blackwell Publishers, Oxford.

Kass, T., 1991, Thematic History of Armidale. Report prepared for Perumal Murphy Pty. Ltd. on behalf of Armidale City Council.

Kerr, J., and and J. Broadbent, 1980, *Gothick Taste in the Colony of New South Wales.* David Ell, Gladesville.

King, H. W. H., 1963, Armidale, NSW; a Standard "Australian" service town: Its Evolution, Morphology and Changing Functional Character. In *New England Essays*, edited by the Department of Geography, pp. 96–114. University of New England, Armidale.

Kneipp, P., 1982, *This Land of Promise: the Ursuline Order in Australia, 1882–1982.* University of New England, Armidale.

Kohl, P. L., 1985, Symbolic Cognitive Archaeology: a New Loss of Innocence. *Dialectical Anthropology* 9:105–117.

Kostoff, S., 1991, *The City Shaped. Urban Patterns and Meanings through History.* Thames and Hudson, London.

Kreckel, R., 1985, Ideology, Culture and Theoretical Sociology. In *Power and Knowledge:*

References

Anthropological and Sociological Approaches, edited by R. Fardon, pp. 151–170. Scottish Academic Press, Edinburgh.

Kryder-Reid, E., 1994, "As Is the Gardener, So Is the Garden": the Archaeology of Landscape as Myth. In Historical Archaeology of the Chesapeake, edited by P. A. Shackel and B. J. Little, pp. 131–148. Smithsonian Institution Press, Washington, D.C.

Kulik, G., 1988, Pawtucket Village and the Strike of 1824: the Origins of Class Conflict in Rhode Island. In Material Life in America 1600–1860, edited by R. B. St. George, pp. 385–401. Northeastern University Press, Boston.

Lake, M., 1994, The Politics of Respectability: Identifying the Masculinist Context. In Pastiche 1. Reflections on Nineteenth-Century Australia, P. Russell and R. White, pp. 263–281. Allen and Unwin, Sydney.

Larrain, J., 1983, Marxism and Ideology. Macmillan Press, London.

Larrain, J., 1994, Ideology and Cultural Identity. Modernity and the Third World Presence. Polity Press, Cambridge.

Layton, R., 1991, The Anthropology of Art. Second edition. Cambridge University Press, Cambridge.

Leone, M. P., 1981, Archaeology's Relationship to the Present and the Past. In Modern Material Culture: the Archaeology of Us, edited by R. A. Gould and M. B. Schiffer, pp. 5–14. Academic Press, New York.

Leone, M. P., 1982, Some Opinions about Recovering Mind. American Antiquity 47(4): 742–760.

Leone, M. P., 1984, Interpreting Ideology in Historical Archaeology: the William Paca Garden in Annapolis, Maryland. In Ideology, Power and Prehistory, edited by D. Miller and C. Tilley, pp. 25–36. Cambridge University Press, Cambridge.

Leone, M. P., 1989, Issues in Historic Landscapes and Gardens. Historical Archaeology 23(1):45–47.

Leone, M. P., 1994, The Archaeology of Ideology: Archaeological Work in Annapolis since 1981. In Historical Archaeology of the Chesapeake, edited by P. A. Shackel and B. J. Little, pp. 219–230. Smithsonian Institution Press, Washington, D.C.

Leone, M. P., 1995, A Historical Archaeology of Capitalism. American Anthropologist 97(2):251–268.

Leone, M. P., and P. Potter, Jr., 1988, The Archaeology of the Georgian Worldview and the 18th Century Beginnings of Modernity. In The Recovery of Meaning: Historical Archaeology in the Eastern United States, edited by M. P. Leone and P. Potter, Jr., pp. 211–217. Smithsonian Institution Press, Washington, D.C.

Leone, M. P., P. Potter, Jr., and P. A. Shackel, 1987, Toward a Critical Archaeology. Current Anthropology 28(3):283–302.

Levy, T., and N. Silberman, 1987, Comments on Leone, Potter and Shackel "Towards a critical archaeology." Current Anthropology 28(3):296.

Little, B. J., 1994, People with History: an Update on Historical Archaeology in the United States. Journal of Archaeological Method and Theory 1(1):5–40.

Longacre, W. A., 1970, A Historical Review. In Reconstructing Prehistoric Pueblo Societies, edited by W. A. Longacre, pp. 1–10. School of American Research, University of New Mexico Press, Albuquerque.

Longacre, W. A., 1972, Archaeology as Anthropology: a Case Study. In Contemporary Archaeology. A guide to Theory and Contributions, edited by M. P. Leone, pp. 316–319. Southern Illinois University Press, Carbondale.

Lowenthal, D., 1985, The Past is a Foreign Country. Cambridge University Press, Cambridge.

McGuire, R., 1988, Dialogues with the Dead. Ideology and the Cemetery. In The Recovery of Meaning. Historical Archaeology in the Eastern United States, edited by M. P.

Leone and P. B. Potter Jr., pp. 435–480. Smithsonian Institution Press, Washington, D.C.

McGuire, R., 1991, Building Power in the Cultural Landscape of Broome County, New York, 1880 to 1940. In *The Archaeology of Inequality*, edited by R. H. McGuire and R. Paynter, pp. 102–124. Basil Blackwell, London.

McLellan, D., 1986, *Ideology*. Open University Press, Milton Keynes.

McMichael, P., 1984, *Settlers and the Agrarian Question. Capitalism in Colonial Australia*. Cambridge University Press, Cambridge.

MacCannell, D., 1976, *The Tourist. A New Theory of the Leisure Class*. Shocken Books, New York.

Macintyre, S., 1994, The Making of the Australian Working Class: an Historical Survey. In *Pastiche 1. Reflections on Nineteenth-Century Australia*, edited by P. Russell and R. White, pp. 123–139. Allen and Unwin, Sydney.

Madgwick, M., 1962, The Schools of Armidale, 1880–1910, with Particular Reference to the Private Schools. *Armidale and District Historical Society Journal and Proceedings* 3:25–34.

Markell, A. B., 1994, Solid Statements. Architecture, Manufacturing and Social Change in Seventeenth-Century Virginia. In *Historical Archaeology of the Chesapeake*, edited by P. A. Shackel and B. J. Little, pp. 51–64. Smithsonian Institution Press, Washington, D.C.

Markus, T. A., 1993, *Buildings and Power. Freedom and Control in the Origin of Modern Building Types*. Routledge, London.

Marx, K., 1902, *Capital. A Critical Analysis of Capitalism Production*. Swan Sonnenschein and Co., London.

Meltzer, D. J., 1981, Ideology and Material Culture. In *Modern Material Culture. The Archaeology of Us*, edited by R. A. Gould and M. Schiffer, pp. 113–125. Academic Press, New York.

Miller, D., 1987, *Material Culture and Mass Consumption*. Blackwell, Oxford.

Miller, D., and C. Tilley, 1984, Ideology, Power and Prehistory: an Introduction. In *Ideology, Power and Prehistory*, edited by D. Miller and C. Tilley, pp. 1–15. Cambridge University Press, Cambridge.

Mitchell, B., 1988, *House on the Hill. Booloominbah, Home and University, 1888–1988*. The University of New England, Armidale.

Mitchell, B., 1995, *Horbury Hunt's Armidale*. Armidale Arts Council, Armidale.

Morphy, H., 1991, *Ancestral Connections: Art and an Aboriginal System of Knowledge*. University of Chicago Press, Chicago.

Morris, B. J., 1986, Cultural Domination and Domestic Dependency: the Dhan-Ghadi and the Protection of the State. Ph.D. dissertation, University of Sydney.

Mrozowski, S., 1991, Landscapes of Inequality. In *The Archaeology of Inequality*, edited by R. H. McGuire and R. Paynter, pp. 79–101. Basil Blackwell, London.

Mullins, P., 1993, "A Bold and Gorgeous Front": The Contradictions of African America and Consumer Culture, 1880–1930. Paper presented at the School of American Research Advanced Seminar, The Historical Archaeology of Capitalism, Santa Fe, NM. Manuscript on file, Department of Anthropology, University of Maryland, College Park.

Mundy, G. C., 1852, *Our Antipodes: or a Residence and Rambles in the Australasian Colonies with a Glimpse of the Gold Fields*. Richard Bentley, London.

National Trust of New South Wales, 1982, *National Trust Register*. National Trust of New South Wales, Sydney, Australia.

Noble, W., and I. Davidson, 1989, On Depiction and Language. *Current Anthropology* 30: 337–342.

References 263

Noble, W., and I. Davidson, 1993, Tracing the Emergence of Modern Human Behaviour: Methodological Pitfalls and a Theoretical Path. *Journal of Anthropological Archaeology* 12:121–149.

Noble, W., and I. Davidson, 1996, *Human Evolution, Language and Mind: a Psychological and Archaeological Inquiry*. Cambridge University Press, Cambridge.

Oppenheimer, J., 1977, Communication Routes and the Pattern of Settlement in New England to 1850. In *An Atlas of New England Volume 2—the Commentaries*, edited by D. A. M. Lea, J. J. J. Pigram, and L. M. Greenwood, pp. 153–170. Department of Geography, University of New England, Armidale.

Oppenheimer, J., 1988, The Dumaresq Brothers and the Settlement of the Armidale District. *Armidale and District Historical Society Journal and Proceedings* 31: 117–124.

Orser, C. E., 1988a, The Archaeological Analysis of Plantation Society: Replacing Status and Caste with Economics and Power. *American Antiquity* 53(4):735–751.

Orser, C. E., 1988b, Toward a Theory of Power for Historical Archaeology. Plantations and Space. In *The Recovery of Meaning: Historical Archaeology in the Eastern United States*, edited by M. P. Leone and P. B. Potter, Jr., pp. 313–343. Smithsonian Institution Press, Washington, D.C.

Orser, C. E., 1996, *A Historical Archaeology of the Modern World*. Plenum Press, New York.

Palkovich, A., 1988, Asymmetry and Recursive Meanings in the Eighteenth Century: The Morris Pound House. In *The Recovery of Meaning: Historical Archaeology in the Eastern United States*, edited by M. P. Leone and P. B. Potter, Jr., pp. 293–306. Smithsonian Institution Press, Washington, D.C.

Patterson, T., 1994, Social Archaeology in Latin America: an Appreciation. *American Antiquity* 59(3):531–537.

Paynter, R., and R. H. McGuire, 1991, The archaeology of Inequality: Material Culture, Domination and Resistance. In *The Archaeology of Inequality*, edited by R. H. McGuire and R. Paynter, pp. 1–27. Basil Blackwell, London.

Peirce, C. S., 1985, Logic as Semiotic; the Theory of Signs. In *Semiotics. An Introductory Anthology*, edited by R. E. Innis, pp. 1–23. Indiana University Press, Bloomington.

Personality Files, Heritage Centre, University of New England, Armidale.

Perumal Murphy Pty. Ltd., 1991, Armidale Heritage Study. Specialist report: Built Heritage. Report prepared for Armidale City Council.

Plamenatz, J., 1970, *Ideology*. Macmillan, London.

Ponzio, A., 1993, *Signs, Dialogue and Ideology*. John Benjamin Publishing Company, Amsterdam.

Potter, P. B., Jr., 1992, Critical Archaeology: in the Ground and on the Street. *Historical Archaeology* 26:117–129.

Potter, P. B., Jr., 1994, *Public Archaeology in Annapolis. A Critical Approach to History in Maryland's Ancient City*. Smithsonian Institution Press, Washington, D.C.

Preucel, R. W. (ed.), 1991, *Processual and Postprocessual Archaeologies: Multiple Ways of Knowing the Past*. Center for Archaeological Investigations, Southern Illinois University Press, Carbondale.

Raszewski, C., 1988, The Armidale School of Arts, or Mechanics' Institute 1859–1871. *Armidale and District Historical Society Journal and Proceedings* 31:35–52.

Rich, B., 1990, Aboriginal Historic Sites in North East New South Wales. Stage 1. Unpublished report to the New South Wales National Parks and Wildlife Service.

Rootes, C., 1981, The Dominant Ideology Thesis and its Critics. *Sociology* 15:436–444.

Sackett, J., 1990, Style and Ethnicity in Archaeology: the Case for Isochrestism. In *The Uses of Style in Archaeology*, edited by M. Conkey and C. Hastorf, pp. 32–43. Cambridge University Press, Cambridge.

Saitta, D., 1994, Agency, Class and Archaeological Interpretation. *Journal of Anthropological Archaeology* 13:201–227.

Shackel, P. A., 1993, *Personal Discipline and Material Culture. An Archaeology of Annapolis, Maryland, 1695–1870*. University of Tennessee Press, Knoxville.

Shanks, M., 1992, *Experiencing the Past. On the Character of Archaeology*. Routledge, London.

Shanks, M., and C. Tilley, 1987, *Re-Constructing Archaeology: Theory and Practice*. Cambridge University Press, Cambridge.

Shennan, S., 1989, Introduction: Archaeological Approaches to Cultural Identity. In *Archaeological Approaches to Cultural Identity*, edited by S. Shennan, pp. 1–32. Unwin Hyman, London.

Siegel, S., and N. J. Castellan, Jr., 1988, *Nonparametric Statistics for the Behavioral Sciences*. McGraw-Hill, New York.

Slotkin, R., 1985, *The Fatal Environment. The Myth of the Frontier in the Age of Industrialization, 1800–1890*. Atheneum, New York.

Smith, C. E., 1994, Situating Style: an Ethnoarchaeological Analysis of Social and Material Context in an Australian Aboriginal Artistic System. Ph.D. dissertation, University of New England, Armidale.

Stannage, C. T., 1994, Uncovering Poverty in Australian History. In *Pastiche 1. Reflections on Nineteenth-Century Australia*, edited by P. Russell and R. White, pp. 143–157. Allen and Unwin, Sydney.

Stapleton, I., 1983, *How to Restore the Old Aussie House*. The Fairfax Library, Sydney.

Stapleton, I., C. Lucas, and partners, 1993, Conservation Plan for *Booloominbah*. Unpublished report for the University of New England.

Steel, N., 1990, Towards the Archaeology of Capital: Assessing the Relationship between Archaeological Visibility and Levels of Capital Investment at Rocky River NSW and Bakers Creek Mine, Hillgrove, NSW. B. A. (Hons.) dissertation, University of New England, Armidale.

Therborn, G., 1980, *The Ideology of Power and the Power of Ideology*. NLB, London.

Thomas, C., 1993, Rosewood Cottage. 144 Allingham St, Armidale, NSW. *Armidale and District Historical Society Journal and Proceedings* 36:31–38.

Thomas, D. H., 1986, *Refiguring Anthropology. First principles of probability and statistics*. Waveland Press, Prospect Heights, IL.

Thomas, J., 1990, Archaeology and the Notion of Ideology. In *Writing the Past in the Present*, edited by F. Baker and J. Thomas, pp. 63–68. St. David's University College, Lampeter.

Thomas, J., and C. Tilley, 1993, The Axe and the Torso: Symbolic Structures in the Neolithic of Brittany. In *Interpretative Archaeology*, edited by C. Tilley, pp. 225–326. Berg Publishers, Oxford.

Thompson, J., 1984, *Studies in the Theory of Ideology*. Polity Press, Cambridge.

Thompson, K., 1986, *Beliefs and Ideology*. Tavistock Publications, London.

Tilley, C., 1989, Discourse and Power: the Genre of the Cambridge Inaugural Lecture. In *Domination and Resistance*, edited by D. Miller, M. Rowlands, and C. Tilley, pp. 41–62. Unwin Hyman, London.

Tilley, C., 1993, Prospecting Archaeology. In *Interpretative Archaeology*, edited by C. Tilley, pp. 395–416. Berg Publishers, Oxford.

Turner, B. S., 1992, Australia: the Debate about Hegemonic Culture. In *Dominant Ideologies*, edited by N. Abercrombie, S. Hill, and B. S. Turner, pp. 158–181. Routledge, London.

Walker, R. B., 1963, The Economic Development of New England in the Nineteenth Century. In *New England Essays*, edited by the Department of Geography, pp. 75–84. University of New England, Armidale.

References

Walker, R. B., 1966, *Old New England. A History of the Northern Tablelands of New South Wales 1818–1900*. Methuen, London.

Wallerstein, I., 1993, *Historical Capitalism*. Verso, London.

Ward, R., 1958, *The Australian Legend*. Oxford University Press, Melbourne.

Ward, R., 1976, The Oldest Home in Armidale? William Bligh in New England. *Armidale and District Historical Society Journal and Proceedings* 19:49.

Wells, A., 1989, *Constructing Capitalism*. Allen and Unwin, Sydney.

Wiessner, P., 1989, Style and Changing Relations between the Individual and Society. In *The Meanings of Things. Material Culture and Symbolic Expression*, edited by I. Hodder, pp. 56–63. Harper Collins Academic, London.

Wiessner, P., 1990, Is There a Unity to Style? In *The Uses of Style in Archaeology*, edited by M. Conkey and C. Hastorf, pp. 105–112. Cambridge University Press, Cambridge.

Wild, R. A., 1978, *Bradstow: a Study of Status, Class and Power in a Small Australian Town*. Angus and Robertson, Sydney.

Williams, R., 1976, *Keywords. A Vocabulary of Culture and Society*. Croom Helm, London.

Williams, R., 1977, *Marxism and Literature*. Oxford University Press, Oxford.

Wilson, G., 1992, Researching the History of Armidale Houses. *Armidale and District Historical Society Journal and Proceedings* 35:79–89.

Wilson, G., and J. Cooper, 1991, From Jessie Street West. *Armidale and District Historical Society Journal and Proceedings* 34:85–100.

Wobst, H. M., 1977, Stylistic Behaviour and Information Exchange. In *For the Director: Research Essays in Honour of James B. Griffin*, edited by C. E. Cleland, pp. 317–342. Museum of Anthropology, University of Michigan, Ann Arbor.

Wolf, E., 1990, Distinguished Lecture: Facing Power—Old Insights, New Questions. *American Anthropologist* 92:586–596.

Wright, E. O., 1978, *Class, Crisis and the State*. New Left Books, London.

Wright, E. O. (ed.), 1989, *The Debate on Classes*. Verso, London.

Wylie, A., 1987, Comments on Leone, Potter and Shackel "Towards a critical archaeology." *Current Anthropology* 28(3):297–298.

Yentsch, A., 1988, Legends, Houses, Families and Myths: Relationships between Material Culture and American Ideology. In *Documentary Archaeology in the New World*, edited by M. C. Beaudry, pp. 5–19. Cambridge University Press, Cambridge.

Yoffee, N., and A. Sherratt, 1993, Introduction: the Sources of Archaeological Theory. In *Archaeological Theory: Who Sets the Agenda?*, edited by N. Yoffee and A. Sherratt, pp. 1–9. Cambridge University Press, Cambridge.

Index

AAC. *See* Australian Agricultural
  Company (AAC)
Aborigines
  exclusions from workforce, 69, 75
  houses, 101
  national flag, creation of, 17
  shepherds, employment as, 47–48
Action-orientation, ideology and, 17
Alienation, 7
Allingham, George, 198
Alteration to physical structure, 96
Anglican cathedral, 195–196. *See also* St.
  Peter's Anglican Cathedral
Anglican church, 184
Antiquity, as a value of the past, 205–206
Armidale Gas Company, 174
Armidale Heritage Society, 93
Armidale Municipal Council, 51
Armidale (New South Wales, Australia)
  Aborigines, exclusions from workforce,
    69, 75
  buildings. *See specific structure and*
    style
    methodology, studies of. *See*
      Methodology, studies of buildings
  capitalism, ideology of, 4–5
  "cathedral city," as, 194–199
  central business district, 94
  Central Park. *See* Central Park
  class
    Colonial times, class systems, 70–71
    distinctions, 72*f*
    status, distinguished, 39–40
  conservation zone, 94
  democracy, 60–65, 69
  exit sign for, 200*f*
  Factory Acts, 62
  flour imports and exports, 66
  freemasonry, 77
  Galloway, John James, grid created by,
    55, 59*f*, 174

Armidale (New South Wales, Australia)
  (*cont.*)
  ideology, overview, 71–80
  industrial capitalism, 65–70
    changing locations, 68*f*
    described, 38
  location and settlement, changes in,
    68*f*, 164–165*f*
  map of (1884), 179*f*, 179–80
  Masonic Lodge, 77
  material for study. *See* Methodology
  Mechanic's Institutes, 54
  mercantile capitalism. *See* Mercantile
    capitalism
  methodology, studies of buildings for
    study. *See* Methodology
  middle class, 70–71
  middling class, 70–71
  New England. *See* New England
    (Armidale)
  North Hill. *See* North Hill
  overview, 37–81
  pastoral capitalism
    described, 38
    ideology, overview, 73–76
    "squattocracy" and, 40–49, 75
  plans for (1848 and 1849), 56*f*
  population increase, 37
  present day, 199–205
  private buildings, 85*f*. *See* Private
    buildings
  public buildings. *See* Public buildings
  public clubs and societies, 77
  railway line, 60
  real estate advertisements, 210*f*
  School of Arts, 54, 77
  South Hill area. *See* South Hill
  spectator sport, 54
  style, contexts of interpretation, 163–
    167
  underclass, 70–71

267

Armidale (New South Wales, Australia)
(*cont.*)
wealth and workforce, spatial
distribution under
mercantile capitalism, 57–58*f*
pastoral capitalism, 50*f*
wealth inheritance, 74
West Armidale. *See* West Armidale
west end, 94
women, exclusions from workforce, 69,
75
working class
Colonial Armidale, 70–71
described, 38–39
education and, 62–64
group, as, 64–65, 66*f*
The Armidale School (TAS), 62
Artifacts, ideology and style, 182–194
capitalist, 183–193
scale, 193–194
strategies, 183–193
workers, 183–189
Asymmetry
Booroolong, 154*f*
distribution of, 121*f*
first example of, 153
ideological expressions of, 182
Violet Hill, 160*f*
wealthy, use by, 149
Aurignacian, 26
Australian Aborigines. *See* Aborigines
Australian Agricultural Company (AAC), 44

Baker, George, 154, 200
Barnes, John, 87
Bay windows, 116*f*, 134*f*
Beaker folk culture, 26
Belief or theory, ideology as, 23, 25
Birida, 154, 156*f*, 157*f*, 190
Bligh, William Richard, 45
Bliss, John, 174
Bona Vista, 171
Booloominbah, 154–155
asymmetry, 154*f*
design of, 149
Gordon window, 190–191, 192*f*
Gothic revival manner, 147*f*
individuality, expression of, 158
medieval design elements, 156*f*
supervision of construction, 146
towers, 157*f*

Booroolong, 153, 154*f*
Bradley, J.D., 171
Brick, distribution of, 118*f*, 124, 125*f*
Brown, John, 87
Buchanan, James, 171
Buildings. *See specific topic*

Capital
effect of, 105–123
early period (1840–1879), 105–108
late period (1900–1930), 121–123
middle period (1880–1889), 108–121
statistically significant results, 106–
107*t*
labor, contradiction between, 6–7, 61
style, spatial distribution, 167–169
Capitalism
See also Industrial capitalism;
Mercantile capitalism; Pastoral
capitalism
artifacts, ideology and style, 183–193
capitalist accumulation, principal form
of, 6
conflicting forms of, 229–230
defined, 6
group membership and, 181
ideology of, 4–5
labor, contradiction between, 6–7
laissez-faire capitalism, 50
social solidarity and, 21
Cartography, 178
Cast-iron verandah decoration
middle period (1880–1889), 111*f*, 115*f*
style and, 171–172
"Cathedral city," Armidale as, 194–199
early period (1840–1879), 194–196
late period (1900–1930), 196–199
middle period (1880–1889), 194–196
Catholic cathedral, 156*f*, 176*f*, 185*f*
Central Park, 188
"ecclesiastical precinct," 166–167
Changing use of style features over time,
104*f*
Chard, J.S., 171
Chilcott, J., 41
Chivalric tradition, 191
City of Armidale Electric Supply
Company Ltd., 174
Class
buildings, methodology for studies, 88
effect of, 123–130

Index

269

Class (*cont.*)
  effect of (*cont.*)
    early period (1840–1879), 123–124
    late period (1900–1930), 128–130
    middle period (1880–1889), 124–128
  status, distinguished, 39–40
  style, spatial distribution, 169–172
  style without space, 172–174
Classical design influences, 113*f*, 127*f*
Clock tower, courthouse, 176
Colonial Armidale, 70–71
Colonial bond, distribution of, 127*f*, 138
Community, sense of, 188–189
Competition, capitalism and, 151
Concealment, ideology and, 7, 181
Constructing workers, mercantile
  capitalism, 53–54
Context
  geographic context, methodology, 92, 95*f*
  identity and, 219–220
  social context variables, methodology,
    86–90
  social identity and, 219–220
  style and, 28, 163–167
    partial social context, 130–135
    production, 103–130
    unknown context, 135–136, 137*f*,
     139–140*t*
Continuity, as a value of the past, 206
Convict labor, 46–48, 53
Cook, William, 87
Cooperation, need for, 151
Corporate paternalism, 178*f*
Cory, Edward Gostwyck, 41, 44
Cotswold, 157*f*, 190
Courthouse, 157*f*
Crown Lands Acts, 43
Curtis, William, 154, 201

Dangar, Albert Augustus, 154
Dangar, Grace, 43
Dangar, Henry, 41, 43, 48
Data collection, studies of buildings, 93
Democracy, 60–65, 69
Denmark House, 95, *96*, 171
Discipline, techniques of, 175–180
Dissimulation, ideology and, 12, 18, 183
Domesticity, 79–80
Domestic servants, property and, 101
Dominant ideology thesis, 3–4, 222–223,
  227

Dominant social power, 12, 182
Drummond, David Henry, 201
Drummond Memorial School, 201
Duality of structure, 22
Dumaresq, Henry, 44–45, 48
Dumaresq, William, 41, 45, 48
Dumaresq Creek, 167

Early period (1840–1879): *See also
  specific topics*
  capital, effect of, 105–108
  "cathedral city," Armidale as, 194–196
  class, effect of, 123–124
  location and settlement in Armidale,
    164*f*
"Ecclesiastical precinct," 166–167
Economized landscapes, 66–67
Education, working class and, 62–64
Efficiency, 66–67
85 Rusden St., 155
Electric power, 174
Elite: *See also* Wealth
  New England (Armidale), 45
Emulation, 220–221
English bond, 131, 138
Everett brothers, 48

Facade setting, 91
Factory Acts, 62
False consciousness, 11
False or deceptive beliefs, definition of
  ideology, 13, 15, 181
Flemish bond, 126*f*, 138, 143
Flour imports and exports, 66
Forecourt space, 91
Freemasonry, 77
French doors, 134*f*
  early period (1840–1879), 105, 108, 151
  middle period (1880–1889), 111*f*, 114,
    151
  social identity creation and, 151–152
Fretted bargeboard, 118, 119–120*f*, 121
Frieze, style and, 180

Galloway, John James
  "cathedral city," Armidale as, 195
  grid created by, 55, 59*f*, 175
  street names, 197–198
Gaslight, 174
Gentleman, manner and accouterments,
  190–191

270 **Index**

Geographic context
  methodology, studies of buildings, 95*f*
Geographic context, studies of buildings,
  92
Georgian architecture, 145–146
Gipps, Sir George, 40–41, 43
Gladdiswoode, 141*f*
Gold
  mining, mercantile capitalism and, 53
  rushes, New England (Armidale), 47
Gordon, General Charles, 190–191
  stained glass window, 192*f*
Gostwyck estate, 41, 44, 142*f*
Gothic Revival, 146, 147*f*
Greece, 184
Gyra, 41

Hargrave, Richard, 198
Harper, John, 87
Heritage, 206–207
  commodification of, 225–226
  ideology of, 209–213
  modern versions of heritage style, 211*f*
Heritage Drive, 199–201, 204*f*
Heritage Study, 199
Heritage Walk, 199–201, 202–203*f*
Highbury, 141*f*, 153, 155*f*, 190
Hospital buildings, Armidale, 146
Hunt, John Horbury, 146, 147*f*, 149

Identity. *See* Individual identity; Social
  identity
Ideology
  action-orientation, 17
  anatomy of, 11–35
  archaeological accounts, criticisms of, 2
  Armidale, overview, 71–80
  belief or theory as, 23, 25
  concealment and, 181
  definitions, studies, 11–17
  dissimulation, 12, 18, 183
  distortion and dissimulation, 12
  dominant ideology thesis, 3–4, 222–
    223, 227
  dominant social power, 12, 182
  duality of structure, 22
  "end of ideology" thesis, 19
  epistemological tradition, 11
  false consciousness, 11
  false or deceptive beliefs, 13, 15, 181
  frieze, style and, 33, 180

Ideology (*cont.*)
  historical archaeology of, 226–230
  institutional analysis, 21–22
  legitimation, 18, 183, 213
  liberal ideology, 76–77
  masculinism, 76, 78
  material constraints to studying, 213–
    214
  naturalization, 18, 183, 193, 213
  rationalization, 18, 183, 213
  resistance, of, 3
  scales of, 223–224
  social groups, definitions, 12, 14
  social identity and
    construction of social identity, 19–25
    style and, 25–35
  socially significant group or class,
    definition, 12, 14
  social practice, as, 23
  sophisticated ideology, 20, 23, 24*f*
  strategic action, 21–22
  style and, 181–216
    artifacts, 182–194
    heritage, 209–213
    material constraints, 213–214
    past as product, 205–209
    public identity, 194–205
  unification, 17, 182, 187–188
  universalization, 18, 183, 184
  unsophisticated ideology, 23, 24*f*
  vulgar and non-vulgar, 21
Imperial Hotel, 171
Indexical marker, style as, 32
Individual identity
  creation of, 153–159
  style and, 226–227
Industrial capitalism, 65–70
  changing locations, 68*f*
  described, 38
Inequality, 230
Inherited ascendancy, 74
Innes, Archibald Clunes, 48
Institutional analysis, 21–22

Jessie & Barney Sts., 173*f*
Justification, 9

Kapunda, 171, 172, 173–174*f*
Kentucky, 41
Kilbucho, 136
Kirkwood, Robert, 55, 198

Index

Label molds, 116*f*

Labor
  capitalism, contradiction between, 6–7, 61
  constructing workers, mercantile capitalism, 53–54
  convicts, 46–48, 53
  women, exclusions from workforce, 69, 75

Laissez-faire capitalism, 50

Lambert Park, 188, 189*f*

Lands Office, 171

Language, style and social identity, 25–26

Lapita culture, 26

Late period (1900–1930): *See also specific topics*
  capital, effect of, 121–123
  "cathedral city," Armidale as, 196–199
  class, effect of, 128–130
  location and settlement in Armidale, 165*f*

Legitimation, ideology and, 18, 183, 213

Liberal ideology, 76–77

Limits of Location, 40–43

Lived experience, 21

Location of industry
  changing, 68*f*
  economized landscapes, 66–67

Location of structures, 94–96

Lonsdale, Edmund, 87, 154–155, 158*f*

Loombra, 153, 155*f*, 171

MacDonald, George, 43

Mallam, Henry, 99, 101, 197, 201

Map of Armidale (1884), 179*f*, 179–80

Markham, George, 198

Marriage, 79–80
  networks, New England (Armidale), 47*f*

Married Women's Property Act (1893), 101

Marsh, Charles, 171

Marsh, Matthew Henry, 46, 51, 153

Martin, Robert George, 55

Marx, Karl, 226
  alienation, 7, 227
  camera obscura analogy, 11
  capitalism, social solidarity and, 21
  pastoral capitalism, on, 42–43
  proletariat, on, 19

Masculinism, 76, 78

Masonic lodge, 173*f*

Massie, Commissioner, 48

Material artifacts, style and, 28, 30

Materials. *See* Methodology, studies of buildings

Mather, John, 55

McIntyre, Peter, 41

McKinlay family, 200

Meaning
  context and identity, 219–220
  dominant ideology, 222–223
  emulation, 220–221
  heritage, commodification of, 225–226
  investments of, 217–230
  persistence and, 224–225
  relation of, 143
  scales of ideology, 223–224
  style and, 34–35
    persistence, 32–34
    stylishness, 220

Medieval design elements, 153–154, 156*f*

Membership, relations of, 143–161

Mercantile capitalism, 49–60
  artifacts and, 189–193
  concentrations of, 52*f*
  constructing workers, 53–54
  described, 38
  gold mining, 53
  ideology, overview, 73–76
  space, construction of, 55–60
  wealth and workforce, spatial distribution under, 57–58*f*

Mercantile structures
  classical design influences, 113*f*
  dominant position of, 176
  early period (1840–1879), 105, 108
  late period (1900–1930), 121–123
  middle period (1880–1889), 108–121
  similarity, movement toward, 146–149

Methodology, studies of buildings, 83–102
  biases in database, 99
  chronological divisions, 98
  construction of buildings, dating, 88–90
  data collection, 93
  grouping of structures, 84
  limitations of study, 99–102
  location of structures, 94–96
  social context variables, 86–90
  statistically significant variables, 100*f*

Methodology, studies of buildings (*cont.*)
  structures
    categories of, 85*f*
    selection of, 83–85
  survival rate of structures, 101*f*
  variables
    class, 88
    composition, 91–92
    geographic context, 92, 95*f*
    purpose of building, 88
    qualities between parts, 92
    scale, 90
    selection of, 85–86
    social context, relating to, 86–90
    style, relating to, 90–92
    use, relating to, 92–93
Micklegate, 142*f*, 171
Middle class
  Colonial Armidale, 70–71
  stylishness, 215
Middle period (1880–1889): *See also*
    specific topics
  capital, effect of, 108–121
  "cathedral city," Armidale as, 194–196
  class, effect of, 124–128
  location and settlement in Armidale,
    164*f*
Middling class, Colonial Armidale, 70–71
Miller, James, 171, 172
Modern versions of heritage style, 211*f*
Mongoola, 171
Montrose, 173*f*
Moore, H. J. P., 87
Moore, John, 159, 171, 174, 201
Morse, George, 201
Moses, Barnett Aaron, 94
  corporate paternalism of, 178*f*
  Heritage Drive, 200–201
  home of, 177
  tannery, 61, 65, 67, 69
Mosman, Archibald, 198
Mott, Charles, 198
Mundy, Godfrey Charles, 46

Names
  streets, 197–198
  structures
    early period (1840–1879), 123, 124*f*
    middle period (1880–1889), 111*f*, 127
Naturalization, ideology and, 18, 183,
    193, 213

NEGS. *See* New England Girls' School
    (NEGS)
Newcastle, 60
New England (Armidale)
  asymmetry in building, 153
  Australian Aborigines, employment as
    shepherds, 47–48
  boundaries of, 15*f*
  capitalism, 38
    mercantile capitalism, 49–60
    pastoral capitalism, 40–49
  convicts, laborers, 46–48, 53
  Crown Lands Acts, 43
  elite, 45
  gold rushes, 47
  history of, 40–70
  magistracy, 45–46
  marriage networks, 47*f*
  pastoral capitalism, 40–49
    "squattocracy" and, 40–49, 75
    wealth and workforce, spatial
      distribution under, 50*f*
  Robertson Lands Acts, 43
  social identity, 161
  "squattocracy," 40–49, 75
    Limits of Location, 40–43
    sheep and cattle running, 41–42
    shepherds and shearers, 46–48, 61
    space, construction of, 48–49
    wool production, 44
    wealth, land, 44–45
New England Building Society, 177
New England Girls' School (NEGS), 62
**New England Permanent Building
    Society,** 102
94 Rusden St., 197
North Hill
  dominance of, 176
  views from, 167, 176*f*
Nott, George, 201

Old System title, 89
155 Allingham St., 136, 139*t*
111 Brown St., 171
163 Jessie St., 150*f*
162 Markham St., 144*f*
104 Douglas St., 144*f*
Oxley, General John, 37

Paca, William
  garden of, 1–2, 4, 92, 217–218, 225

Index

Palmerston, 142*f*, 156*f*
Past as product, 205–209
Pastoral buildings
dominant position of, 176
early period (1840–1879), 105, 108
middle period (1880–1889), 114, 118
similarity, movement toward, 146–149
Pastoral capitalism
artifacts and, 189–193
described, 38
ideology, overview, 73–76
"squattocracy" and, 40–49, 75
Limits of Location, 40–43
sheep and cattle running, 41–42
shepherds and shearers, 46–48, 61
space, construction of, 48–49
wealth and workforce, spatial
distribution under, 50*f*
Pearson, Richard, 157
Persistence, style and, 32–34, 206, 212,
224–225
Piers, distribution of, 122*f*, 128–129, 131*f*
Porticoes, 109*f*
Postprocessualism, 228
Power
four modes of, 8–9
"power over," 8
"power to," 8
style and, 30, 174–180
discipline, techniques of, 175–180
production, techniques of, 174
Presbyterian Church, 156*f*
Presbyterian Manse, 173*f*
Private buildings
classical design influences, 113*f*
methodology, studies of, 85*f*
middle and upper classes, emulation
of, 183–184
Private pastoral dwellings. *See* Pastoral
buildings
Production
capitalism as mode of, 6
techniques, style and, 174
Proletariat, 19
Public buildings, 85*f*
methodology, studies of, 85*f*
middle and upper classes, emulation
of, 183–184
middle period (1880–1889), 108–121
social identity creation and, 145–146
stained glass, 171

Public clubs and societies, 77
Public identity, ideology and style, 194–
205
"cathedral city," Armidale as, 194–199
present-day Armidale, 199–205

Railroads, 60
Railway Hotel, 171
Rate books, 89
Ratings maps, 89
Rationalization, ideology and, 18, 183,
213
Real estate advertisements. Armidale,
210*f*
Resistance, ideologies of, 3
Respectability, 73, 77–80
Richardson, John, 197
Richardson, Russell, 136
Roberts, Mark, 159
Robertson Lands Acts, 43, 77, 94
Roman Catholic cathedral, 195–196
Rome, 184
Roof settings, 91
Rugby League Park, 167

Salisbury Court, 142*f*
Salmon, James, 201
Saumarez, 44, 142*f*, 171
Scale
artifacts, ideology and style, 193–194
ideology, scales of, 223–224
methodology for studies of buildings,
90
School of Arts, 54, 77
Scored ashlar brickwork, 111*f*, 132*f*
Seabrook, William, 87
Semphill, Hamilton Collins, 41, 44
72 Beardy St., 136, 139*t*
77 Barney St., 136, 138*f*, 139*t*
Sheep and cattle running, 41–42
Shepherds and shearers, 46–48, 61
Sidelights, distribution of, 132*f*
Single-pitch verandah roofs, 117*f*, 135,
187
66 Ohio St., 150*f*
Slade, Joseph, 200
Social context, studies of buildings, 86–
90
Social identity
construction of, 19–25, 218
lived experience, 21

274 Index

Social identity (*cont.*)
  construction of (*cont.*)
    sophisticated ideology, 20, 23, 24*f*
    style and, 25–30
    unsophisticated ideology, 23, 24*f*
  context and, 219–220
  creating, 143–153
  language, 25–26
  semiotics of, 31–35, 103–142
  style and, 7–8
    buildings, Armidale, 103–136
    construction of social identity, 25–30
    friezes, 33
    meaning, 34–35
    semiotics of social identity, 31–35
    sign as relational element, 31
Social practice, ideology as, 23
Solomon, Henry, 200
Solutrean, 26
South Hill
  asymmetry, 190
  capital, spatial distribution and
    features of buildings, 167–169
  Central Park and, 188
  class, spatial distribution and features
    of buildings, 169–171
  Conservation Zone, 208
  dominance of, 176, 191, 193, 208
  exclusivity of, 165–166
  Heritage Walk, 200
  symmetrical working class houses,
    186–187*f*
  workers' houses, 220
Space
  construction of
    mercantile capitalism, 55–60
    pastoral capitalism, 48–49
  style and
    capital, 167–169
    class, 169–172
    style without space, 172–174
Spasshatt, Angela, 171
Speare, Peter, 95, 171
Spectator sports, 54
"Squattocracy," pastoral capitalism and,
    40–49
  anti-squatter push, 75
  sheep and cattle running, 41–42
  shepherds and shearers, 46–48, 61
  space, construction of, 48–49
St. Cuthbert's, 173*f*

St. John's Theological College, 146
St. Mary and Joseph's Catholic
    Cathedral, 166
  spire of, 166
St. Paul's Presbyterian, 171
St. Peter's Anglican Cathedral, 146, 147*f*,
    156*f*, 166, 185*f*
  stained glass, 171
St. Peter's Deanery, 146, 147*f*
Stained glass, 103, 133*f*
  church buildings, 185*f*
  early period (1840–1879), 105
  Gordon window, 192*f*
  late period (1900–1930), 129–130
  middle period (1880–1889), 110*f*
  public buildings, 171
Stop-chamfered verandah columns, 143
  middle period (1880–1889), 117*f*, 128*f*,
    152–153
  social identity creation and, 152–153
Strategic action, 21–22
Street names, 197–198
Structures
  categories of, 85*f*
  selection of, 83–85
    private buildings, 85*f*
    public buildings, 85*f*
Sturry, 141*f*
Style
  architectural terms, 29–30
  buildings, methodology for studies of,
    90–92
  context and, 28
    interpretation, 163–167
    partial social context, 130–135
    production, 103–130
    unknown context, 135–136, 137*f*,
      139–140*t*
  emulation, 220–221
  identity and, 7–8, 25–30
    friezes, 33
    language, 25–26
    meaning, 34–35
    semiotics of social identity, 31–35
    sign as relational element, 31
  ideology and, 181–216
    artifacts, 182–194
    heritage, 209–213
    material constraints, 213–214
    past as product, 205–209
    public identity, 194–205

Index 275

Style (*cont.*)
 indexical marker, as, 32
 individual and society, as balance
  between, 228
 material artifacts and, 28, 30
 persistence of, 32–34, 224–225
 power and, 30, 174–180
  discipline, techniques of, 175–180
  production, techniques of, 174
 social identity and. *See* Social identity
 spatial distribution, 167–174, 217
  capital, 167–169
  class, 169–172
  style without space, 172–174
 symbolic reference, 26
Stylishness, 215–216
 meaning and, 220
Substance, individual as, 227
Survival rate of buildings, 101f
Symmetry distribution
 early period (1840–1879), 124, 125f
 late period (1900–1930), 128, 149–151
 middle period (1880–1889), 114f
 workers' houses and, 170–171

Tablelands. *See* Armidale (New South
  Wales, Australia)
TAS. *See* The Armidale School (TAS)
Taylor, W. T., 198
Termination, 206
32 Tancredi St., 144f, 150f
Thomas, Henry Arding, 44
307 Beardy St., 150f, 201
Tilbuster, 41
Torrens title, 89
Tregara, 171
Trelawney, 153, 155f
Trevenna, 146, 147f, 190
Trim, John, 201
Turned timber finials, 122–23, 123f, 128,
  130f
The Turrets, 153, 155f, 190
204 Barney St., 150f
261 Dumaresq St., 144f, 150f
Tysoe, James, 171

Underclass, Colonial Armidale, 70–71
Unification, ideology and, 17, 182, 187–188
Uniting Church, 171
Universalization, ideology and, 18, 183,
  184

Unrespectability, 78–80
Unsophisticated ideology, 23, 24f
Use, studies of buildings, 92–93

Variables, methodology for studies of
  buildings
 class, 88
 composition, 91–92
 construction of buildings, dating, 88–
  90
 geographic context, 92, 95f
 purpose of building, 88
 qualities between parts, 92
 scale, 90
 selection of, 85–86
 social context, relating to, 86–90
 style, relating to, 90–92
 use, relating to, 92–93
Verandah, 91
Violet Hill, 144f, 155, 157–158, 158–160f
Vulgar and non-vulgar ideology, 21

Wealth
 architectural decoration and, 221–222
 inheritance, 74
 New England (Armidale)
  land, 44–45
  spatial distribution under, 50f, 57–
  58f
Weatherboard, 119f, 126f, 143
Wesleyan Methodist church, 166
West Armidale
 Central Park, 188
 generally, 166
 Heritage Drive, 201
 Lambert Park, 188, 189f
 workers' houses, 220
West Armidale School, 201
Westholme, 171, 173f
White, Frederick Robert, 146, 149, 190–
  191, 201
White, Harold, 198
White, James, 45
White-collar employees, property and,
  101
Wilson, Charles, 171, 200
Wolka, 41
Women
 exclusions from workforce, 69, 75
 Married Women's Property Act (1893),
  101

Women (*cont.*)
  respectability, 73, 77–80
Wool production, 44
Workers
  artifacts, ideology and style, 183–189
  constructing, mercantile capitalism,
    53–54
  surveillance of, 177–178
Workers' houses
  early period (1840–1879), 186*f*
  French doors, 152
  late period (1900–1930), 144*f*, 145, 187*f*
  middle period (1880–1889), 110, 114,
    118, 143–144, 144*f*, 186*f*
  social identity creation and, 143–145

Workers' houses (*cont.*)
  South Hill, 167–169
  symmetry, 149–151, 150*f*, 170–171
Working class
  challenge, 60–65
  Colonial Armidale, 70–71
  described, 38–39
  education and, 62–64
  group, as, 64–65, 66*f*
  stylishness, 215–216
Wright, Elizabeth, 146
Wyevale, 159

Yolngu paintings, 34

Printed by Books on Demand, Germany